To my beloved pare

First published in Korea in 2003 by GCK Book
English translation rights arranged with GCK Book, Ltd.
through Orange Agency

Translation by Joe Johnson
Lettering by Ortho
Printed in China

3 2 1

ComicsLit is an imprint
and trademark of

NANTIER • BEALL • MINOUSTCHINE
Publishing inc.
new york

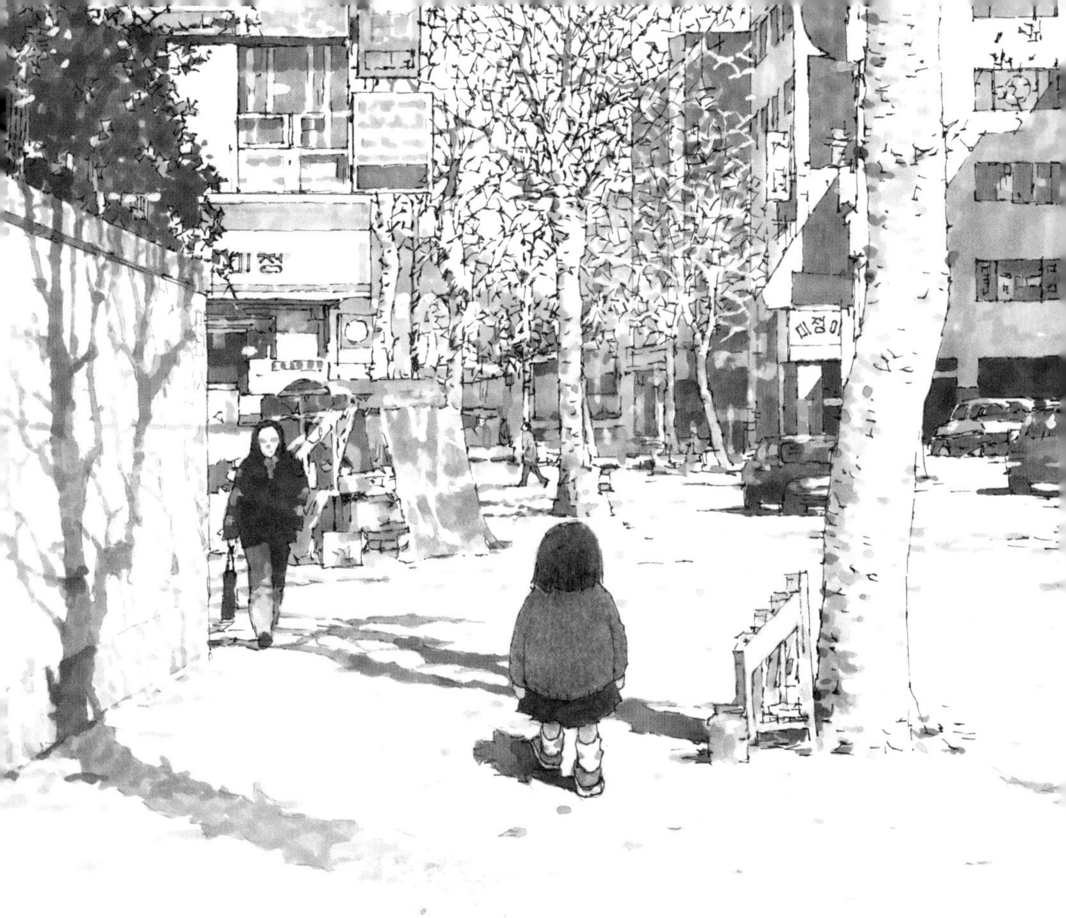
미정
미정이

Run, Bong-Gu, Run!

a little manhwa graphic novel by

Byun Byung-Jun

CONTENTS

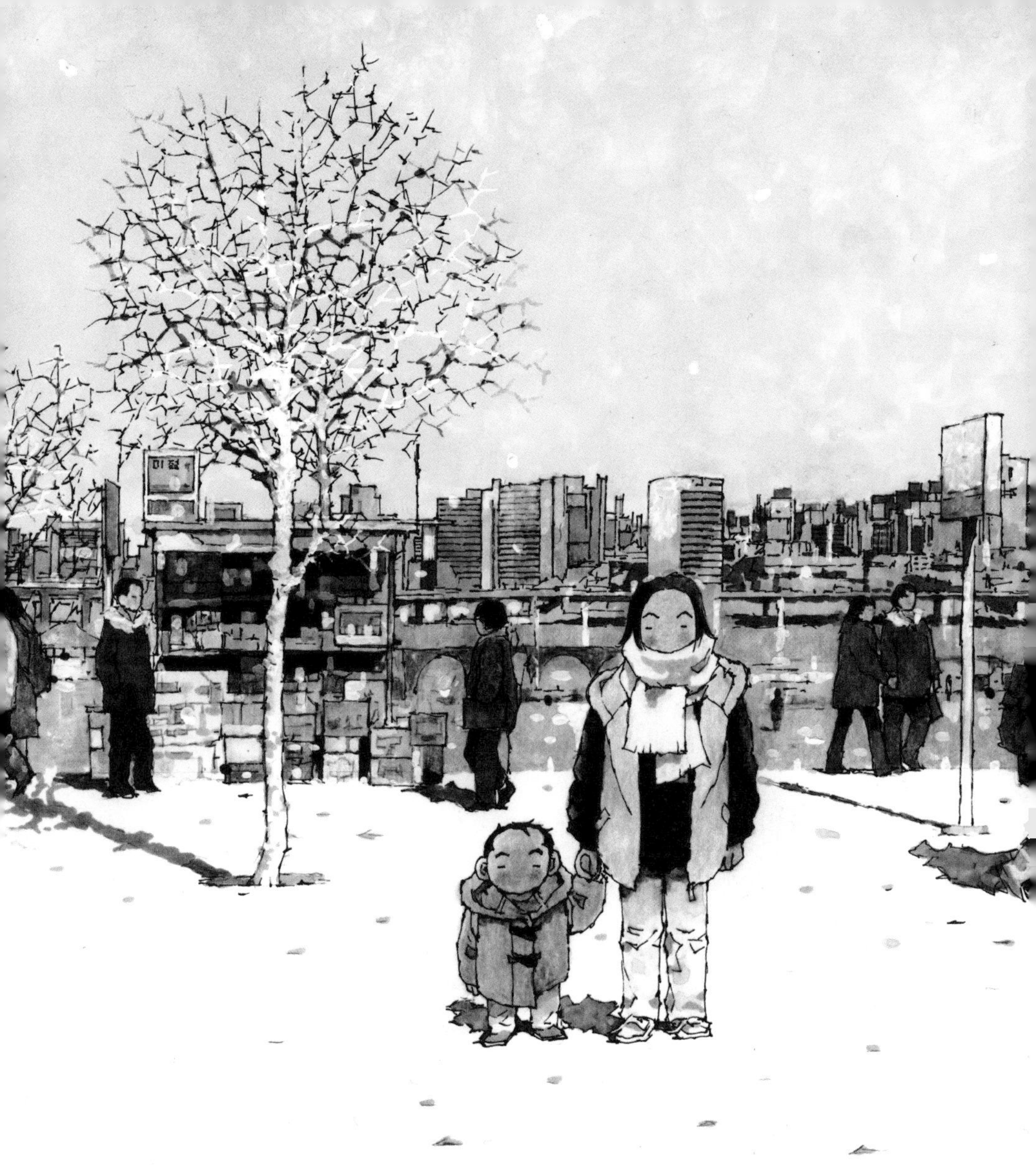

Run, Bong-Gu, Run!

a little manhwa graphic novel by

Byun Byung-Jun

NBM ComicsLit

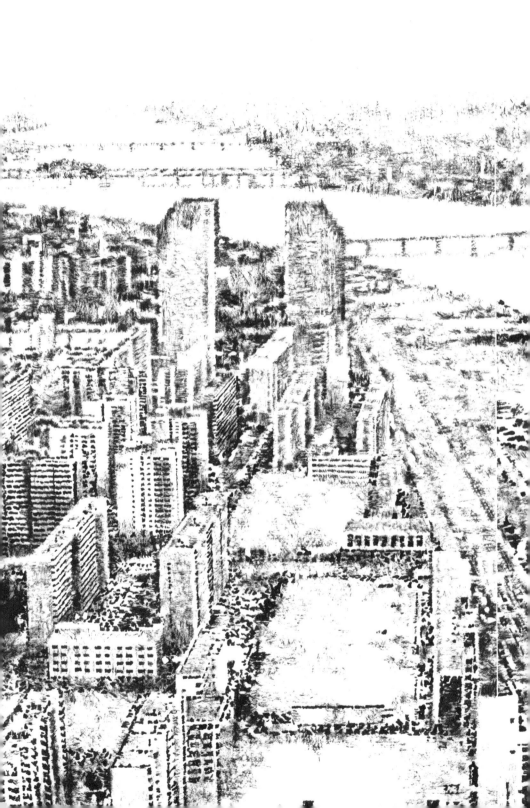

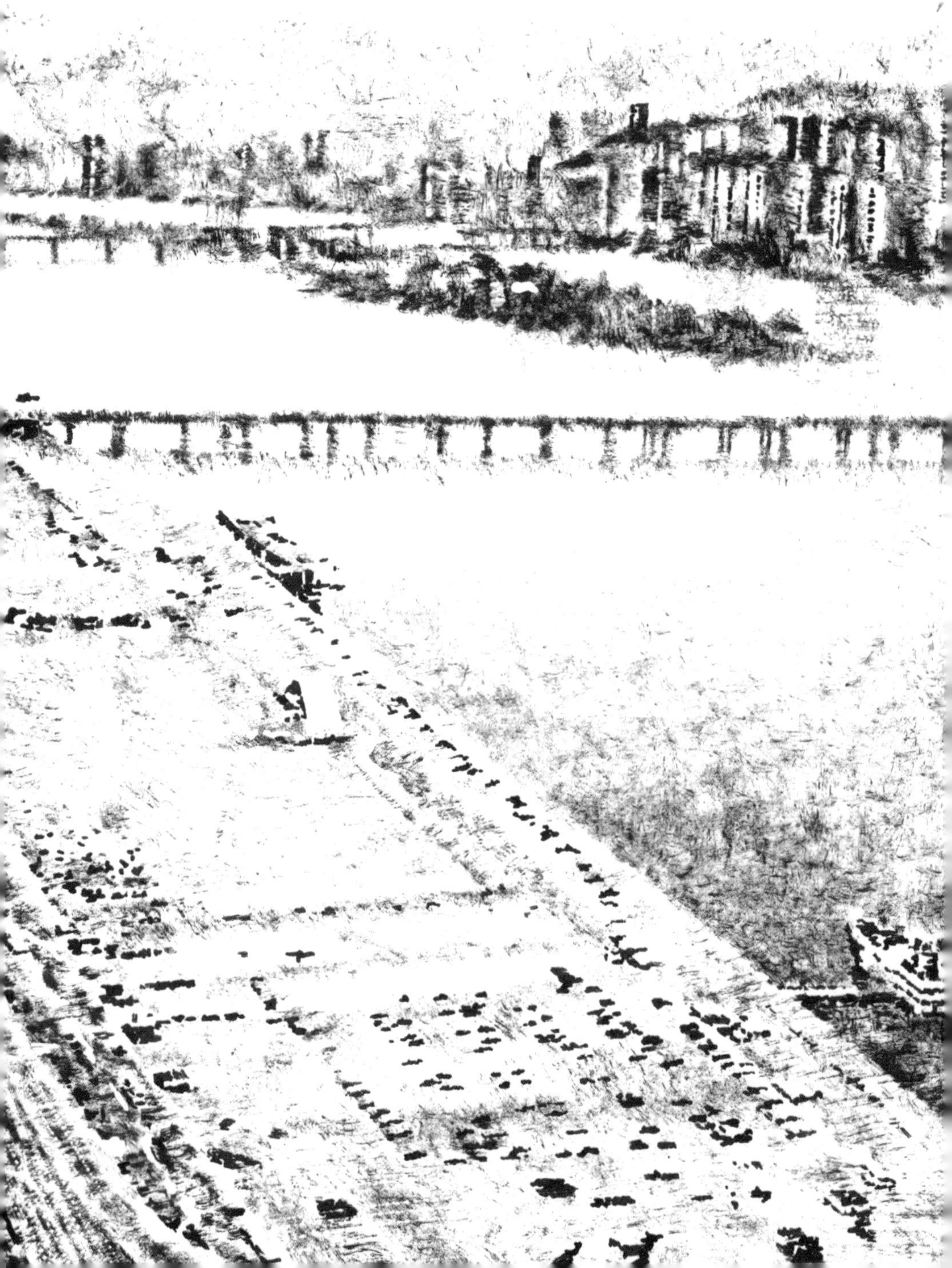

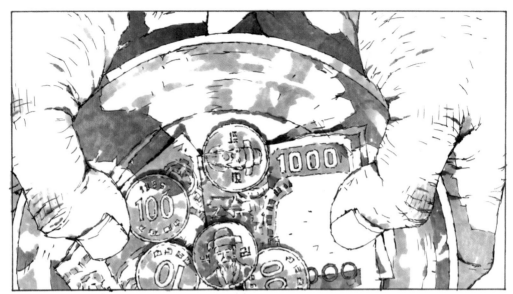

WHHW
하
아.

....

FROM THE
KINDNESS OF
YOUR HEART,
PLEASE, FOR A
POOR, WRETCHED,
HOMELESS
PERSON.

덜
컹 CLICK
CLACK

덜 컹 CLICK
CLACK

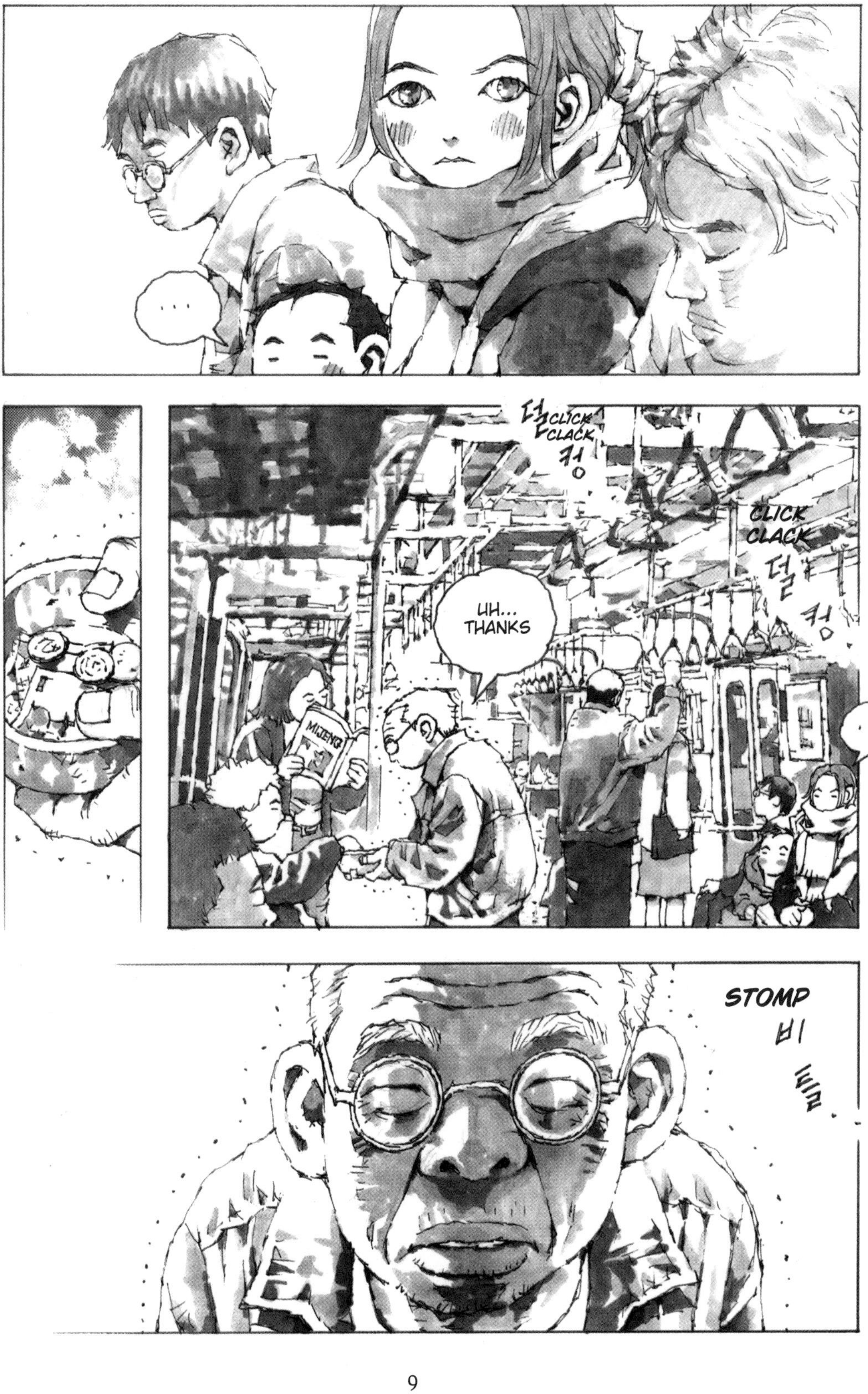
...
덜 CLICK CLACK 컹
CLICK CLACK 덜 컹
UH... THANKS
...
STOMP
비 틀

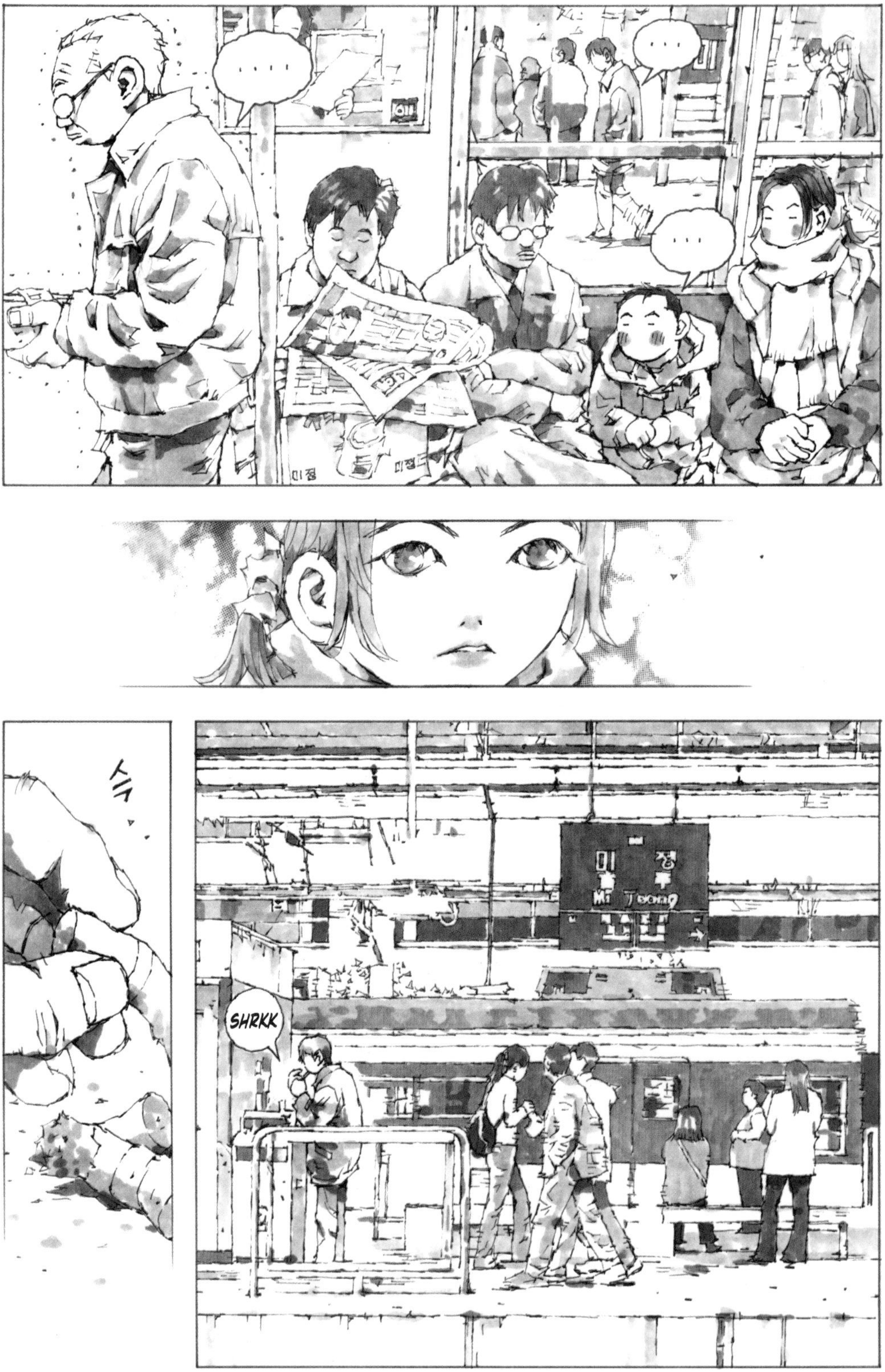
SHRKK

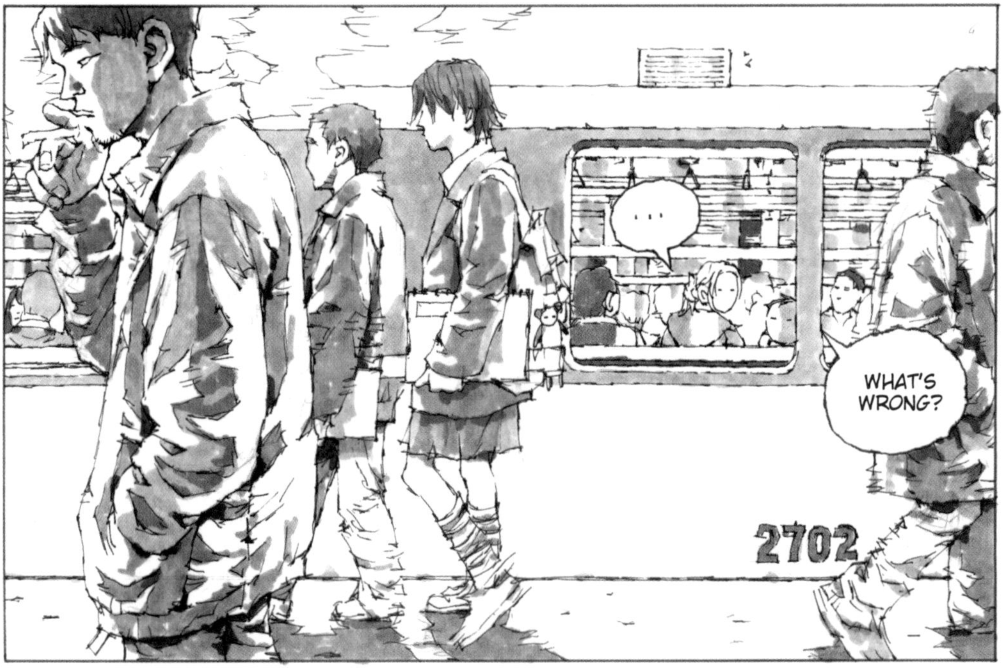
...
WHAT'S WRONG?
2702

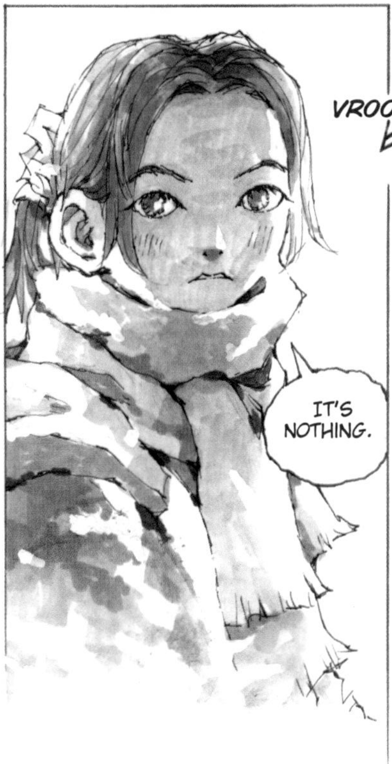
IT'S NOTHING.

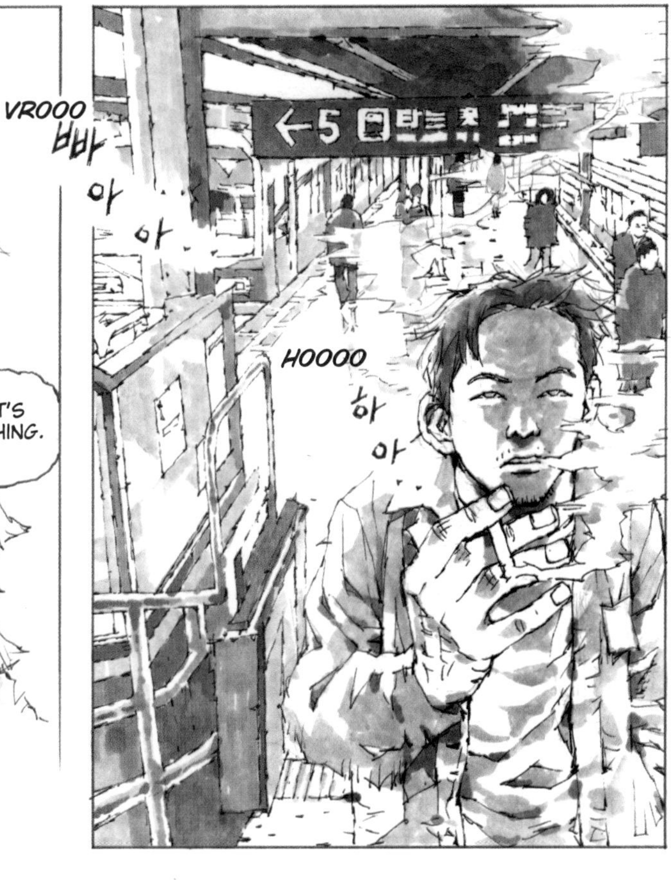
VROOO
빠
아
아
HOOOO
하
아

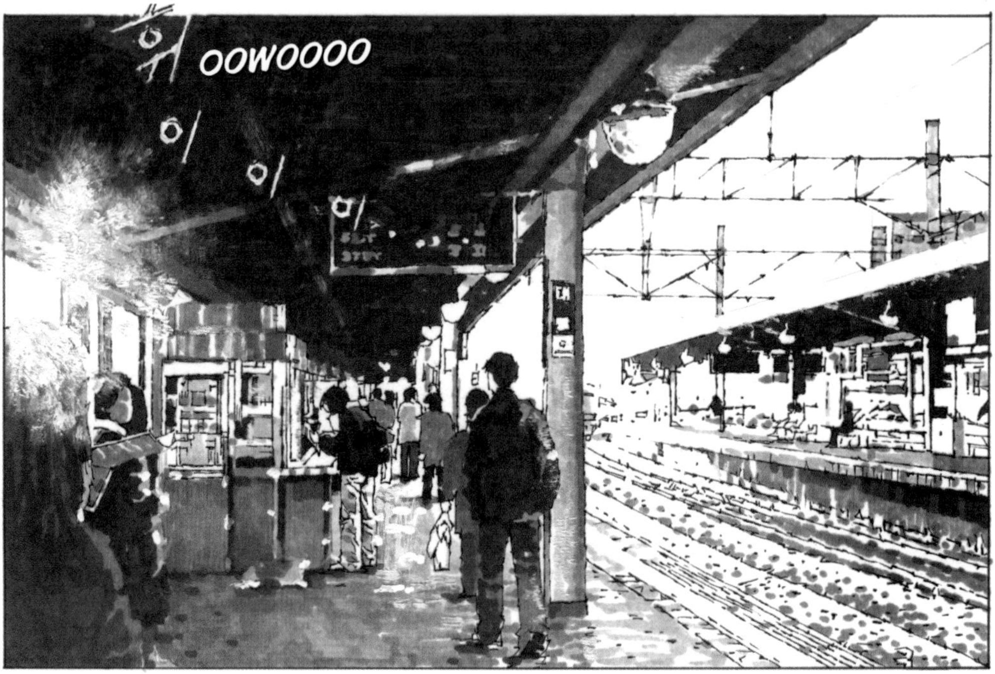
OOWOOOO

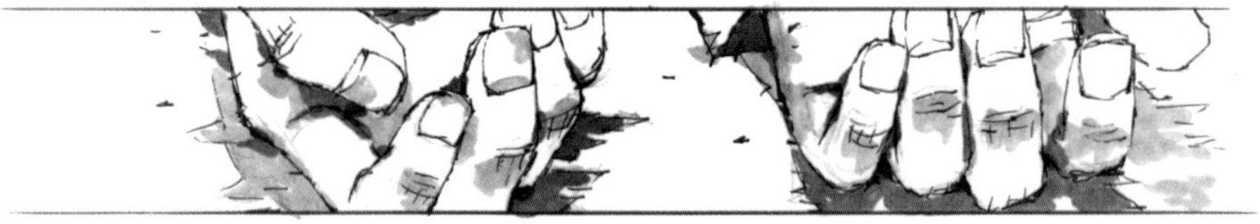

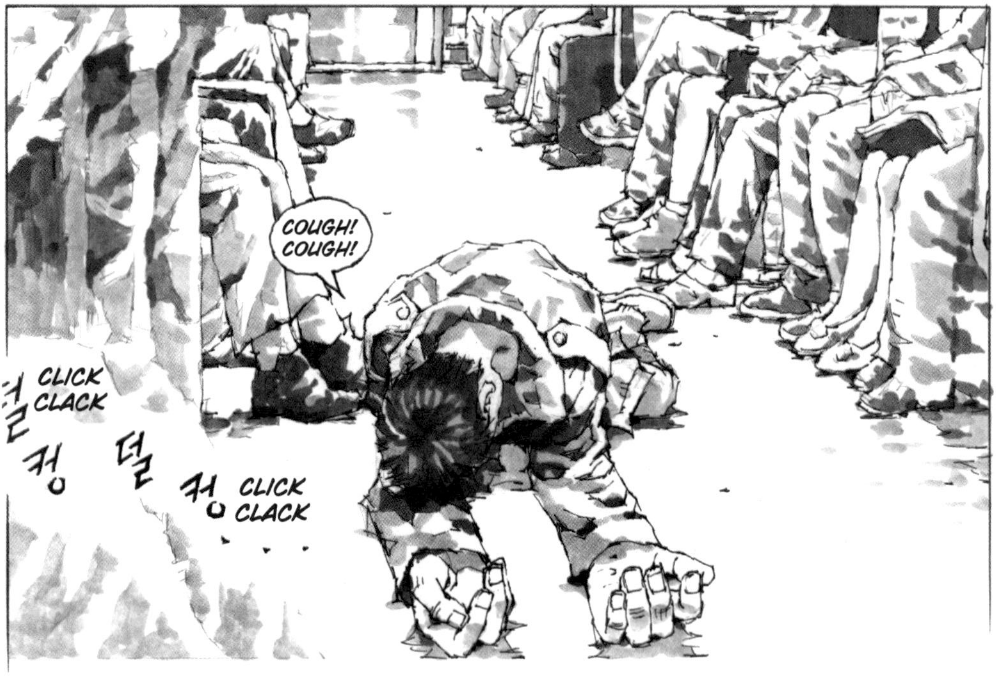
COUGH! COUGH!
덜컹
CLICK CLACK
덜컹
CLICK CLACK

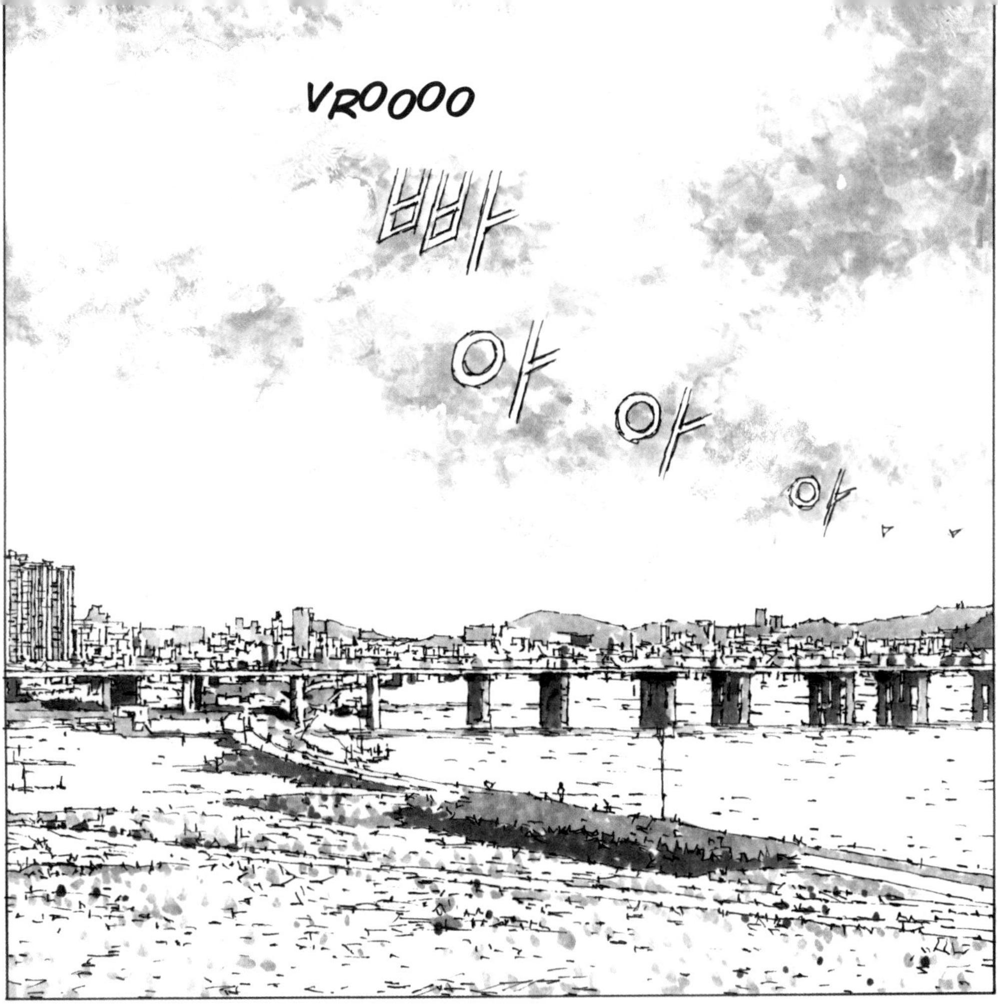
VROOOO
빠
야
야
야

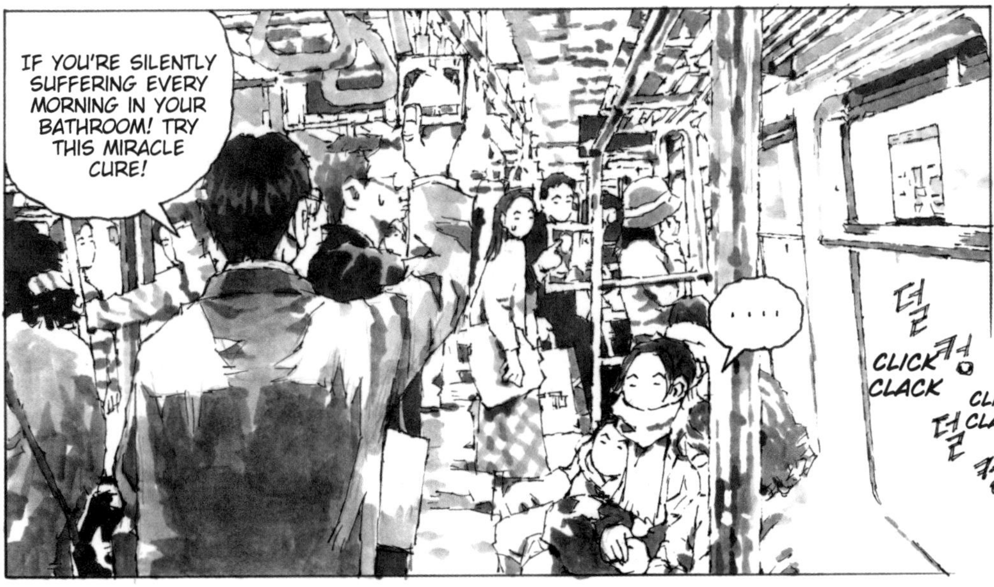
IF YOU'RE SILENTLY SUFFERING EVERY MORNING IN YOUR BATHROOM! TRY THIS MIRACLE CURE!
. . . .
덜컹
CLICK CLACK
덜컹
CLICK CLACK

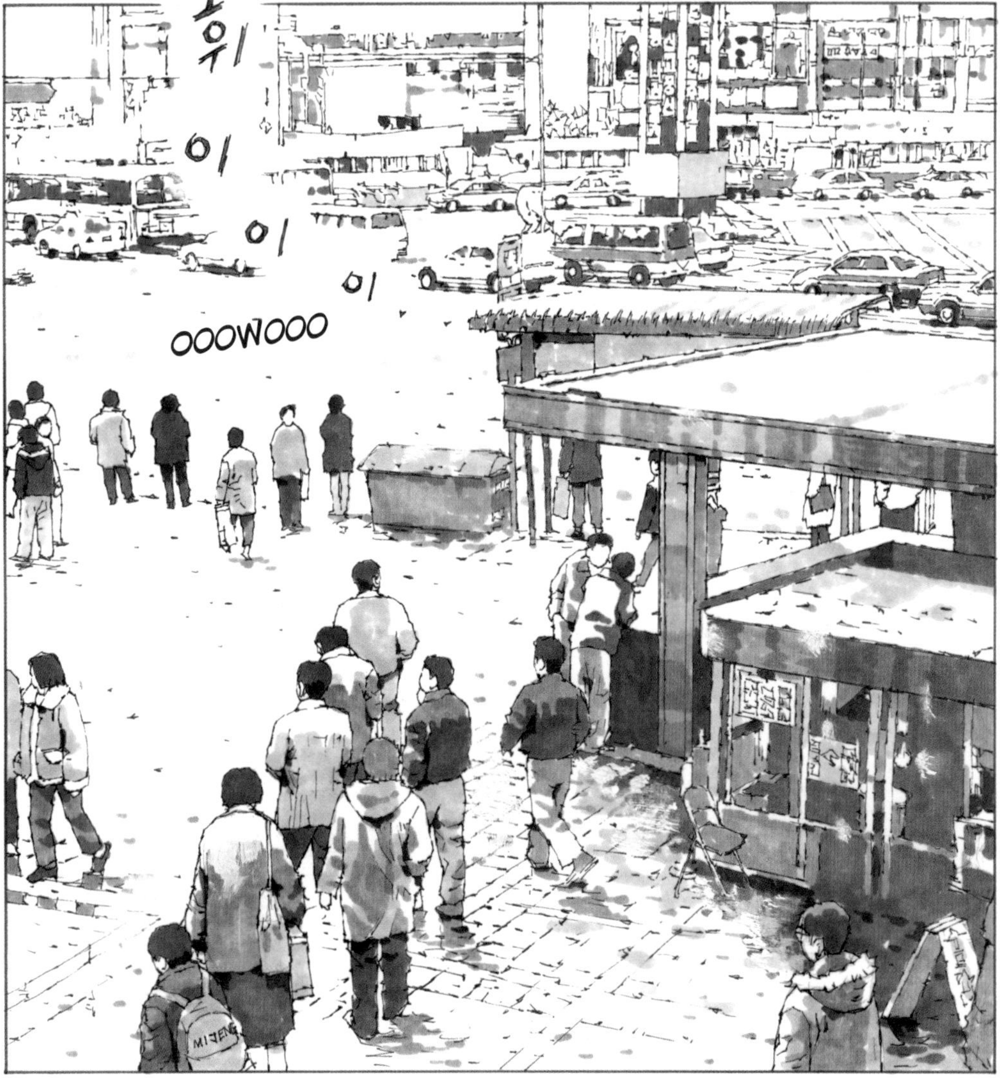
휘이이이
OOOWOOO

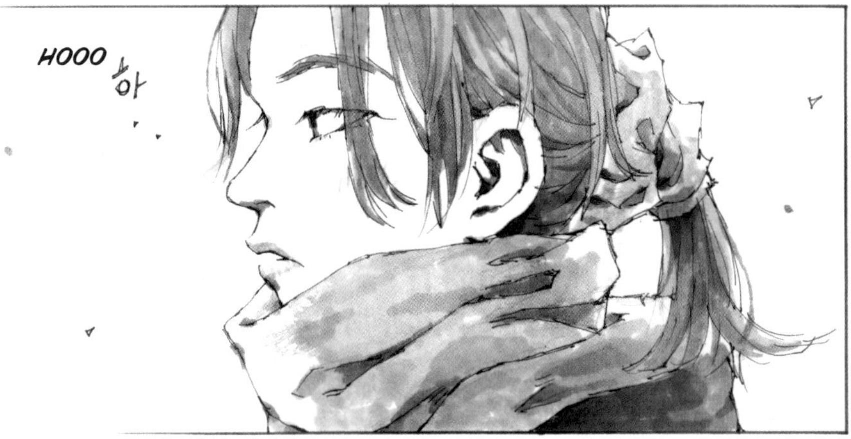
HOOO
하

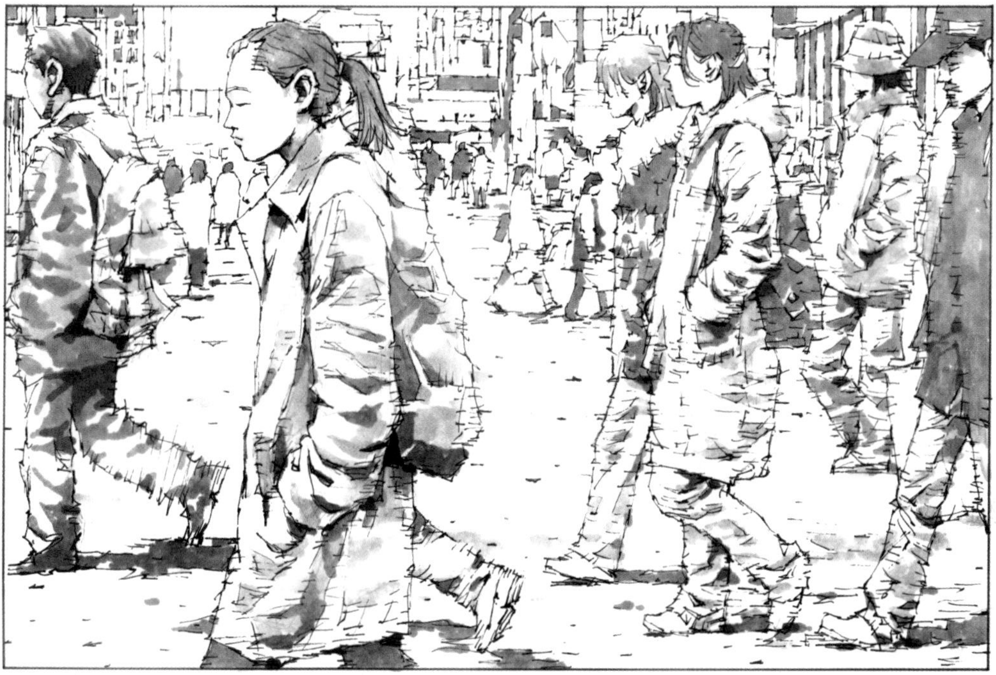

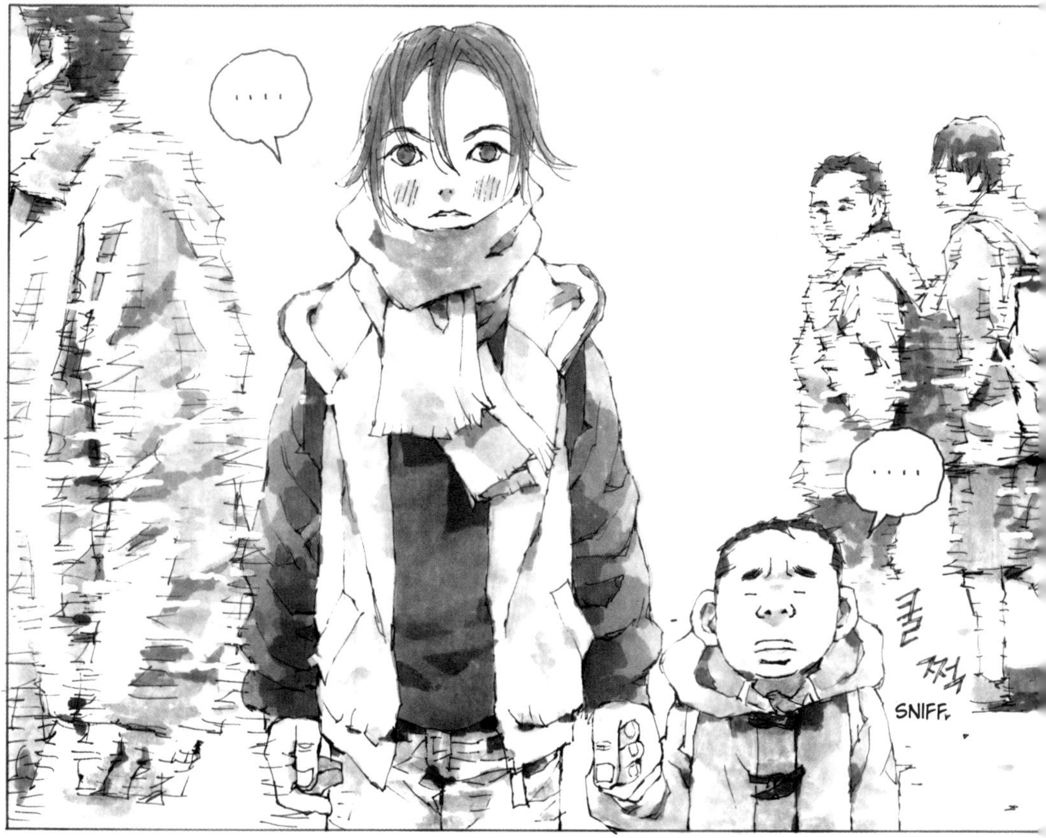
. . . .
. . . .
훌쩍
SNIFF.

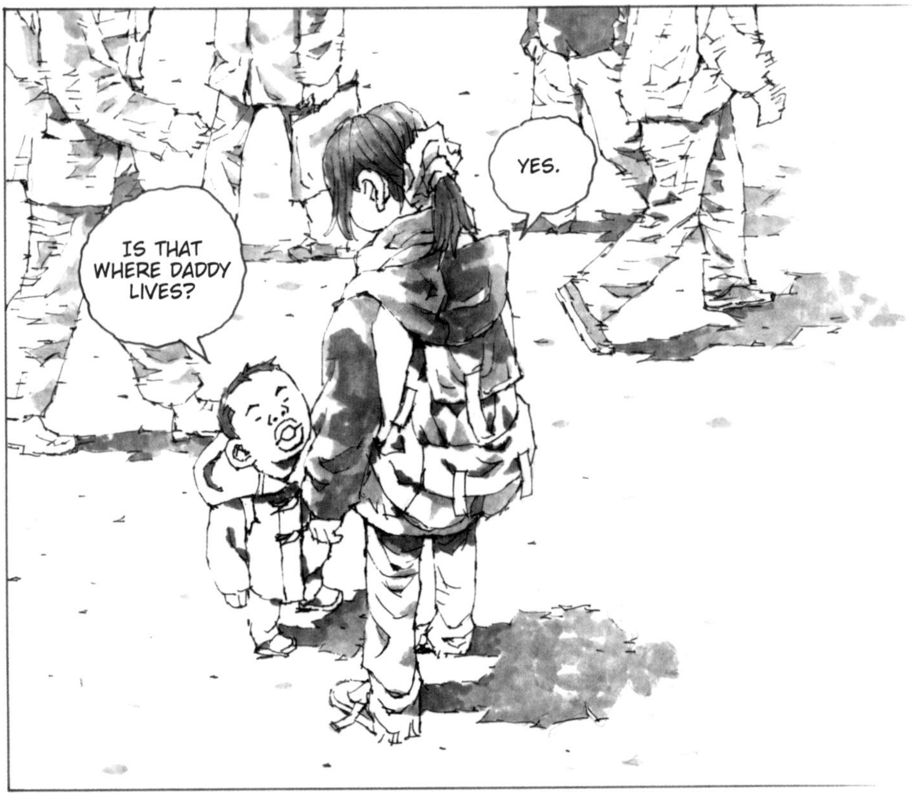
IS THAT WHERE DADDY LIVES?
YES.

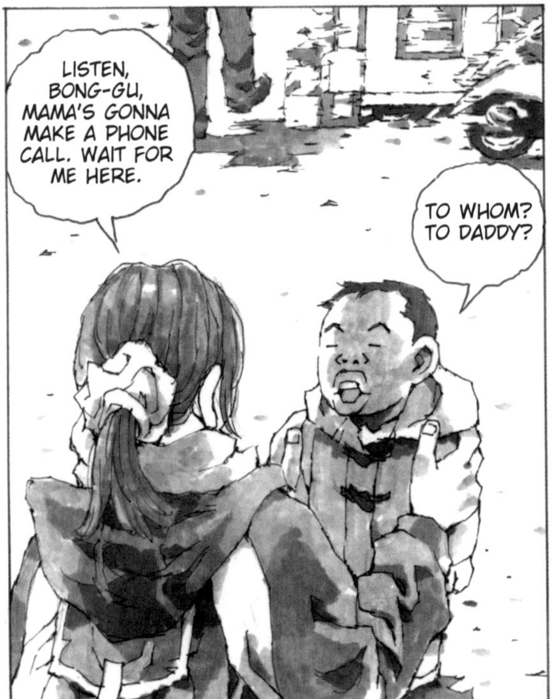
LISTEN, BONG-GU, MAMA'S GONNA MAKE A PHONE CALL. WAIT FOR ME HERE.
TO WHOM? TO DADDY?

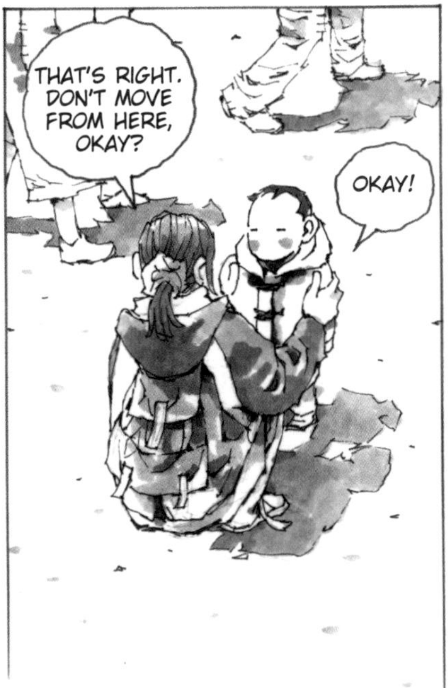
THAT'S RIGHT. DON'T MOVE FROM HERE, OKAY?
OKAY!

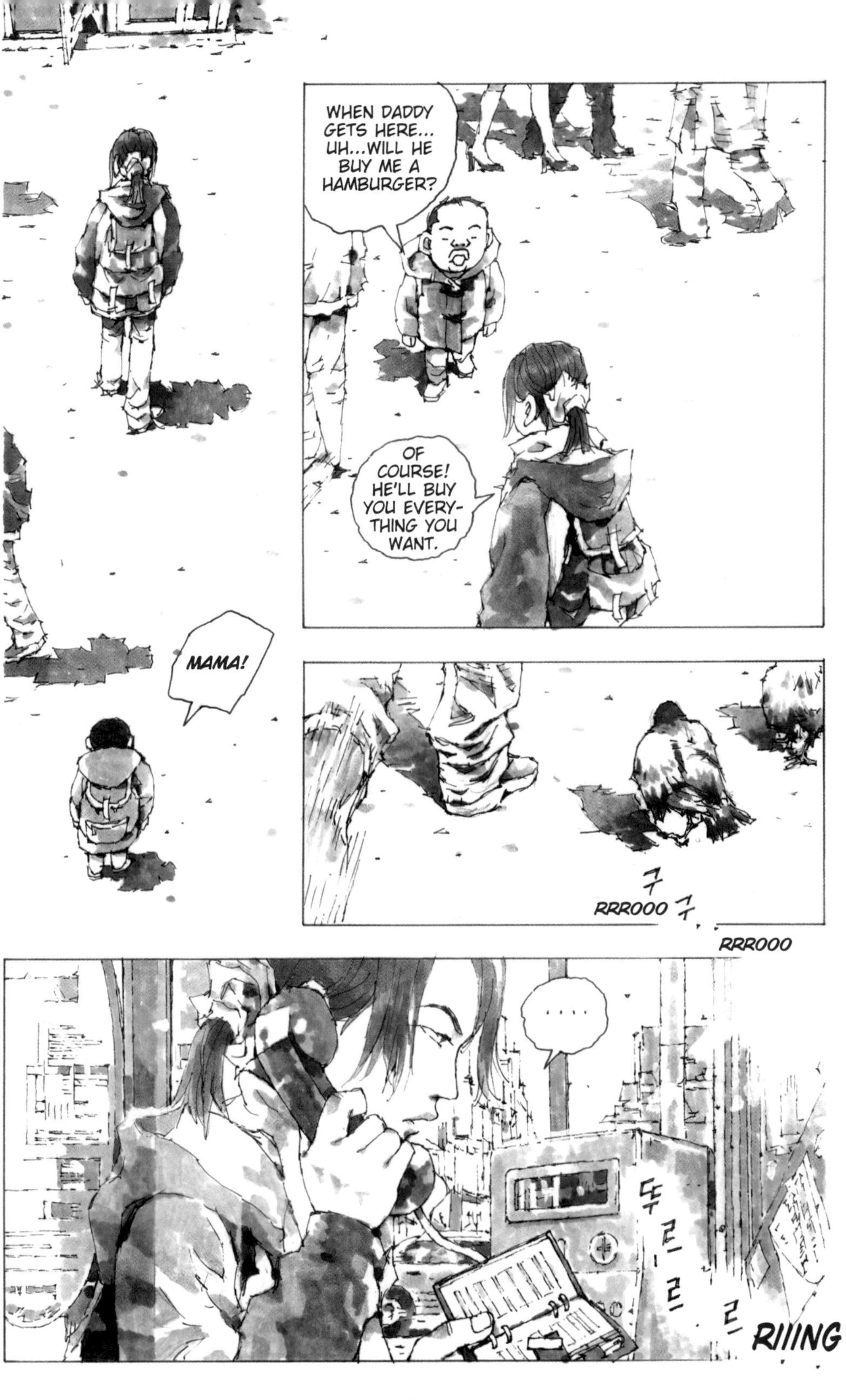
WHEN DADDY GETS HERE... UH...WILL HE BUY ME A HAMBURGER?
OF COURSE! HE'LL BUY YOU EVERY-THING YOU WANT.
MAMA!
RRROOO
RRROOO
....
RIIING

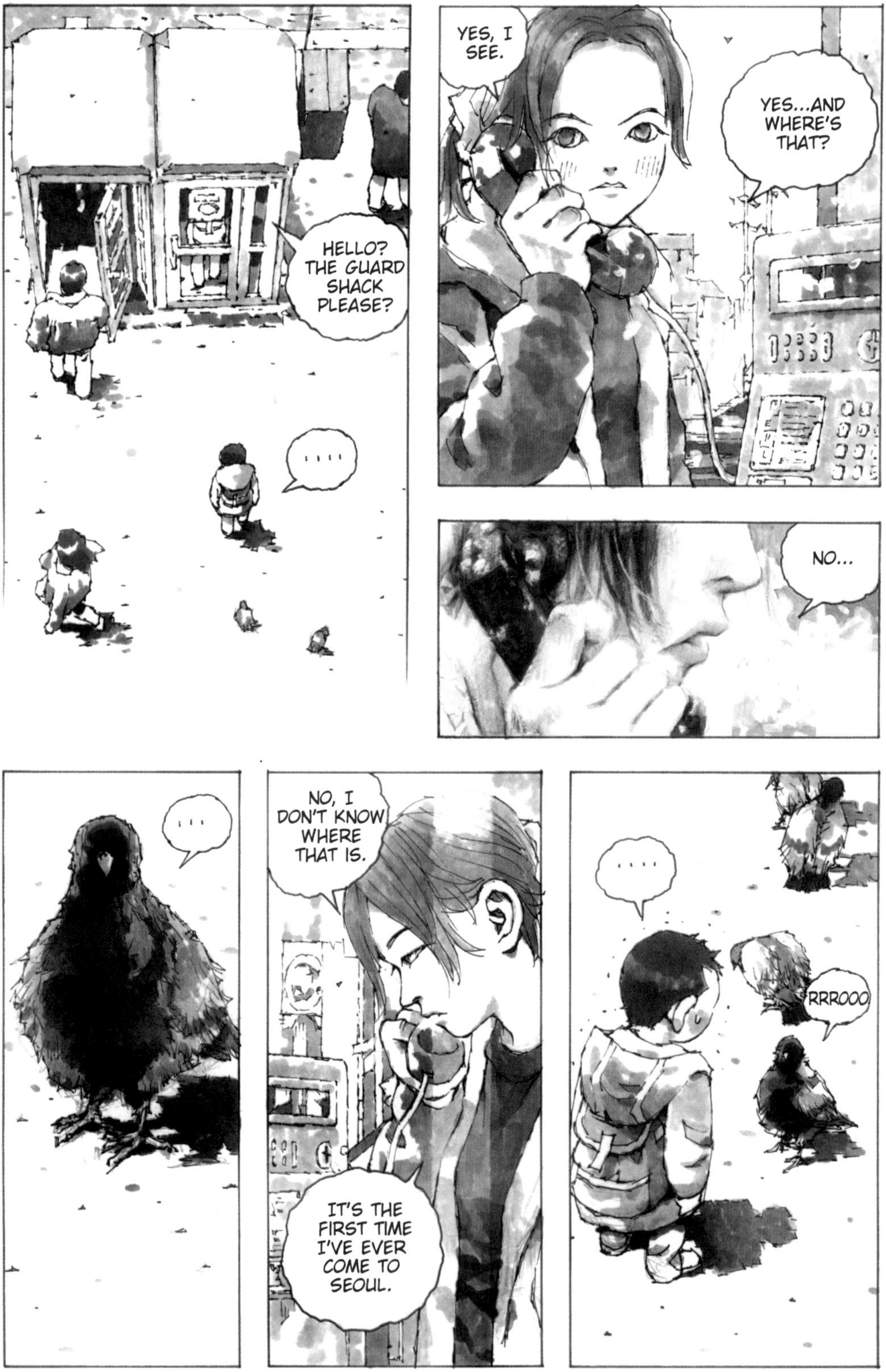
HELLO? THE GUARD SHACK PLEASE?
....
YES, I SEE.
YES...AND WHERE'S THAT?
NO...
...
NO, I DON'T KNOW WHERE THAT IS.
IT'S THE FIRST TIME I'VE EVER COME TO SEOUL.
....
RRROOO

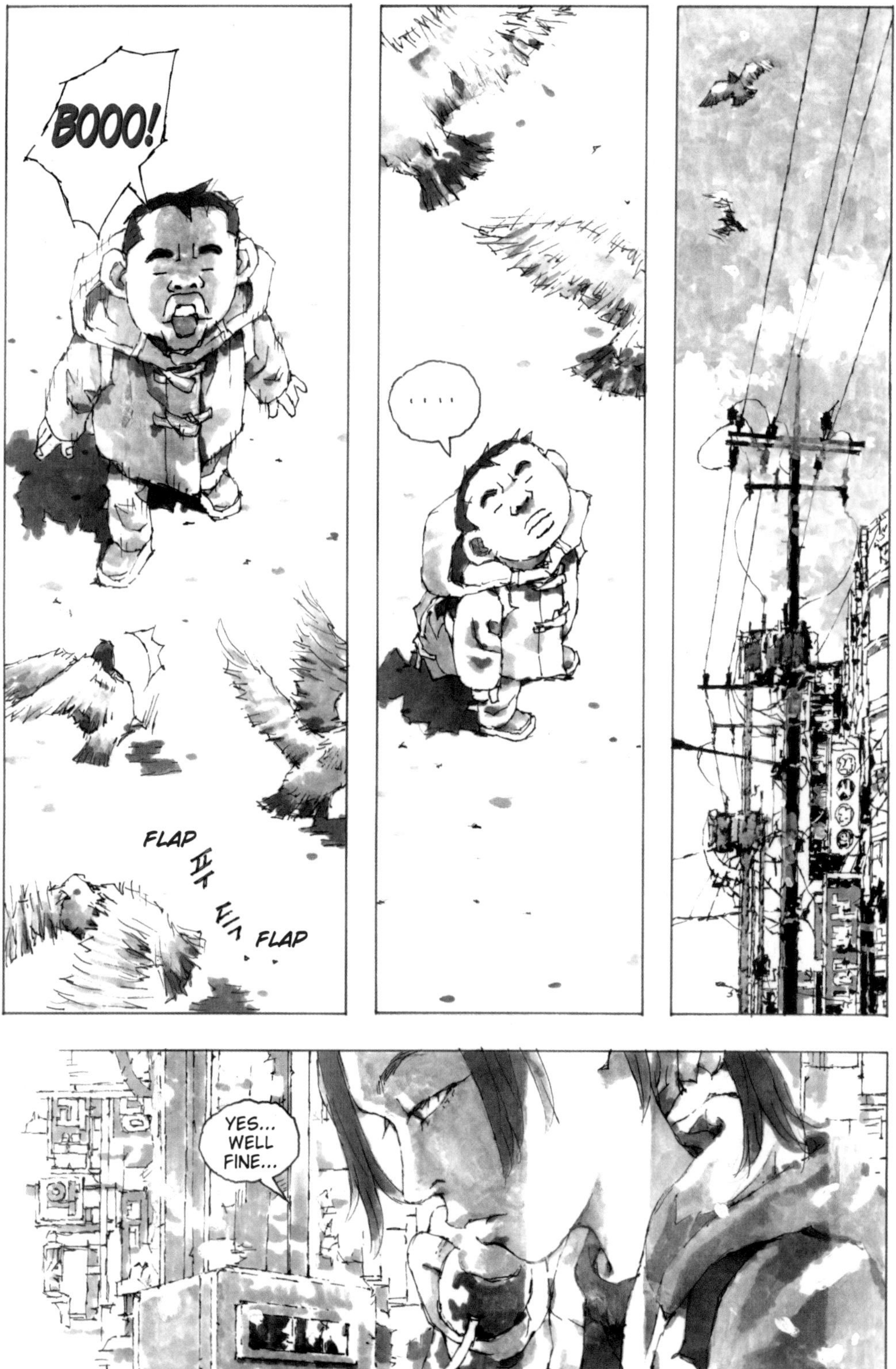
BOOO!
FLAP
FLAP
....
YES... WELL FINE...

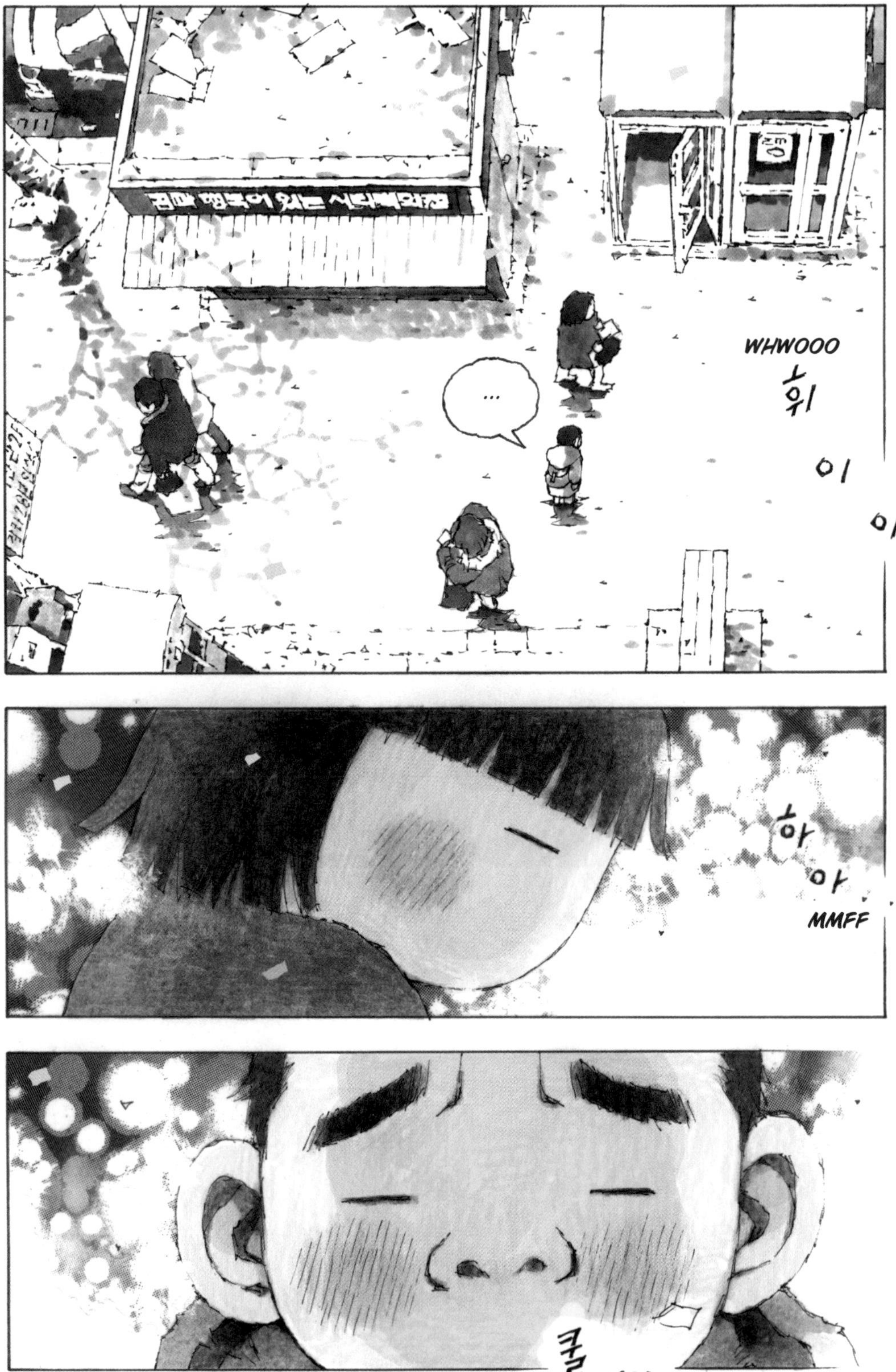
...
WHWOOO
휘
이
이
하
아
MMFF
훌
SNIFF 쩍

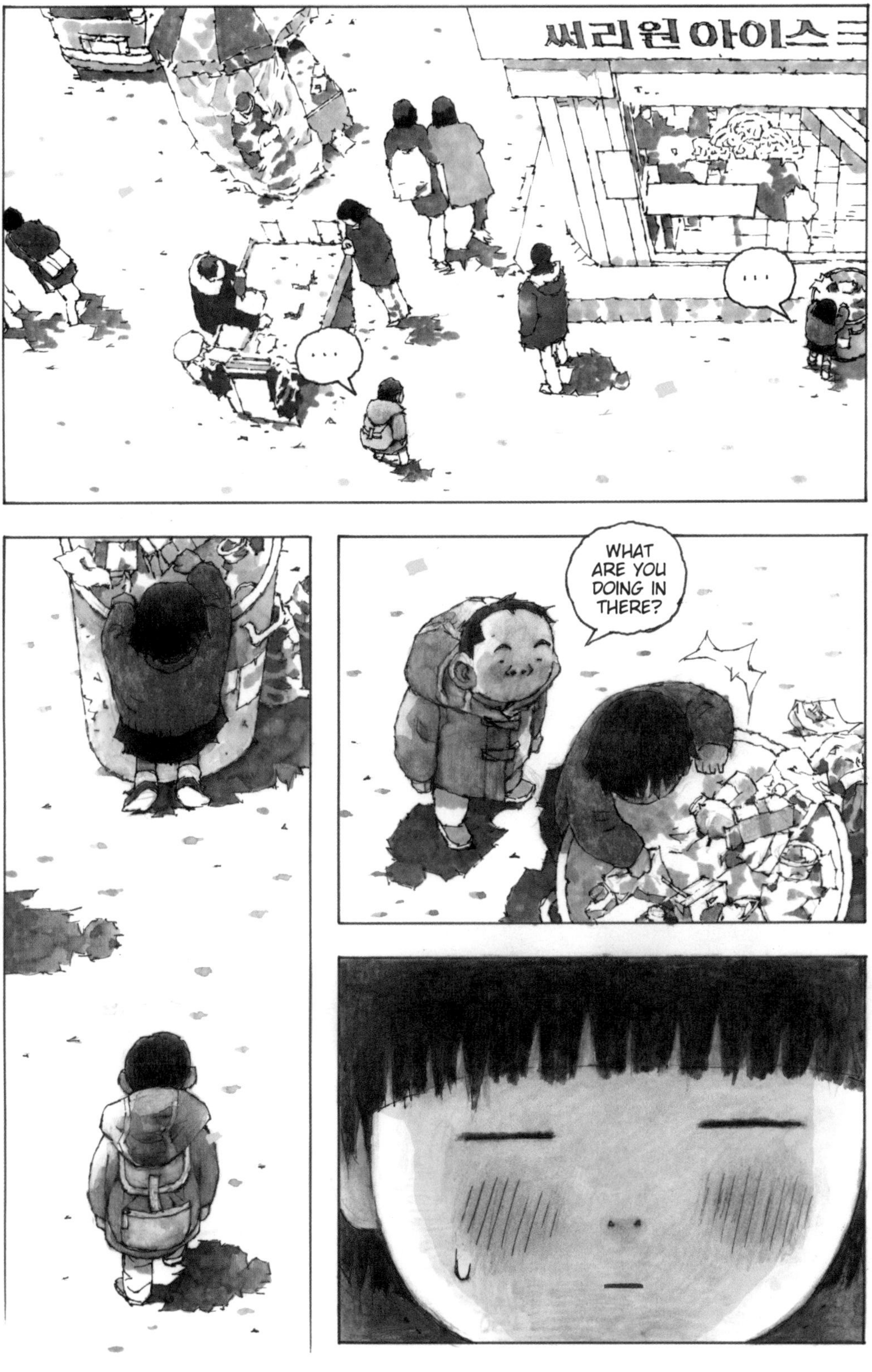
써리원아이스
...
...
WHAT ARE YOU DOING IN THERE?

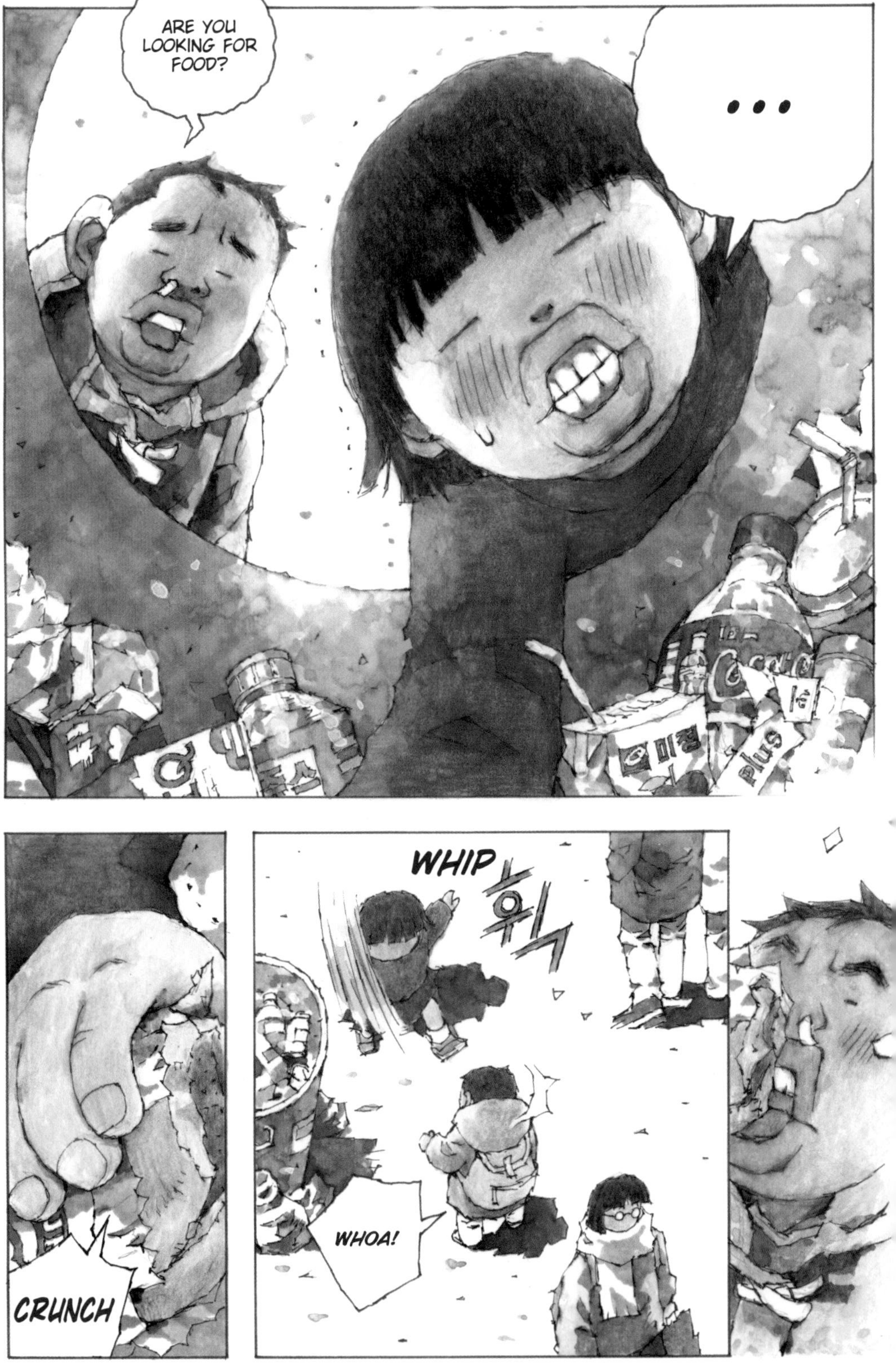
ARE YOU LOOKING FOR FOOD?
• • •
CRUNCH
WHIP
WHOA!

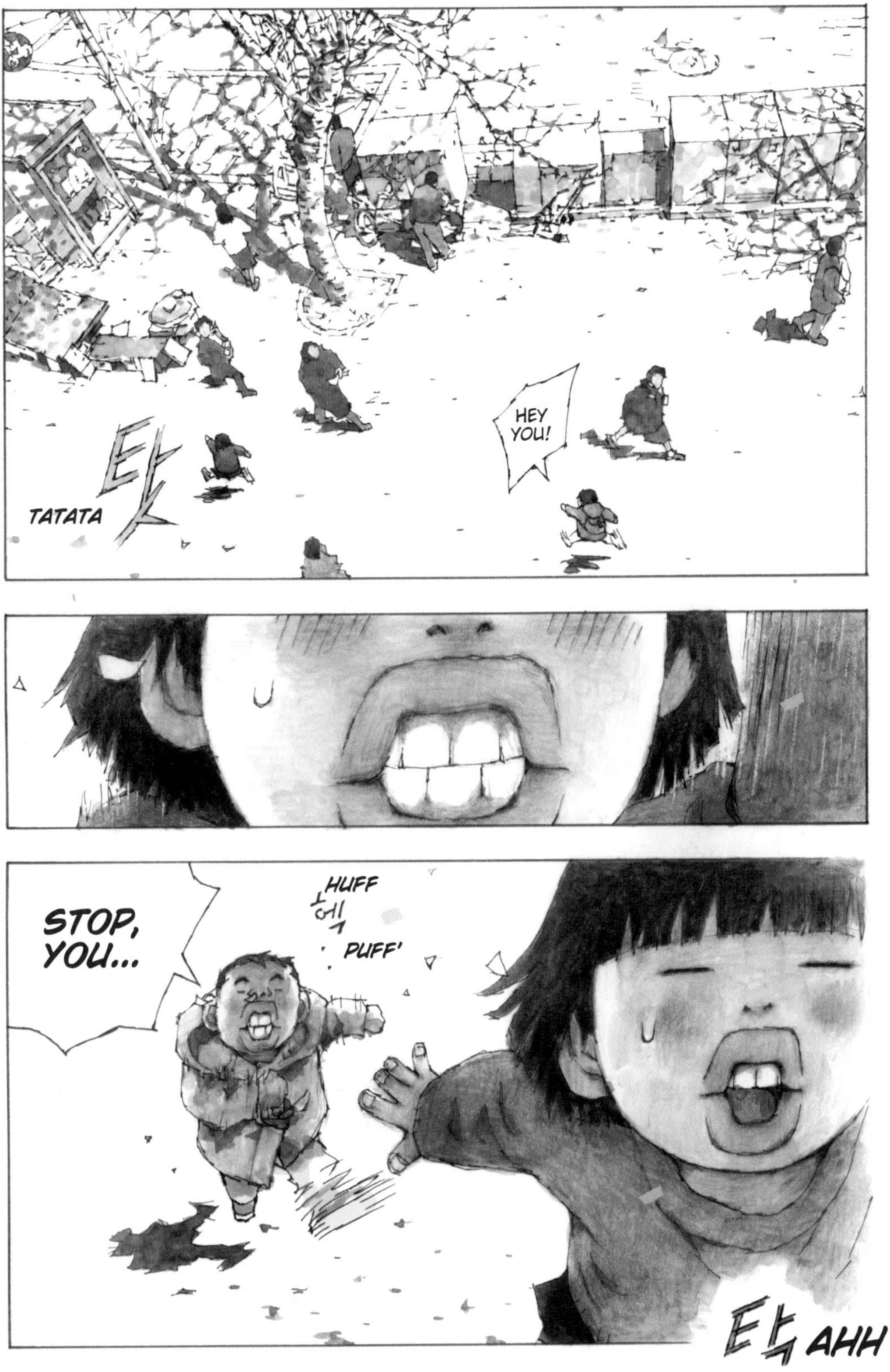
HEY YOU!
탁
TATATA
STOP, YOU...
HUFF
PUFF'
탁
AHH

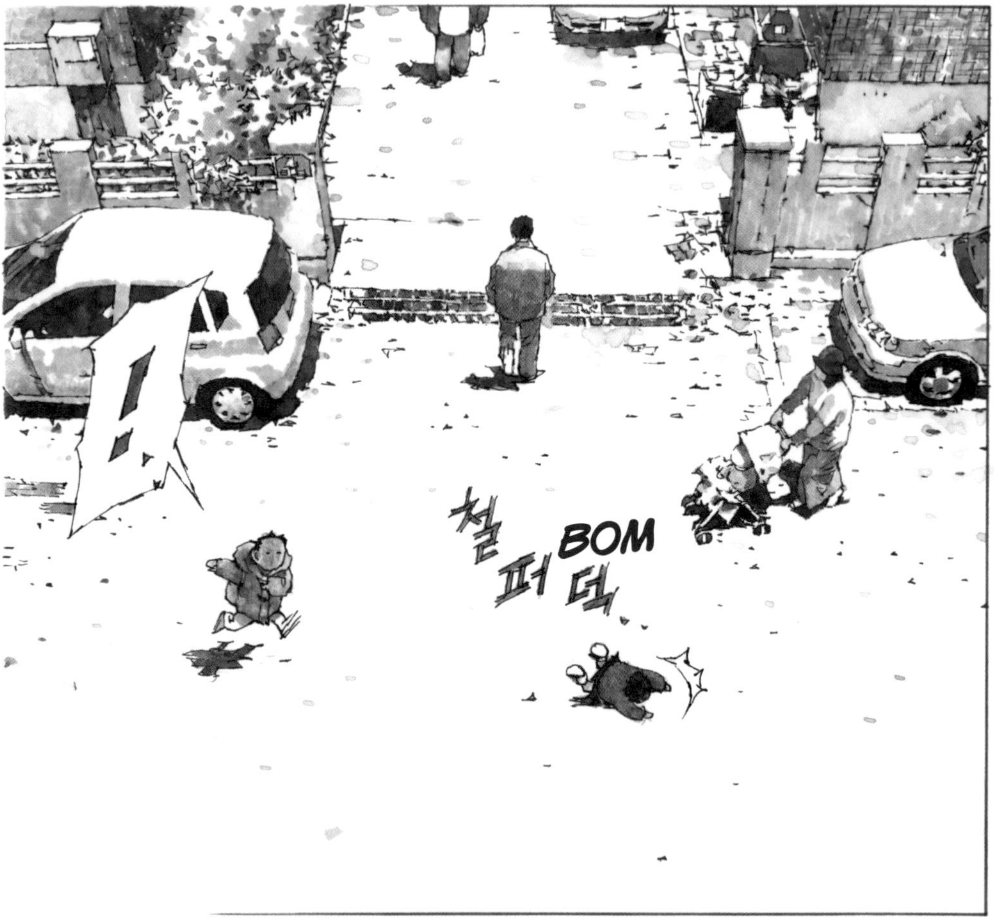
철퍼덕
BOM

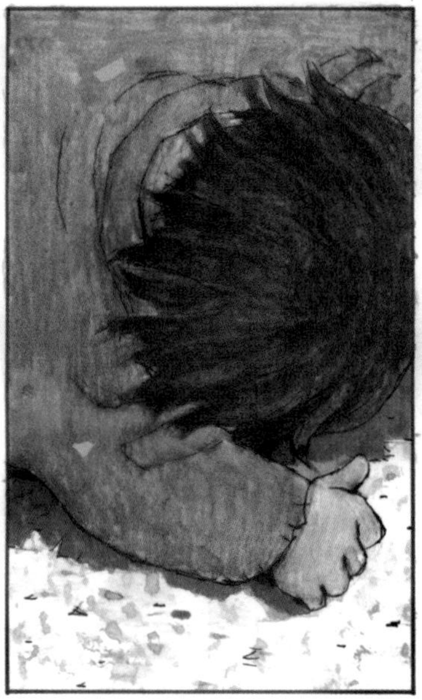

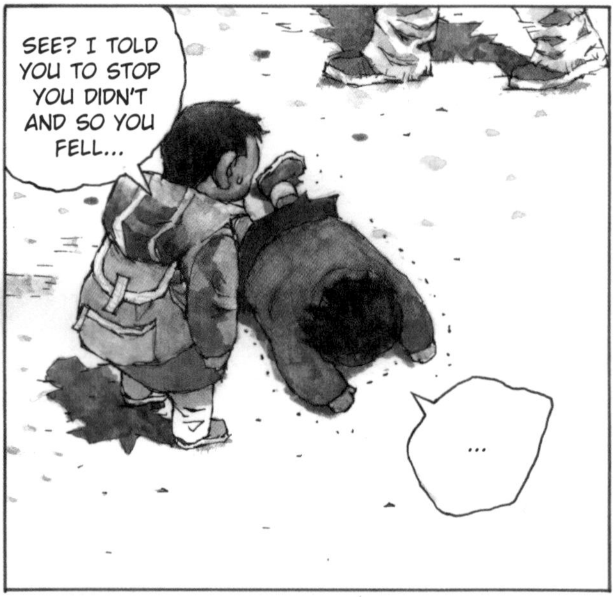
SEE? I TOLD YOU TO STOP YOU DIDN'T AND SO YOU FELL...
...

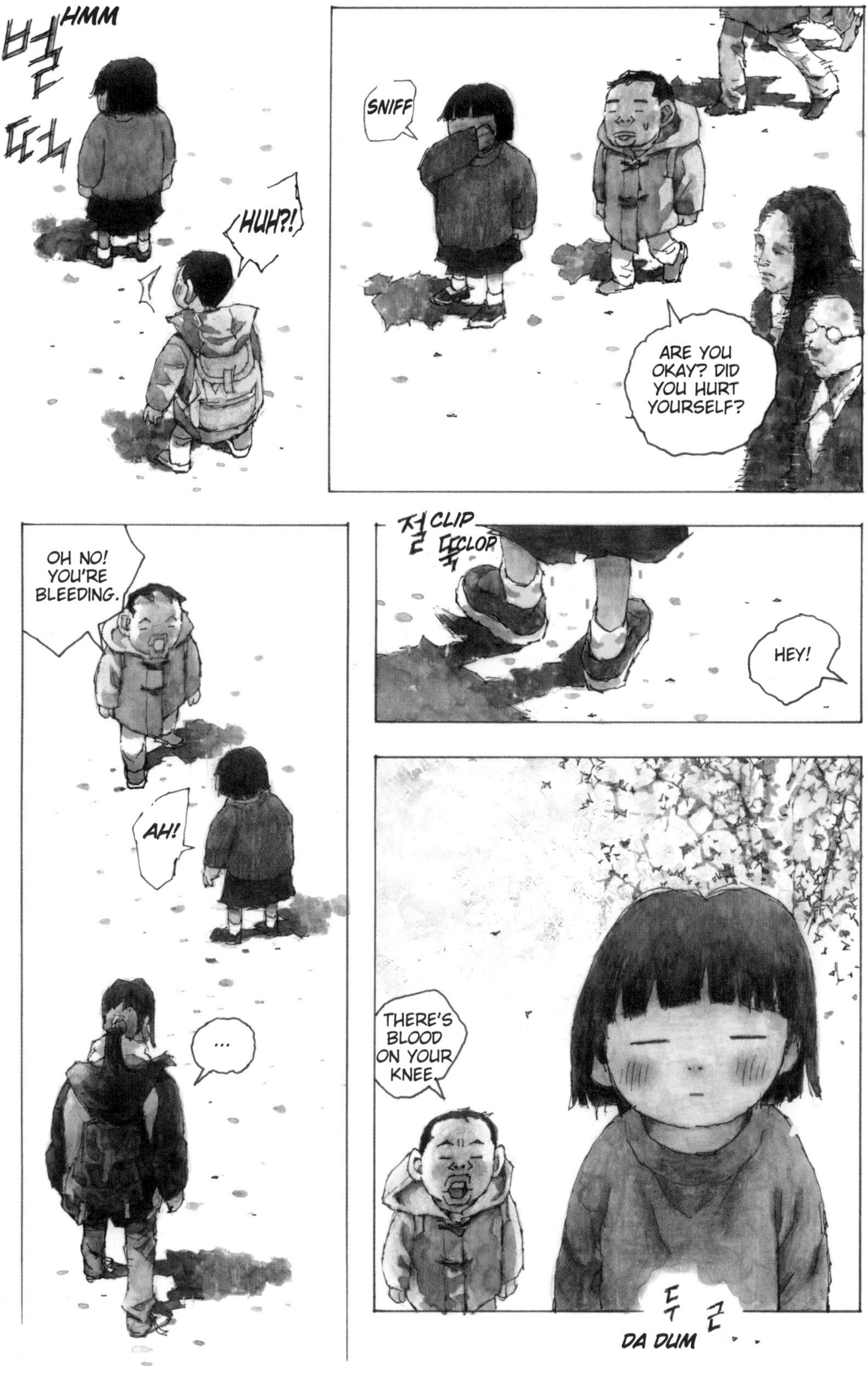
벌떡
HMM
HUH?!
SNIFF
ARE YOU OKAY? DID YOU HURT YOURSELF?
OH NO! YOU'RE BLEEDING.
AH!
...
절뚝
CLIP CLOP
HEY!
THERE'S BLOOD ON YOUR KNEE.
두근
DA DUM

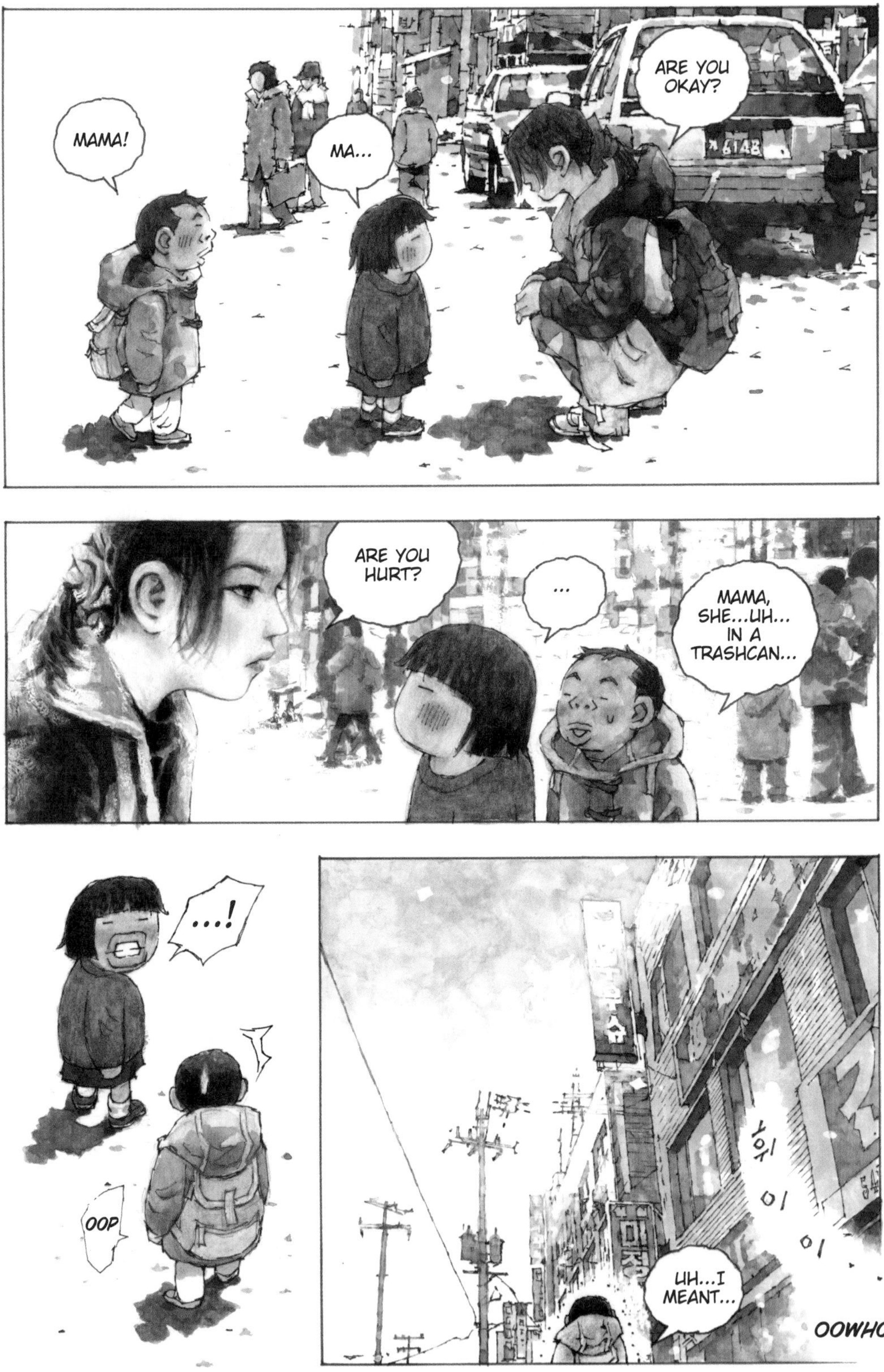
MAMA!
MA...
ARE YOU OKAY?
ARE YOU HURT?
...
MAMA, SHE...UH... IN A TRASHCAN...
...!
OOP
휘이이
UH...I MEANT...
OOWHO

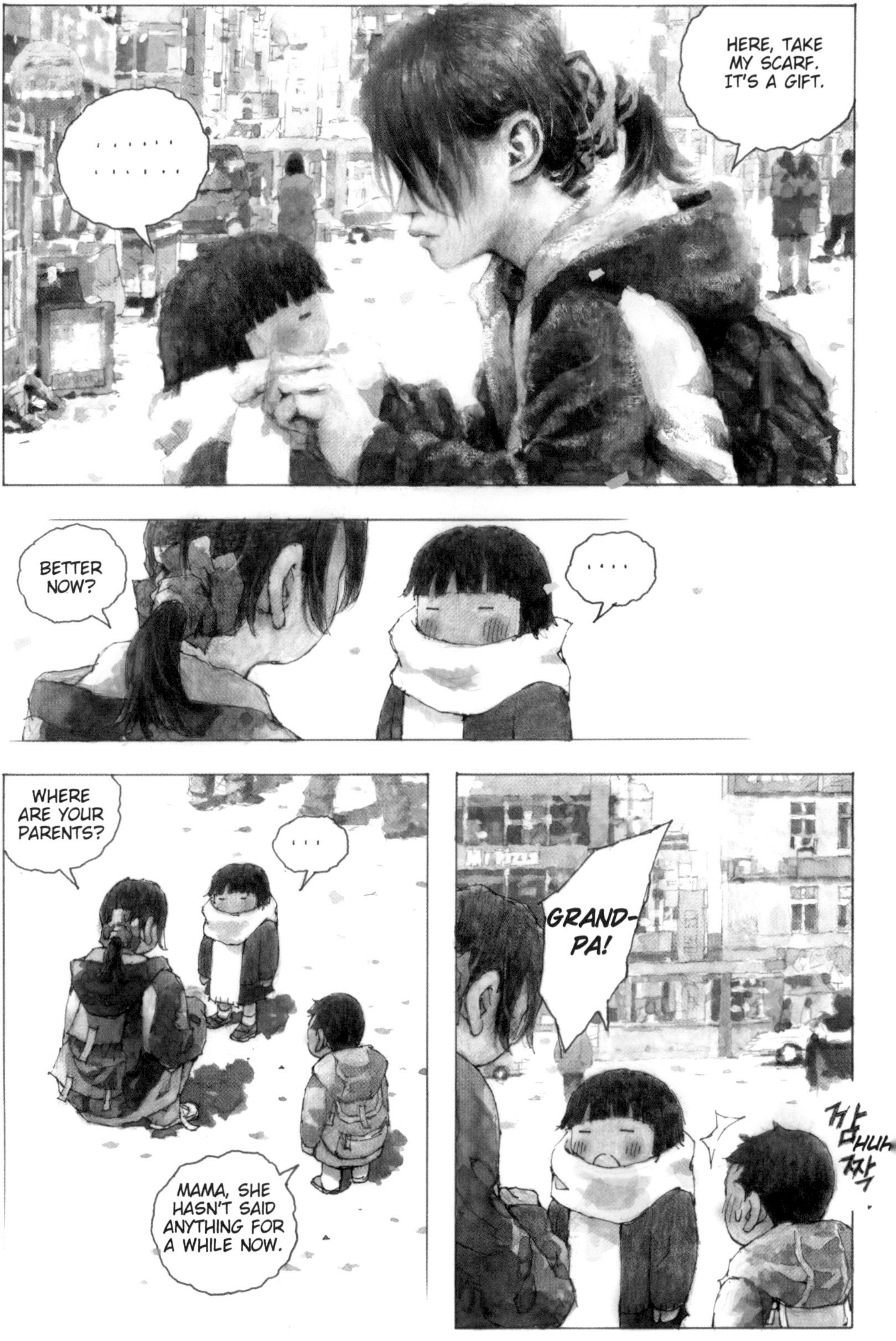

....
....
HERE, TAKE MY SCARF. IT'S A GIFT.
BETTER NOW?
....
WHERE ARE YOUR PARENTS?
...
MAMA, SHE HASN'T SAID ANYTHING FOR A WHILE NOW.
GRAND-PA!

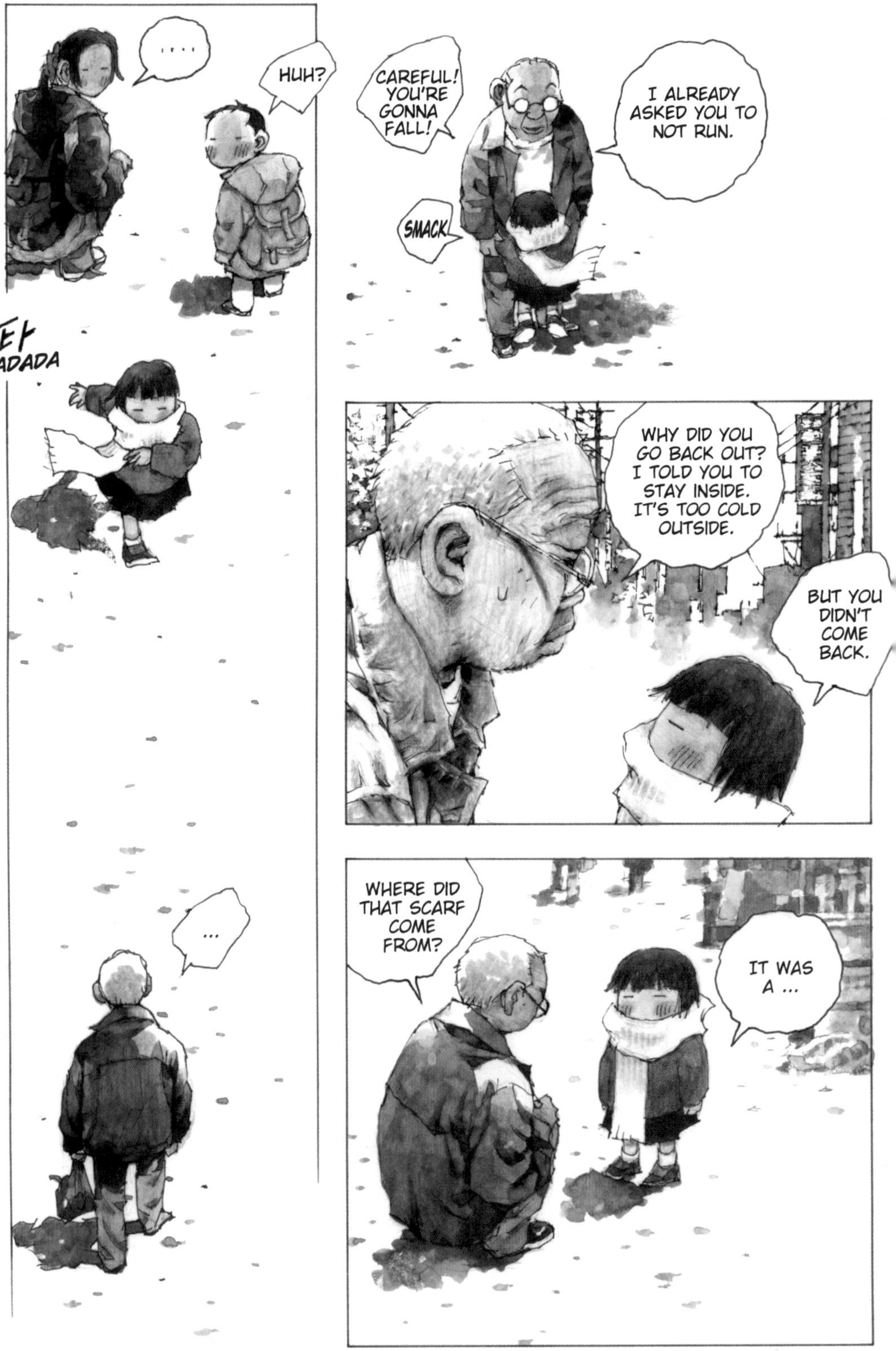
. . . .
HUH?
TADADA
...
CAREFUL! YOU'RE GONNA FALL!
SMACK
I ALREADY ASKED YOU TO NOT RUN.
WHY DID YOU GO BACK OUT? I TOLD YOU TO STAY INSIDE. IT'S TOO COLD OUTSIDE.
BUT YOU DIDN'T COME BACK.
WHERE DID THAT SCARF COME FROM?
IT WAS A ...

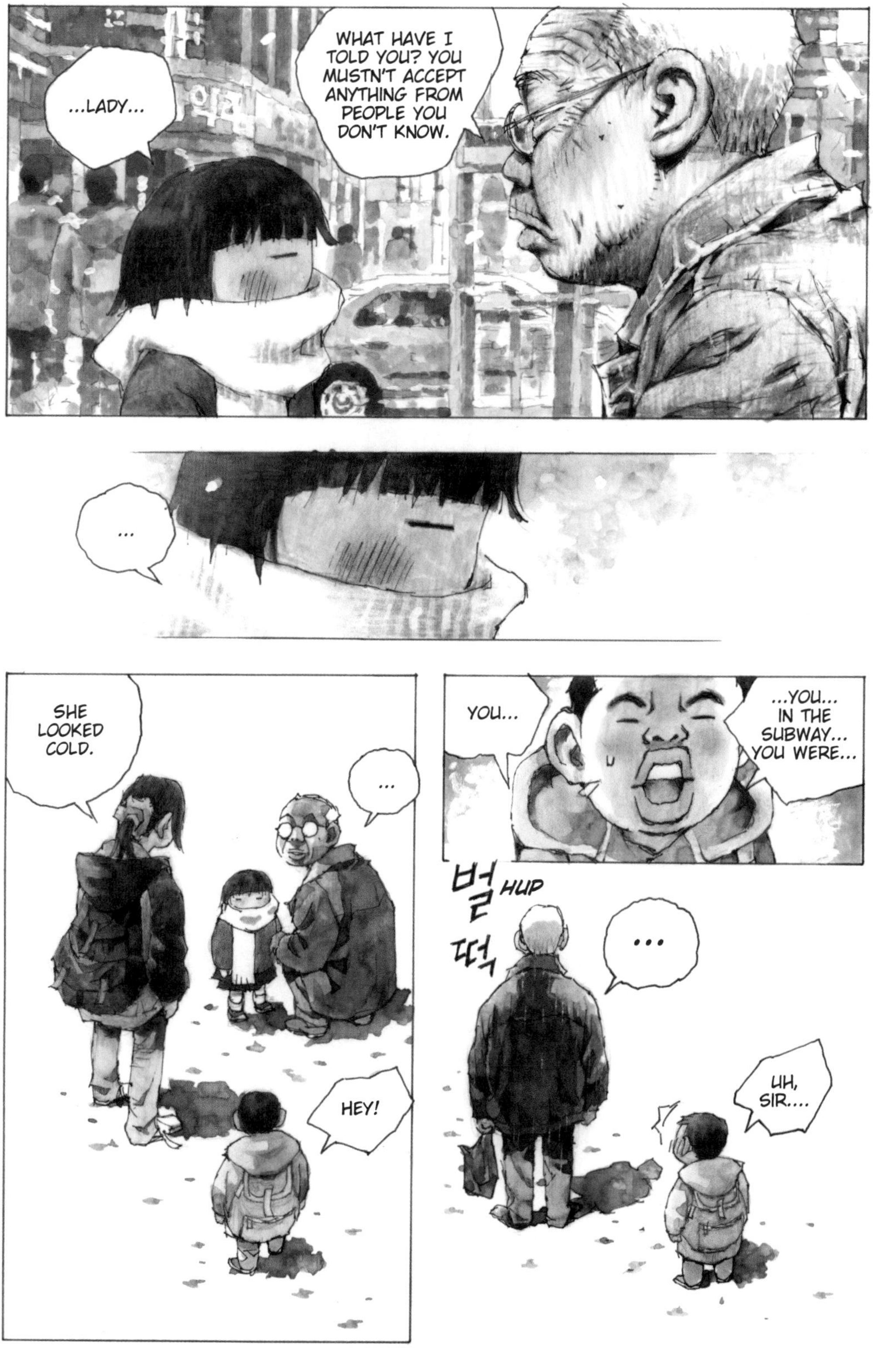
...LADY...
WHAT HAVE I TOLD YOU? YOU MUSTN'T ACCEPT ANYTHING FROM PEOPLE YOU DON'T KNOW.
...
SHE LOOKED COLD.
...
HEY!
YOU...
...YOU... IN THE SUBWAY... YOU WERE...
벌떡
HUP
...
UH, SIR....

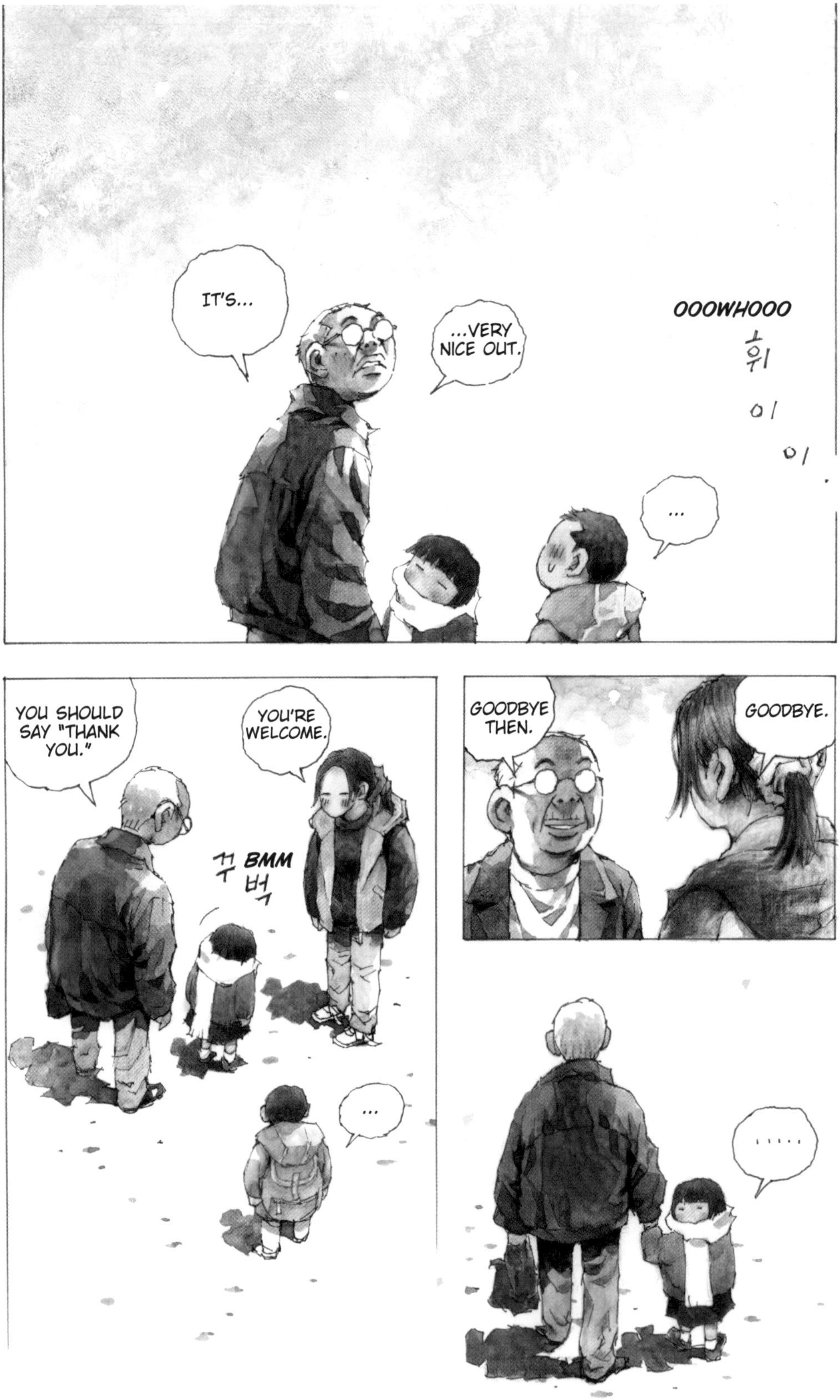
IT'S...
...VERY NICE OUT.
OOOWHOOO
휘
이
이
...
YOU SHOULD SAY "THANK YOU."
YOU'RE WELCOME.
BMM
꾸벅
...
GOODBYE THEN.
GOODBYE.
.....

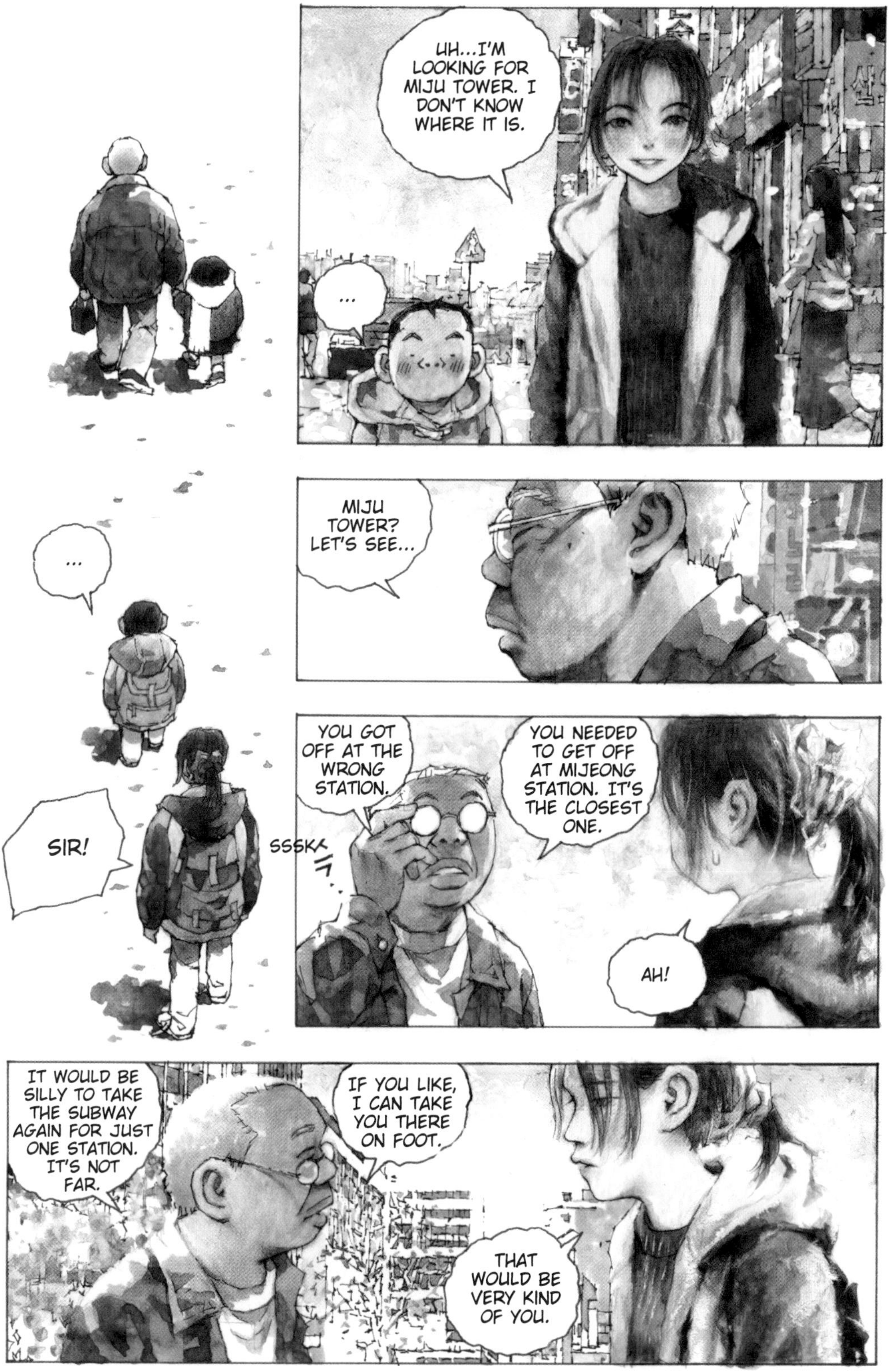
UH...I'M LOOKING FOR MIJU TOWER. I DON'T KNOW WHERE IT IS.
...
MIJU TOWER? LET'S SEE...
...
SIR!
SSSKK
YOU GOT OFF AT THE WRONG STATION.
YOU NEEDED TO GET OFF AT MIJEONG STATION. IT'S THE CLOSEST ONE.
AH!
IT WOULD BE SILLY TO TAKE THE SUBWAY AGAIN FOR JUST ONE STATION. IT'S NOT FAR.
IF YOU LIKE, I CAN TAKE YOU THERE ON FOOT.
THAT WOULD BE VERY KIND OF YOU.

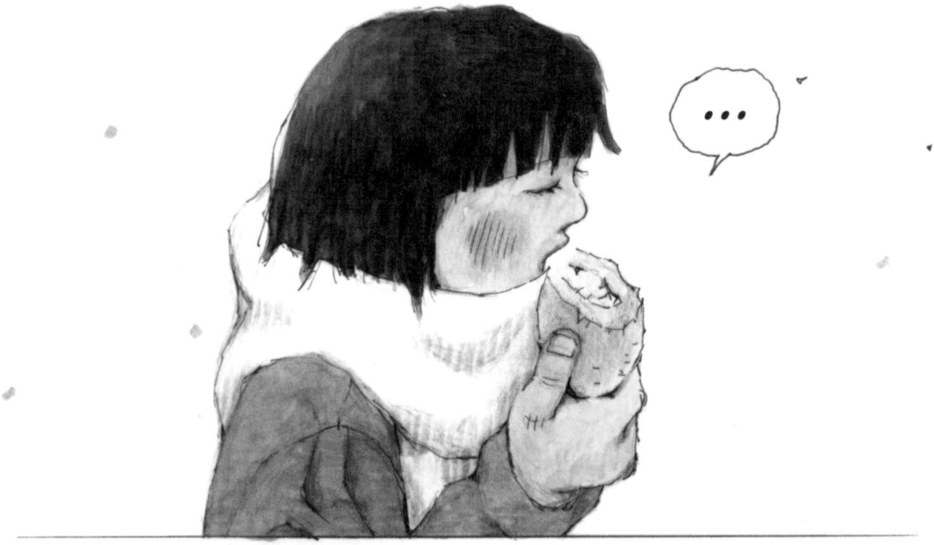
...

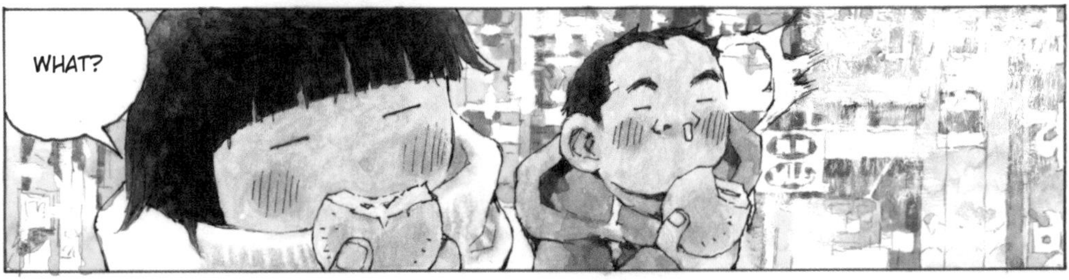
WHAT?

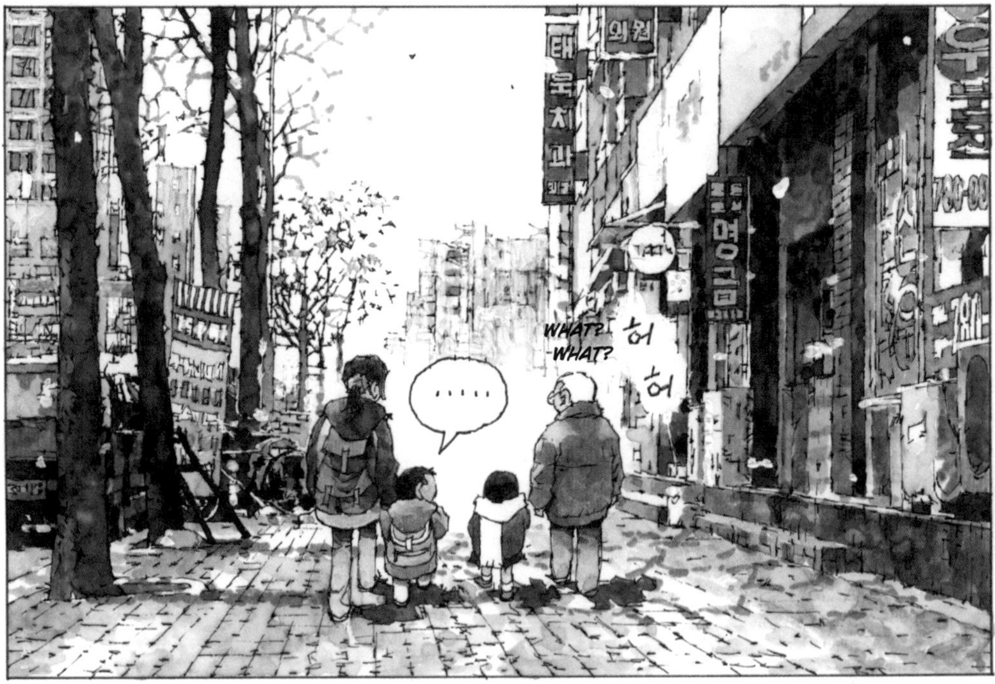
.....
WHAT? WHAT?
허 허

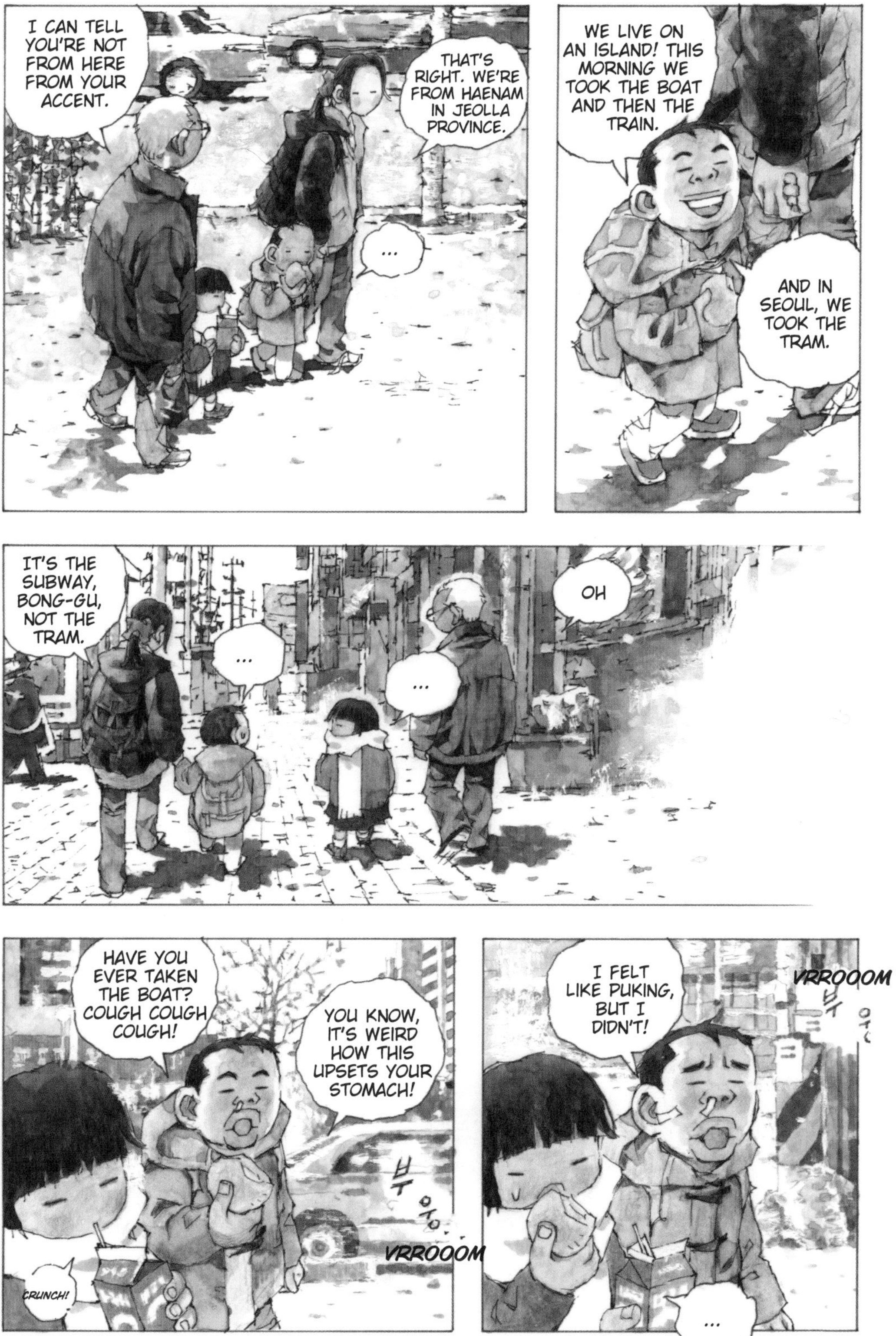
I CAN TELL YOU'RE NOT FROM HERE FROM YOUR ACCENT.
THAT'S RIGHT. WE'RE FROM HAENAM IN JEOLLA PROVINCE.
...
WE LIVE ON AN ISLAND! THIS MORNING WE TOOK THE BOAT AND THEN THE TRAIN.
AND IN SEOUL, WE TOOK THE TRAM.
IT'S THE SUBWAY, BONG-GU, NOT THE TRAM.
...
...
OH
HAVE YOU EVER TAKEN THE BOAT? COUGH COUGH COUGH!
YOU KNOW, IT'S WEIRD HOW THIS UPSETS YOUR STOMACH!
VRROOOM
CRUNCH!
I FELT LIKE PUKING, BUT I DIDN'T!
VRROOOM
...

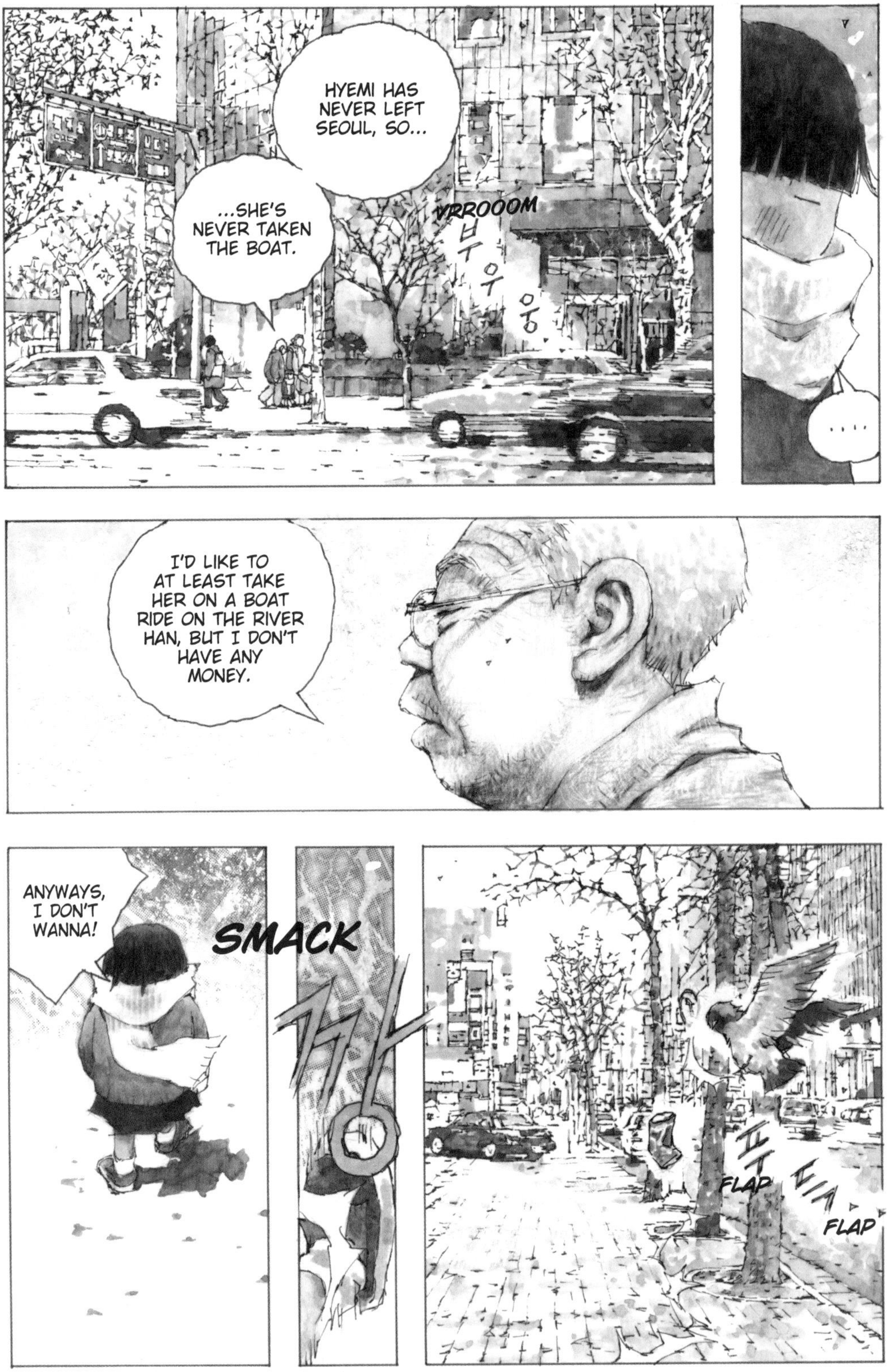
HYEMI HAS NEVER LEFT SEOUL, SO...
...SHE'S NEVER TAKEN THE BOAT.
VRROOOM
부우웅
. . . .
I'D LIKE TO AT LEAST TAKE HER ON A BOAT RIDE ON THE RIVER HAN, BUT I DON'T HAVE ANY MONEY.
ANYWAYS, I DON'T WANNA!
SMACK
FLAP
FLAP

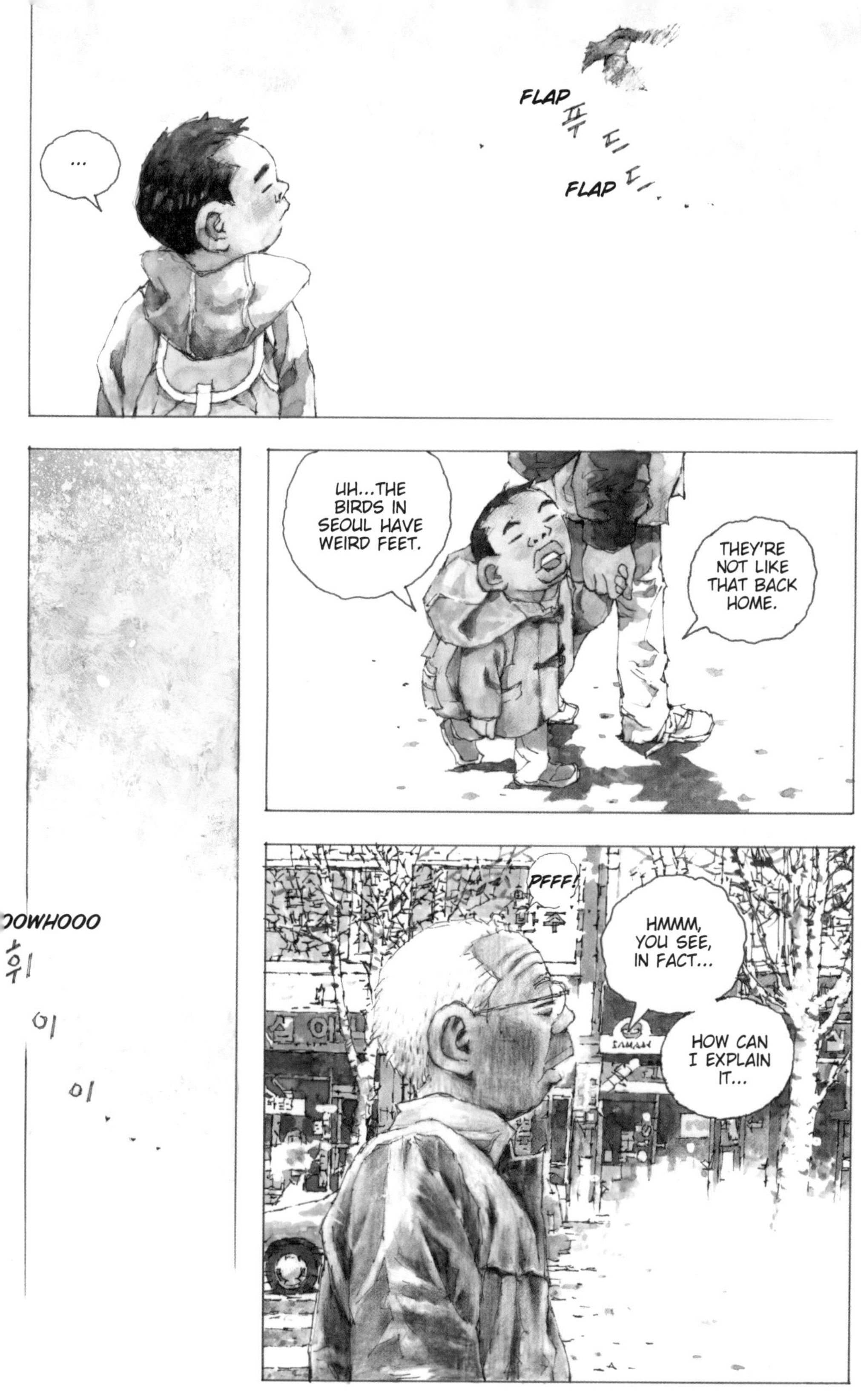
FLAP
푸드드
FLAP
...
OWHOOO
휘이이
UH...THE BIRDS IN SEOUL HAVE WEIRD FEET.
THEY'RE NOT LIKE THAT BACK HOME.
PFFF!
HMMM, YOU SEE, IN FACT...
HOW CAN I EXPLAIN IT...

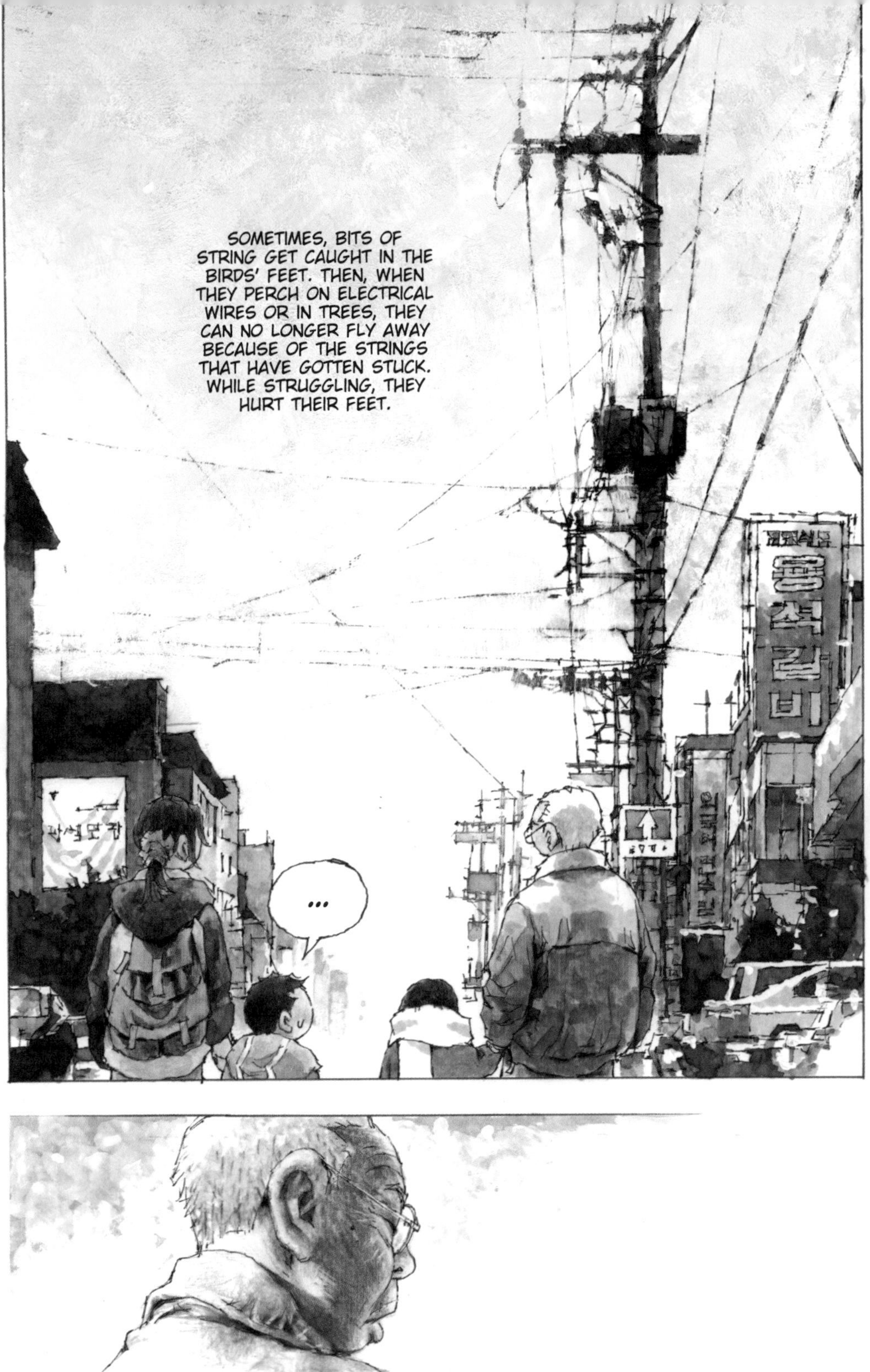
SOMETIMES, BITS OF STRING GET CAUGHT IN THE BIRDS' FEET. THEN, WHEN THEY PERCH ON ELECTRICAL WIRES OR IN TREES, THEY CAN NO LONGER FLY AWAY BECAUSE OF THE STRINGS THAT HAVE GOTTEN STUCK. WHILE STRUGGLING, THEY HURT THEIR FEET.
...

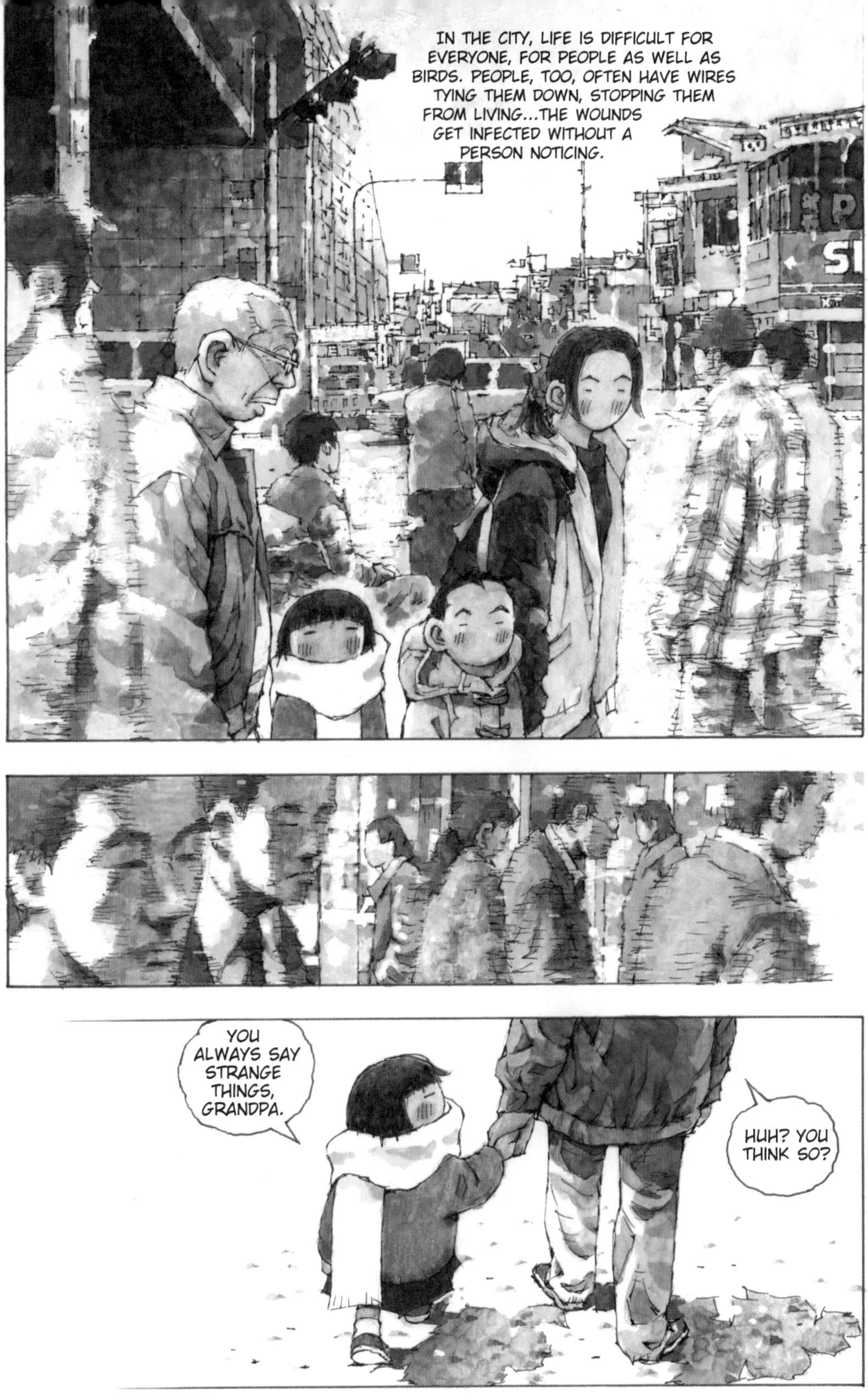
IN THE CITY, LIFE IS DIFFICULT FOR EVERYONE, FOR PEOPLE AS WELL AS BIRDS. PEOPLE, TOO, OFTEN HAVE WIRES TYING THEM DOWN, STOPPING THEM FROM LIVING...THE WOUNDS GET INFECTED WITHOUT A PERSON NOTICING.
YOU ALWAYS SAY STRANGE THINGS, GRANDPA.
HUH? YOU THINK SO?

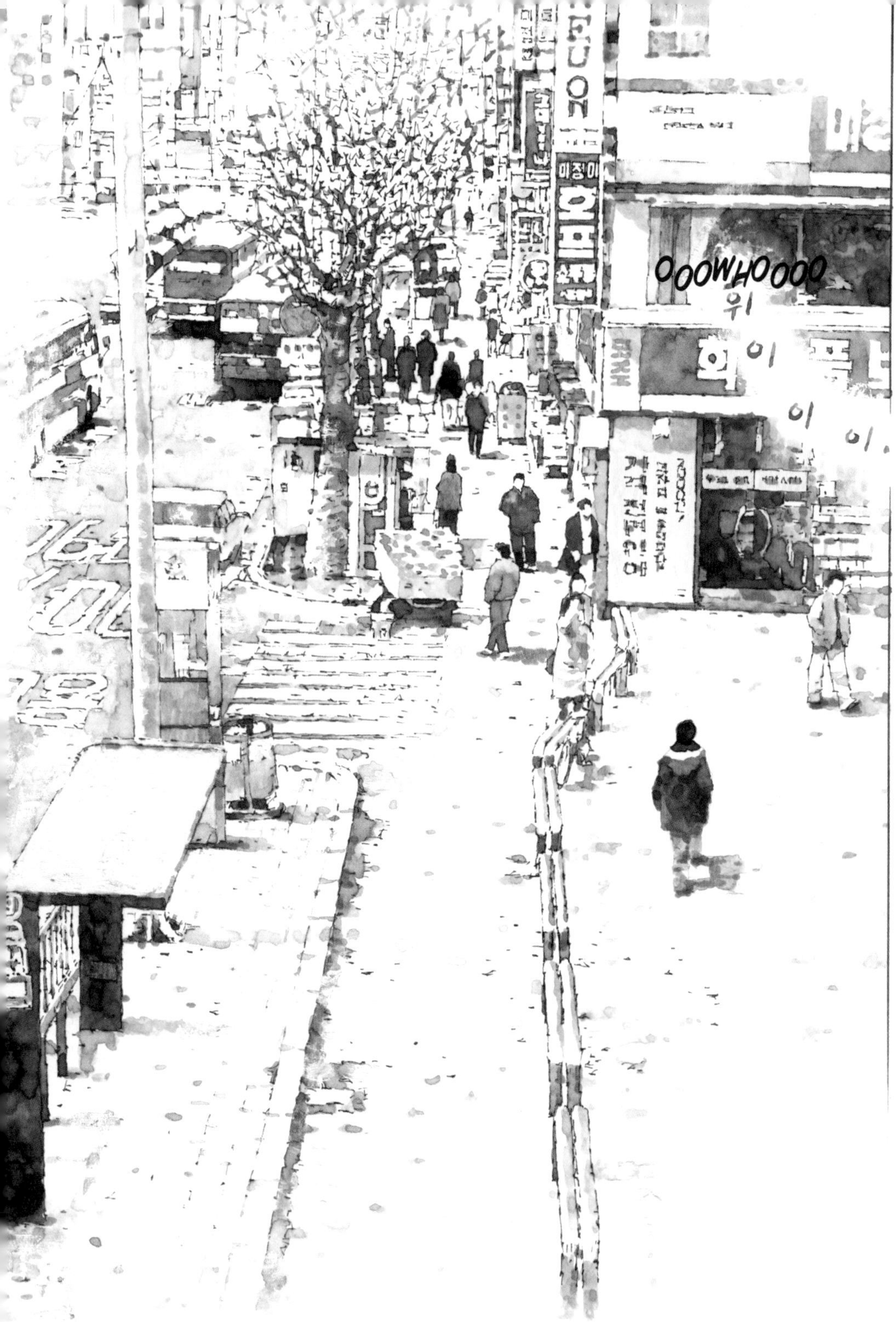
OOOWHOOOO
위
이
이
이.

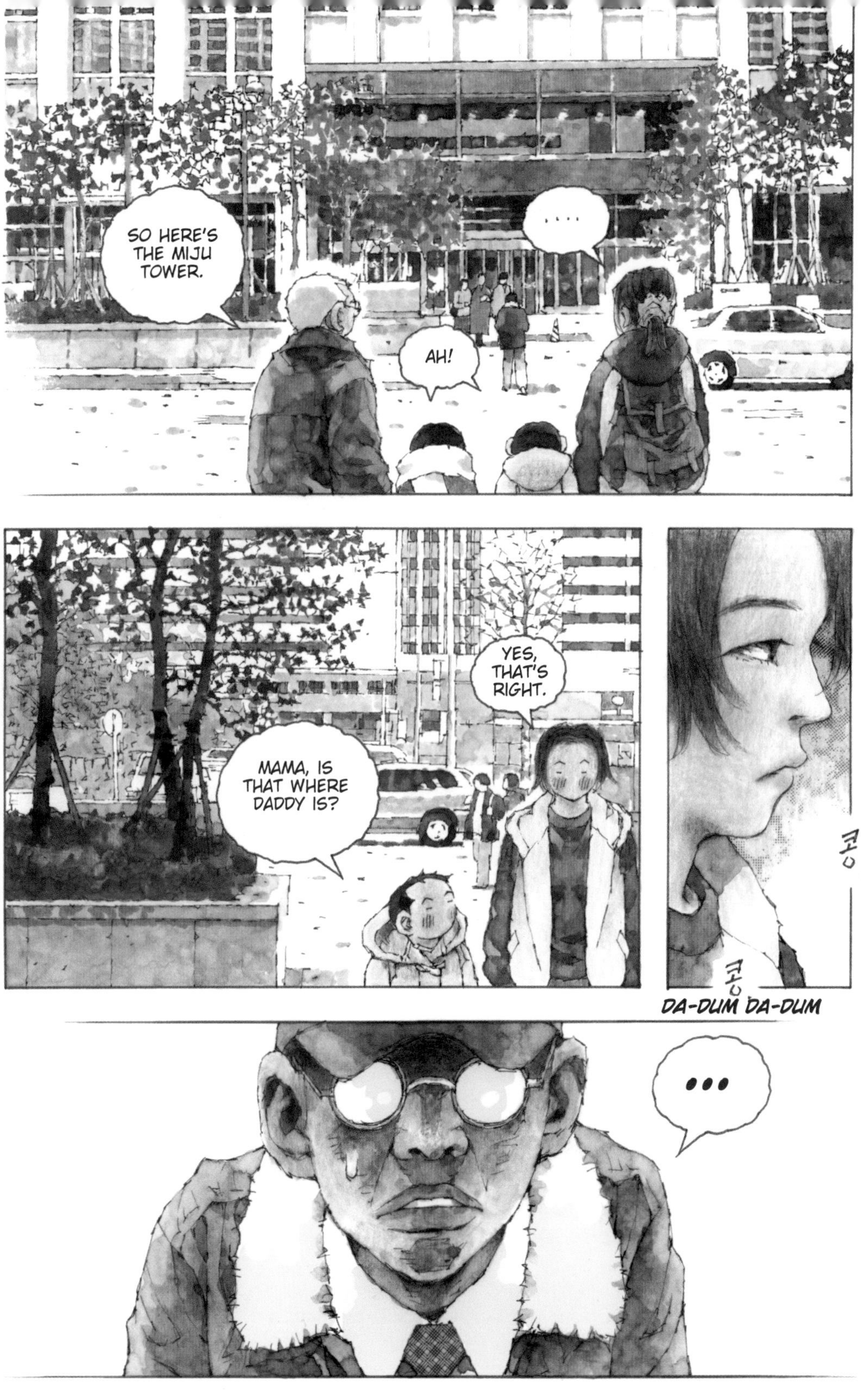
SO HERE'S THE MIJU TOWER.
....
AH!
YES, THAT'S RIGHT.
MAMA, IS THAT WHERE DADDY IS?
콩..
콩
DA-DUM DA-DUM
•••

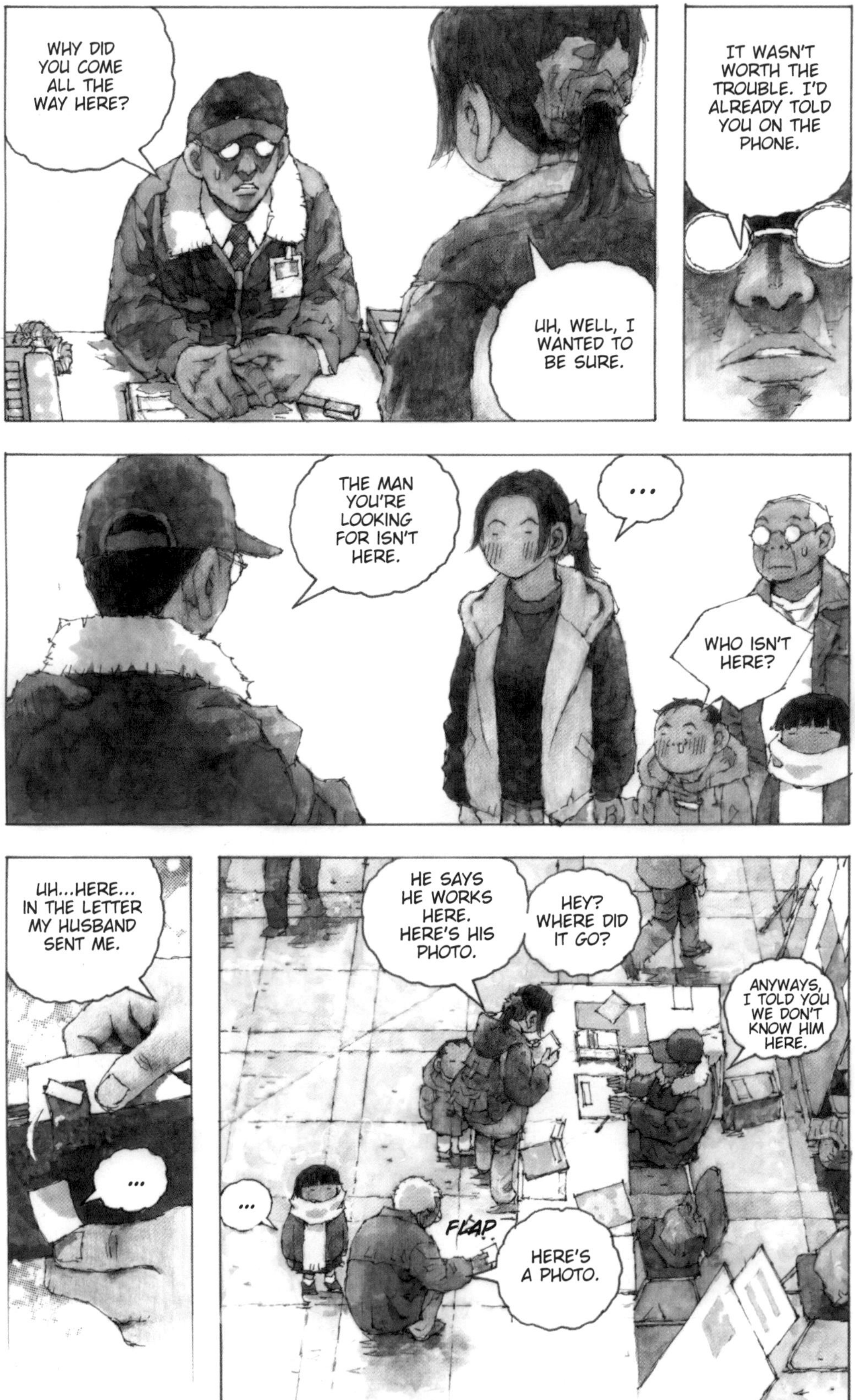
WHY DID YOU COME ALL THE WAY HERE?
UH, WELL, I WANTED TO BE SURE.
IT WASN'T WORTH THE TROUBLE. I'D ALREADY TOLD YOU ON THE PHONE.
THE MAN YOU'RE LOOKING FOR ISN'T HERE.
...
WHO ISN'T HERE?
UH...HERE... IN THE LETTER MY HUSBAND SENT ME.
...
HE SAYS HE WORKS HERE. HERE'S HIS PHOTO.
HEY? WHERE DID IT GO?
ANYWAYS, I TOLD YOU WE DON'T KNOW HIM HERE.
...
FLAP
HERE'S A PHOTO.

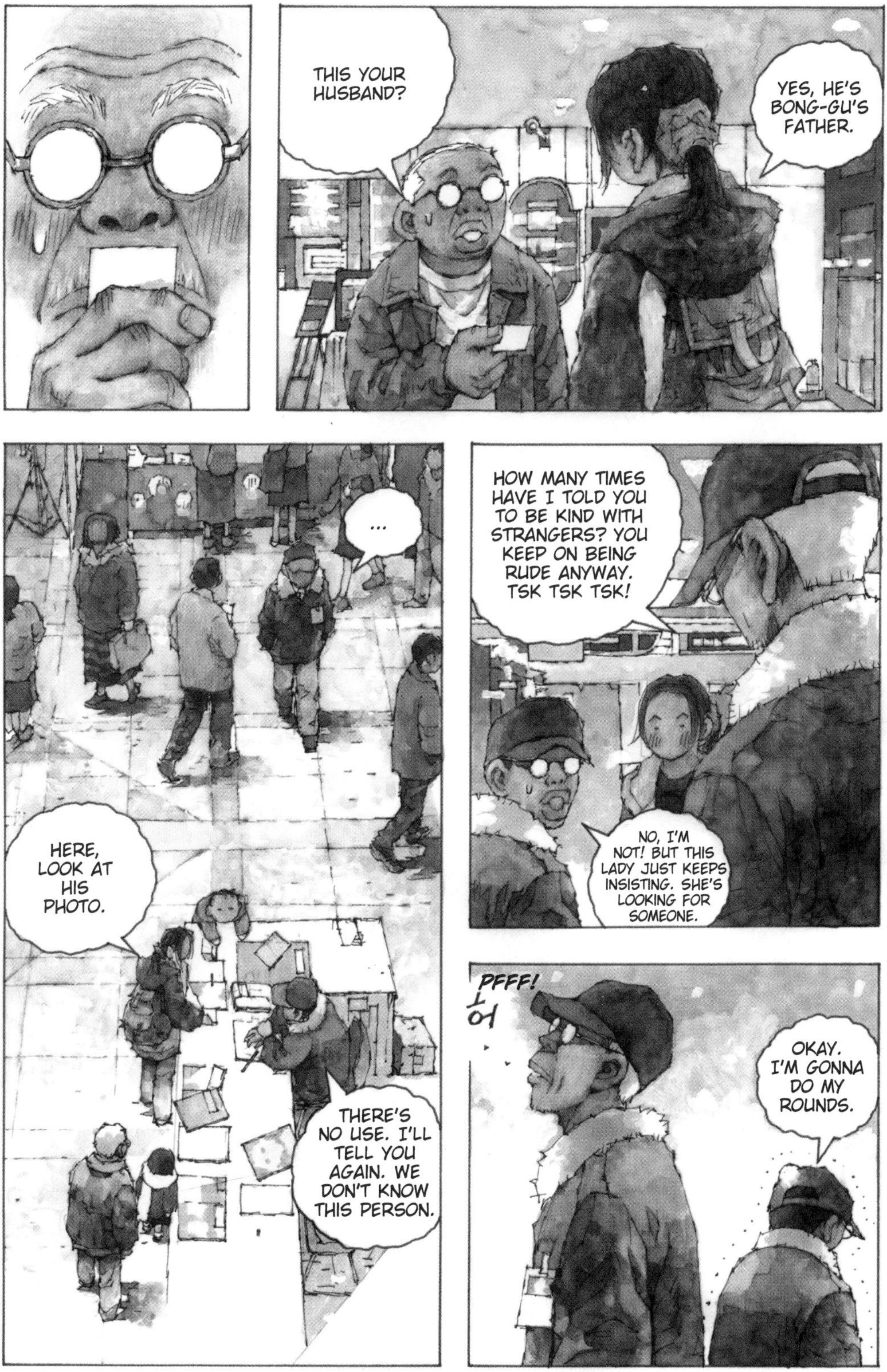
THIS YOUR HUSBAND?
YES, HE'S BONG-GU'S FATHER.
...
HERE, LOOK AT HIS PHOTO.
THERE'S NO USE. I'LL TELL YOU AGAIN. WE DON'T KNOW THIS PERSON.
HOW MANY TIMES HAVE I TOLD YOU TO BE KIND WITH STRANGERS? YOU KEEP ON BEING RUDE ANYWAY. TSK TSK TSK!
NO, I'M NOT! BUT THIS LADY JUST KEEPS INSISTING. SHE'S LOOKING FOR SOMEONE.
PFFF!
흐
어
OKAY. I'M GONNA DO MY ROUNDS.

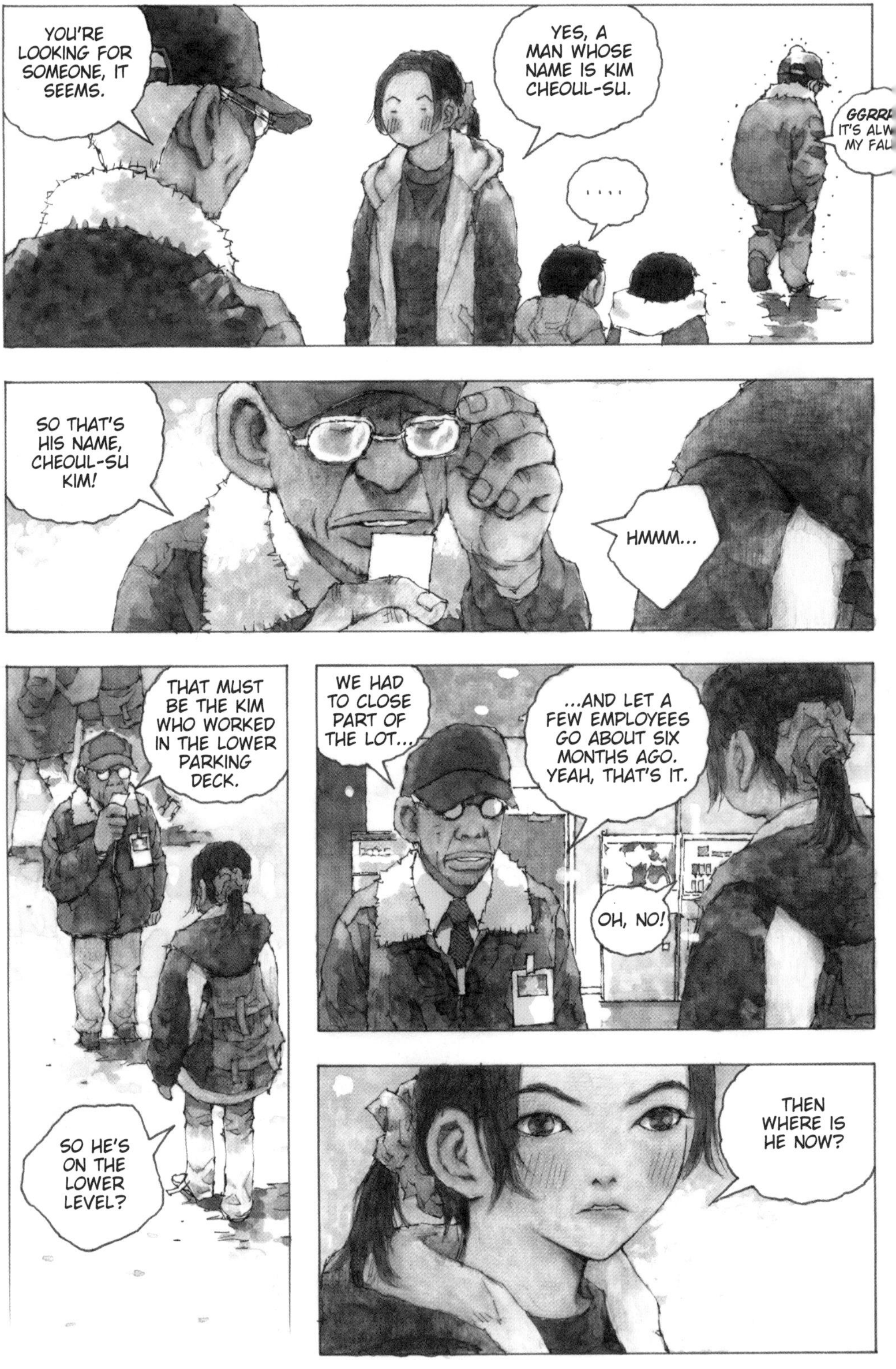
YOU'RE LOOKING FOR SOMEONE, IT SEEMS.
YES, A MAN WHOSE NAME IS KIM CHEOUL-SU.
. . . . .
GGRR
IT'S ALW
MY FA
SO THAT'S HIS NAME, CHEOUL-SU KIM!
HMMM...
THAT MUST BE THE KIM WHO WORKED IN THE LOWER PARKING DECK.
SO HE'S ON THE LOWER LEVEL?
WE HAD TO CLOSE PART OF THE LOT...
...AND LET A FEW EMPLOYEES GO ABOUT SIX MONTHS AGO. YEAH, THAT'S IT.
OH, NO!
THEN WHERE IS HE NOW?

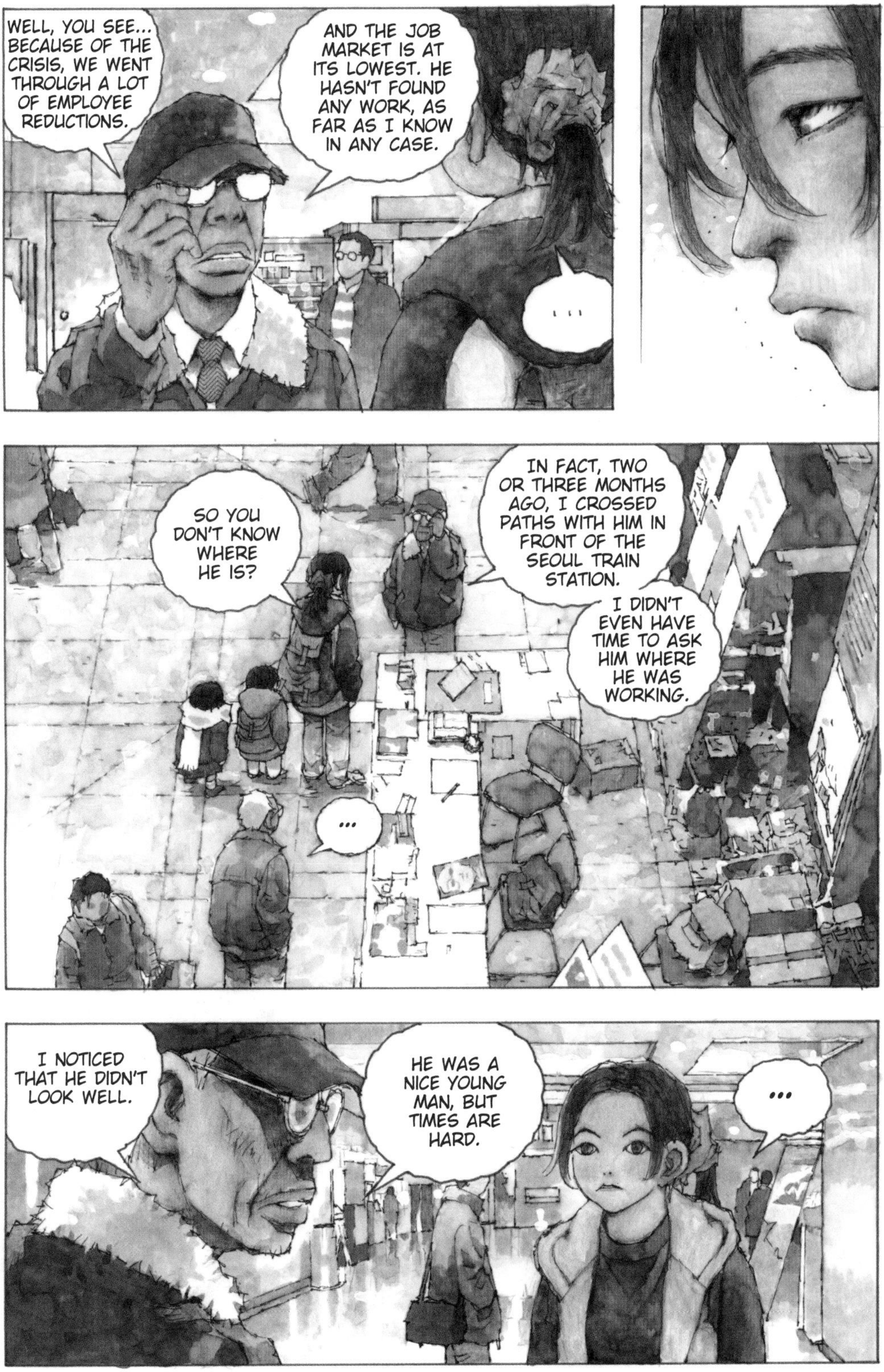
WELL, YOU SEE... BECAUSE OF THE CRISIS, WE WENT THROUGH A LOT OF EMPLOYEE REDUCTIONS.
AND THE JOB MARKET IS AT ITS LOWEST. HE HASN'T FOUND ANY WORK, AS FAR AS I KNOW IN ANY CASE.
...
SO YOU DON'T KNOW WHERE HE IS?
IN FACT, TWO OR THREE MONTHS AGO, I CROSSED PATHS WITH HIM IN FRONT OF THE SEOUL TRAIN STATION.
I DIDN'T EVEN HAVE TIME TO ASK HIM WHERE HE WAS WORKING.
...
I NOTICED THAT HE DIDN'T LOOK WELL.
HE WAS A NICE YOUNG MAN, BUT TIMES ARE HARD.
...

I'M SORRY I WASN'T ABLE TO HELP YOU.

IT'S ALL RIGHT. THANKS ALL THE SAME.

UH...

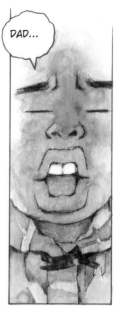

DAD...

BONG-GU!

DADDY! WHERE IS HE?

UHM... HE...

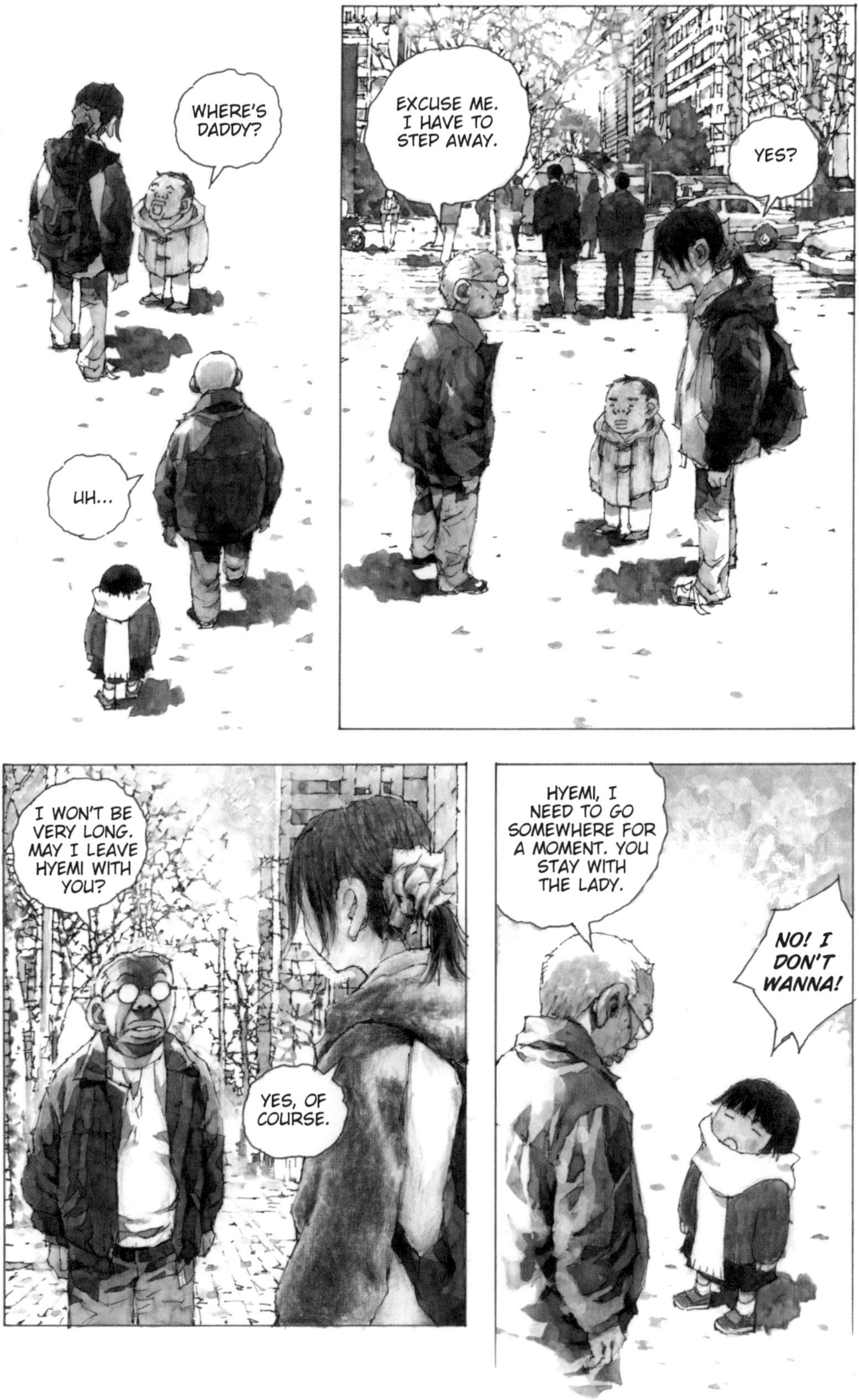
WHERE'S DADDY?
UH...
EXCUSE ME. I HAVE TO STEP AWAY.
YES?
I WON'T BE VERY LONG. MAY I LEAVE HYEMI WITH YOU?
YES, OF COURSE.
HYEMI, I NEED TO GO SOMEWHERE FOR A MOMENT. YOU STAY WITH THE LADY.
NO! I DON'T WANNA!

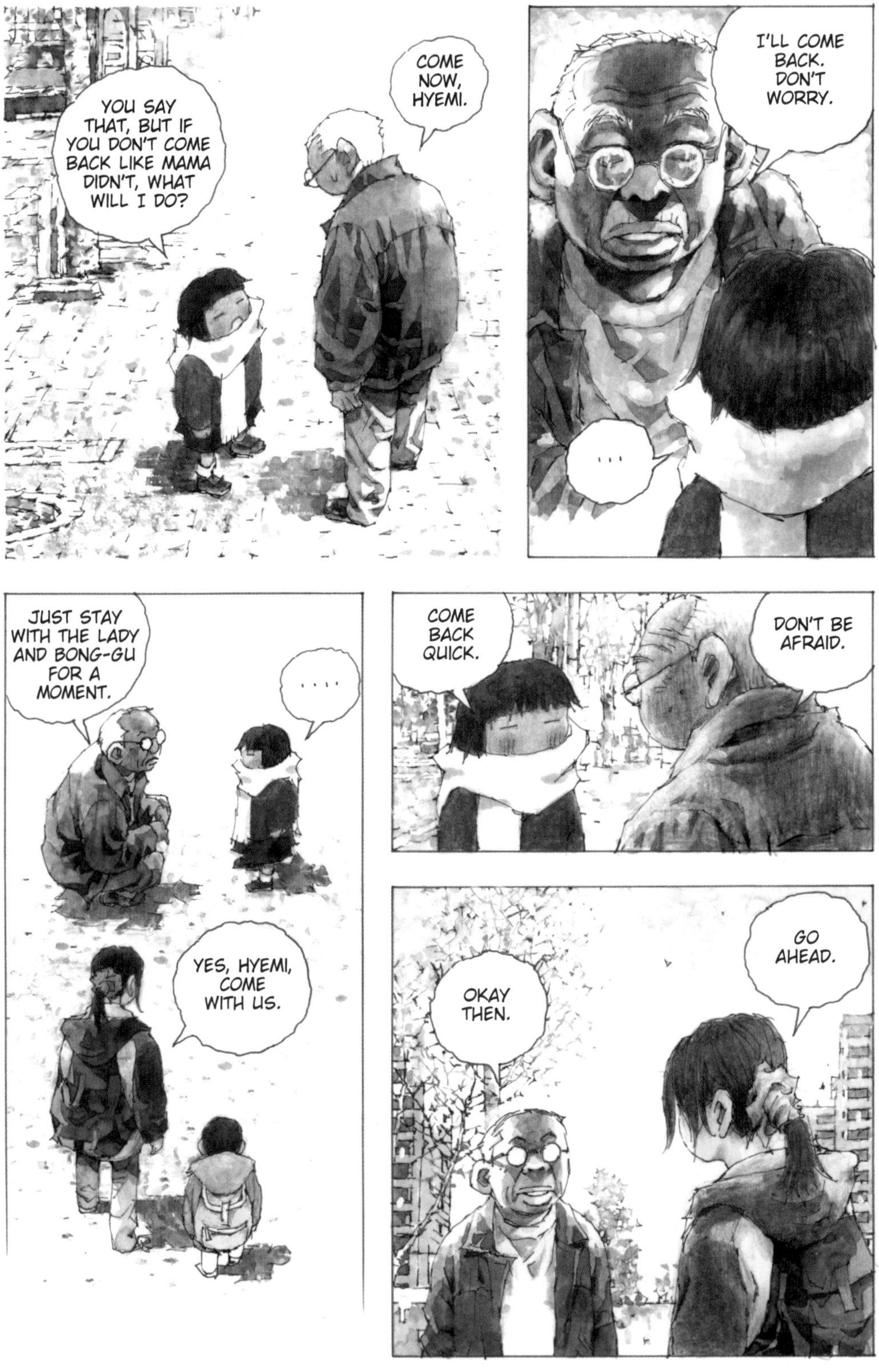
YOU SAY THAT, BUT IF YOU DON'T COME BACK LIKE MAMA DIDN'T, WHAT WILL I DO?
COME NOW, HYEMI.
I'LL COME BACK. DON'T WORRY.
...
JUST STAY WITH THE LADY AND BONG-GU FOR A MOMENT.
....
YES, HYEMI, COME WITH US.
COME BACK QUICK.
DON'T BE AFRAID.
OKAY THEN.
GO AHEAD.

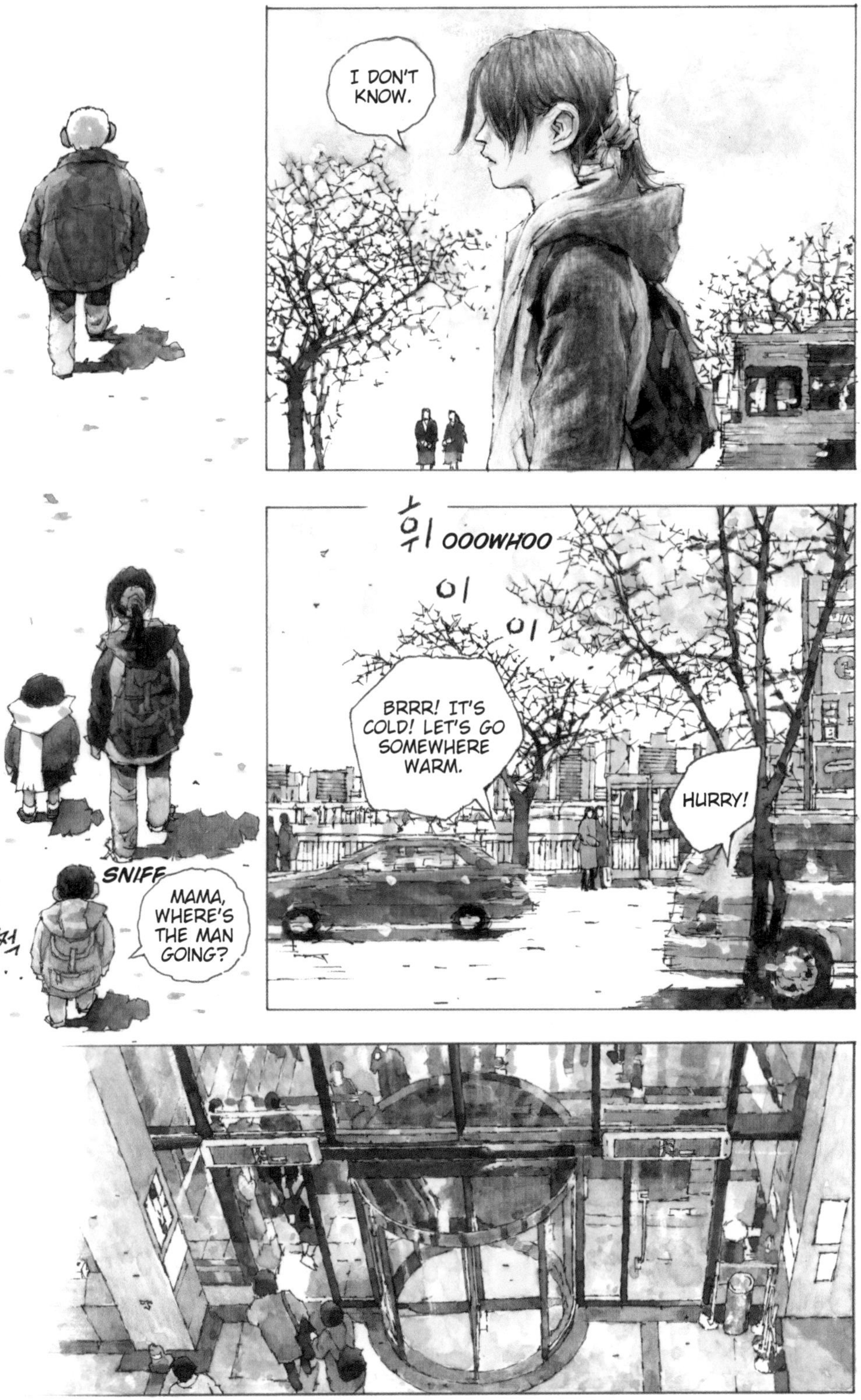
I DON'T KNOW.
휘 이 이 OOOWHOO
BRRR! IT'S COLD! LET'S GO SOMEWHERE WARM.
HURRY!
훌쩍 SNIFF
MAMA, WHERE'S THE MAN GOING?

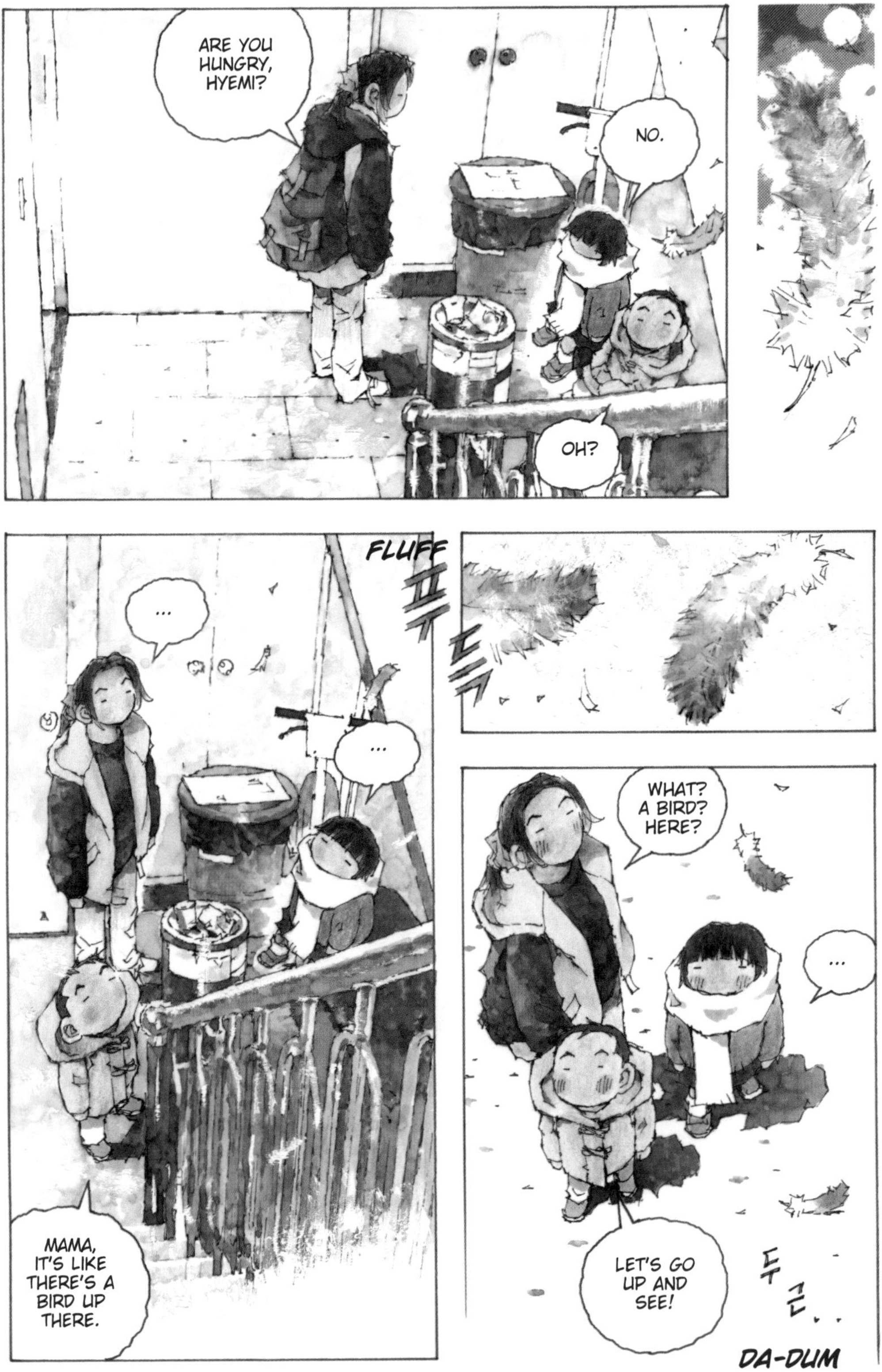
ARE YOU HUNGRY, HYEMI?
NO.
OH?
...
...
FLUFF
MAMA, IT'S LIKE THERE'S A BIRD UP THERE.
WHAT? A BIRD? HERE?
...
LET'S GO UP AND SEE!
두근
DA-DUM

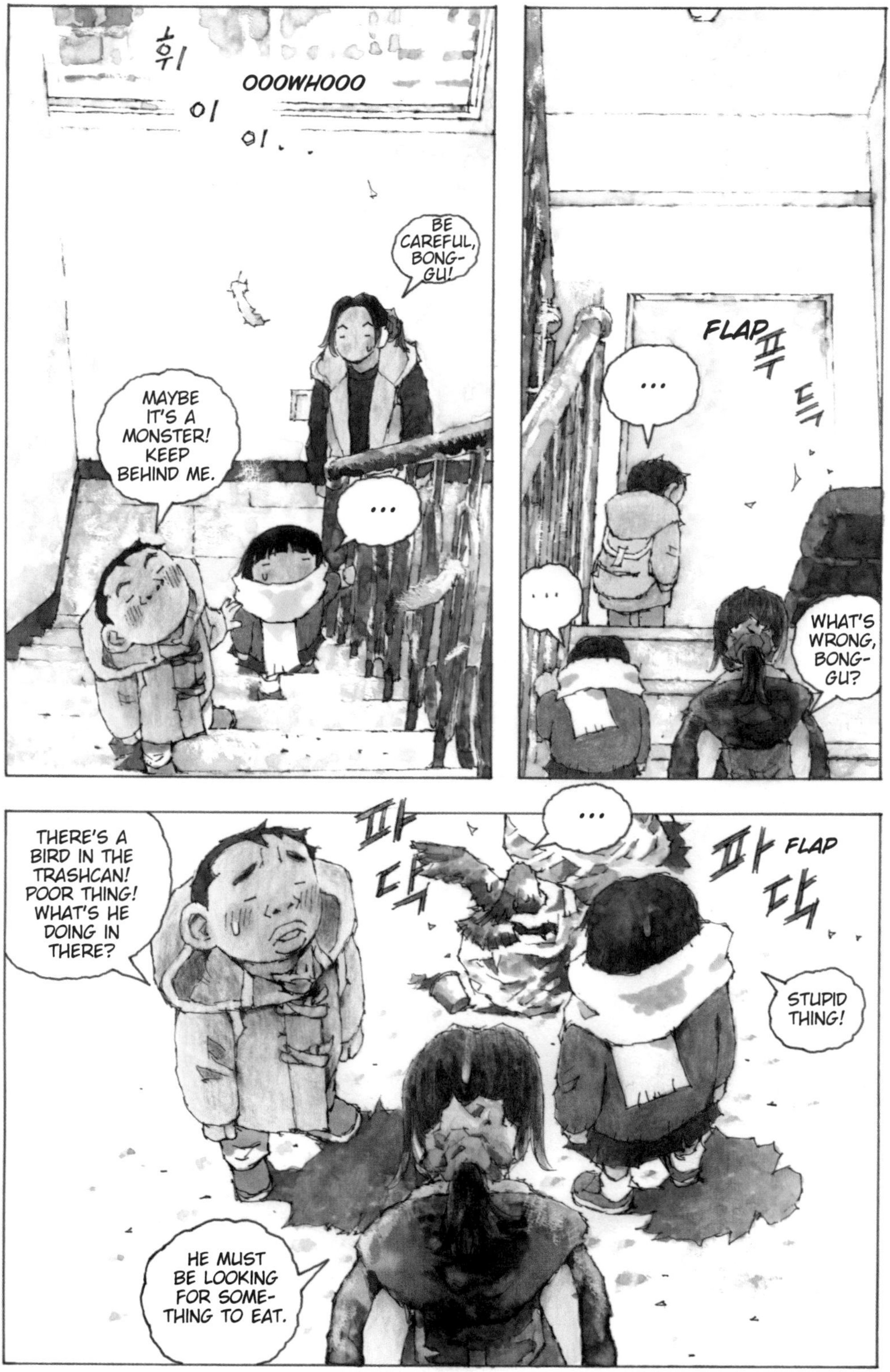
휘
OOOWHOOO
이
이 . .
BE CAREFUL, BONG-GU!
MAYBE IT'S A MONSTER! KEEP BEHIND ME.
...
FLAP
푸드득
...
...
WHAT'S WRONG, BONG-GU?
THERE'S A BIRD IN THE TRASHCAN! POOR THING! WHAT'S HE DOING IN THERE?
파닥
...
파닥
FLAP
STUPID THING!
HE MUST BE LOOKING FOR SOME-THING TO EAT.

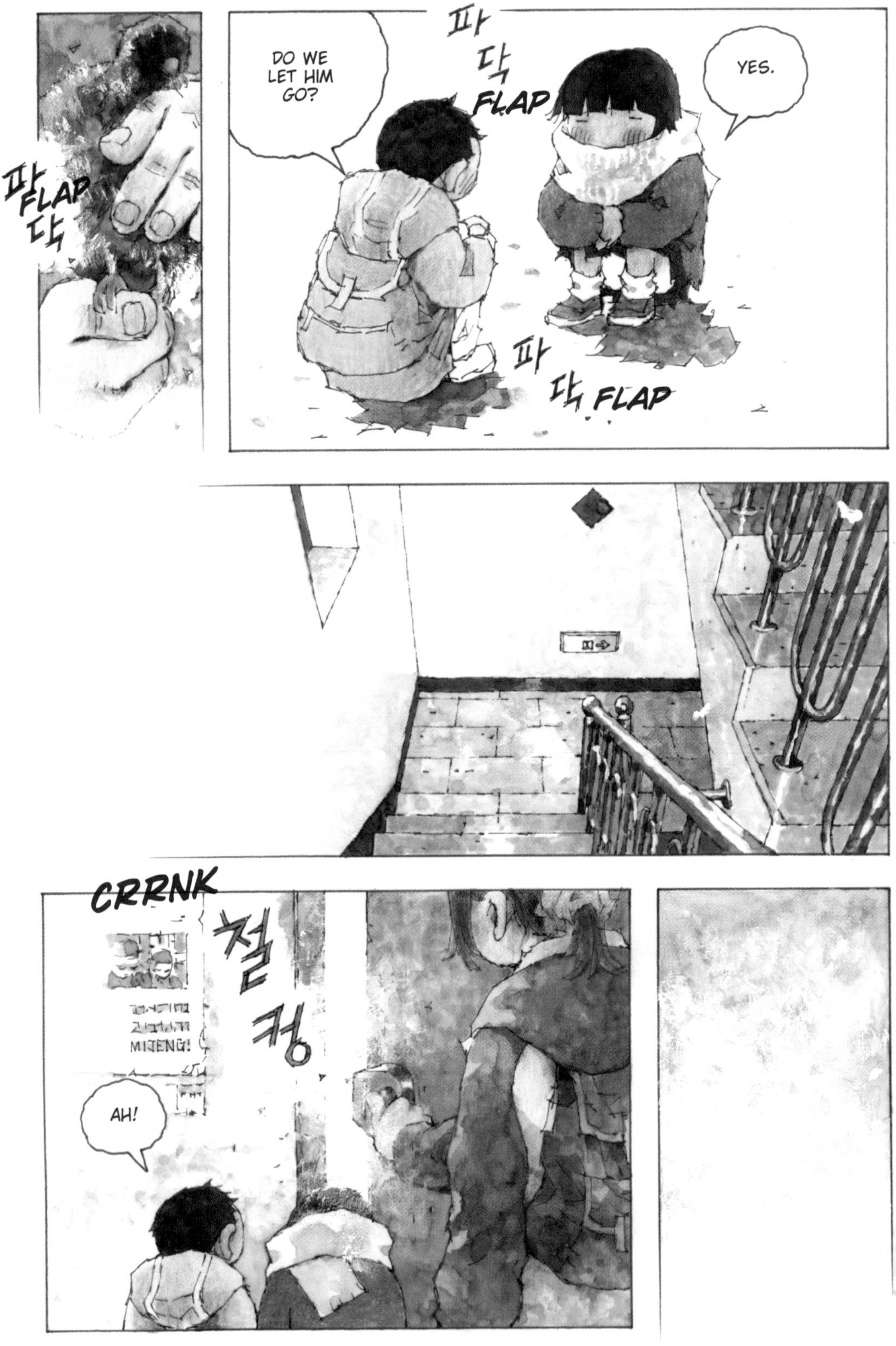

파
FLAP
닥
DO WE LET HIM GO?
파
닥
FLAP
YES.
파
닥
FLAP
CRRNK
철
컹
MIJENG!
AH!

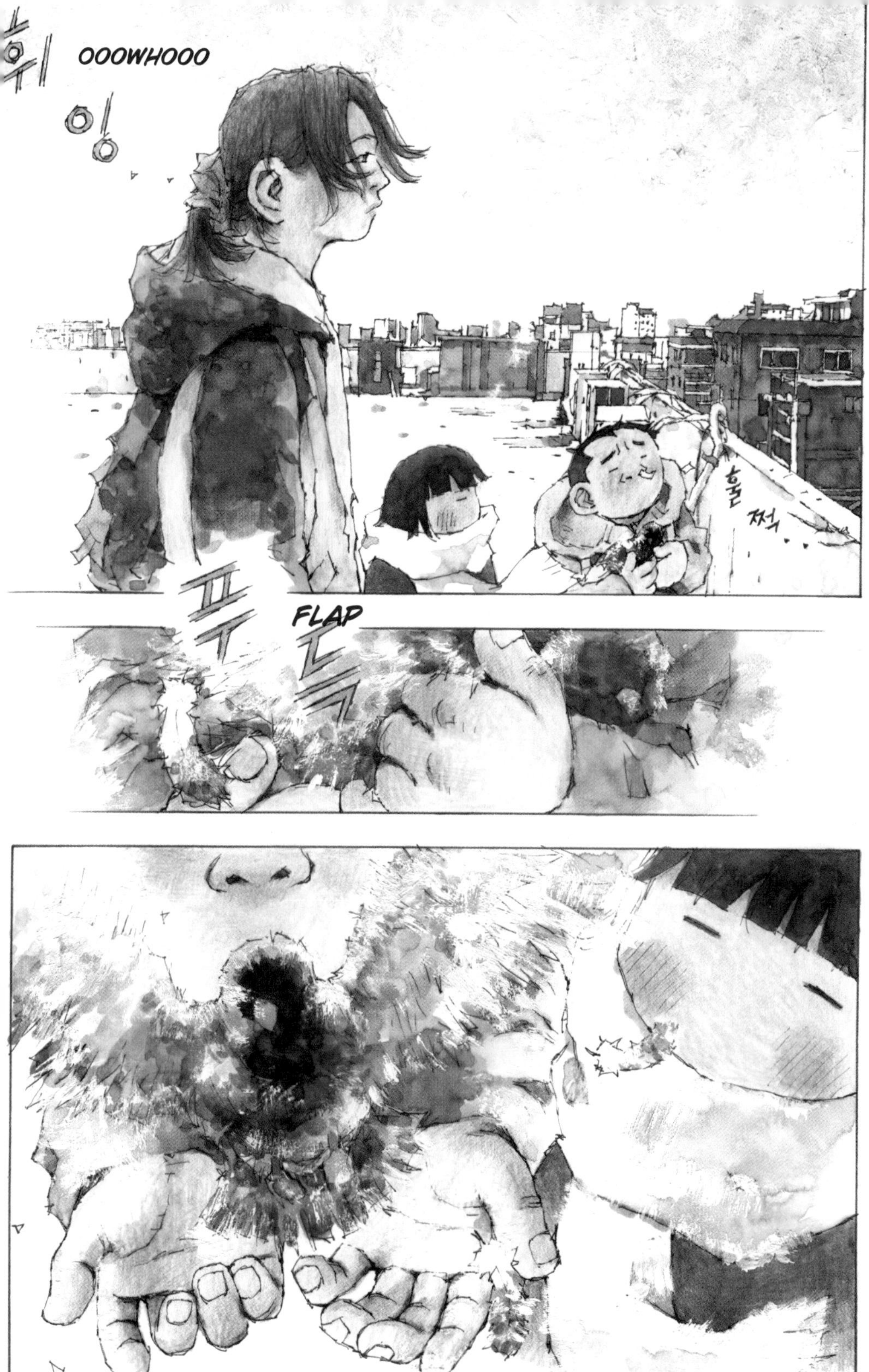
휘잉
OOOWHOOO
훌쩍
푸드득
FLAP

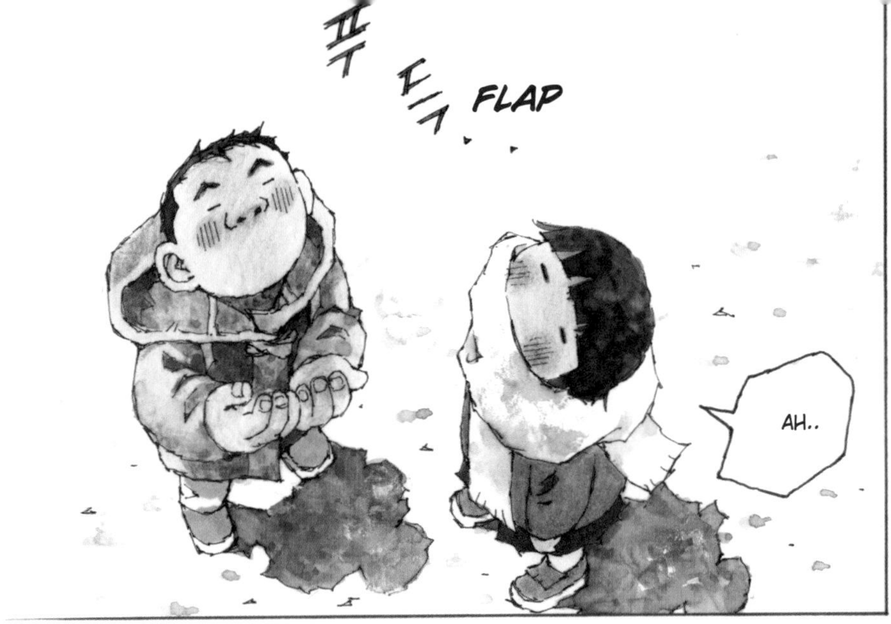
FLAP
AH..

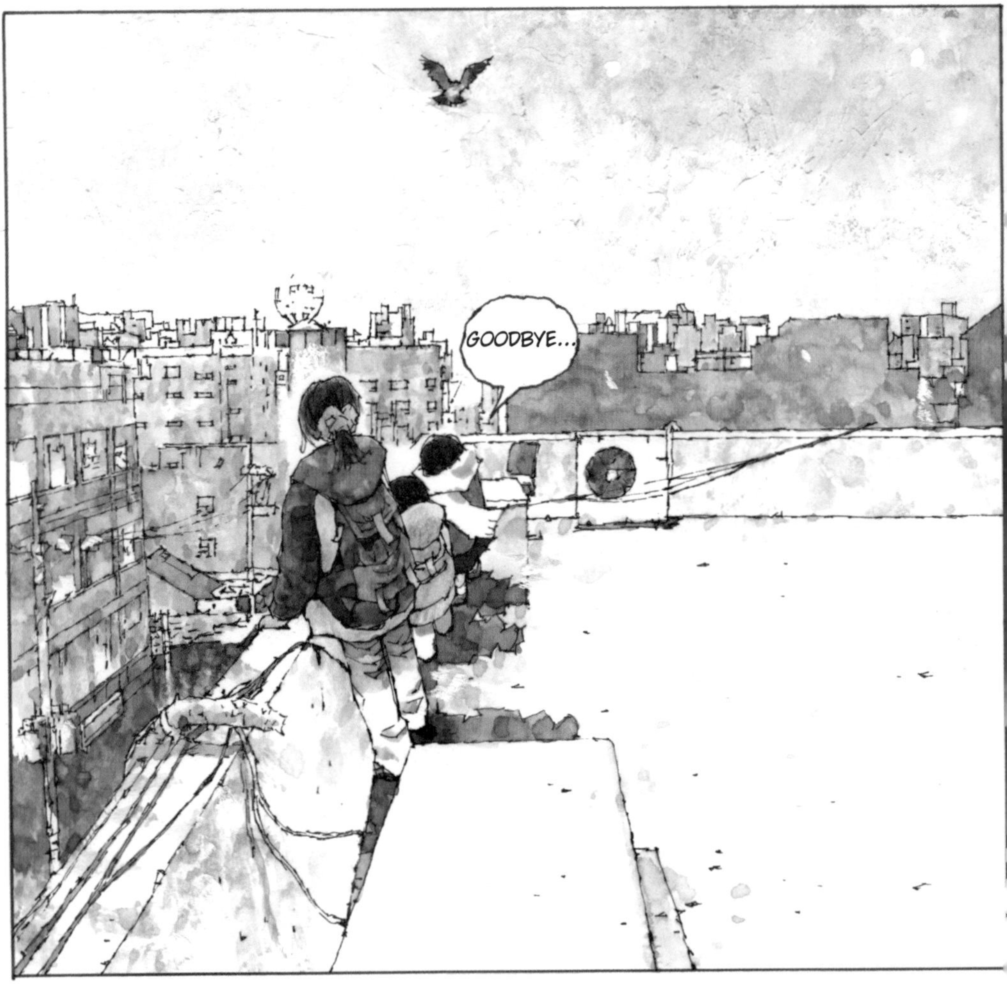
GOODBYE...

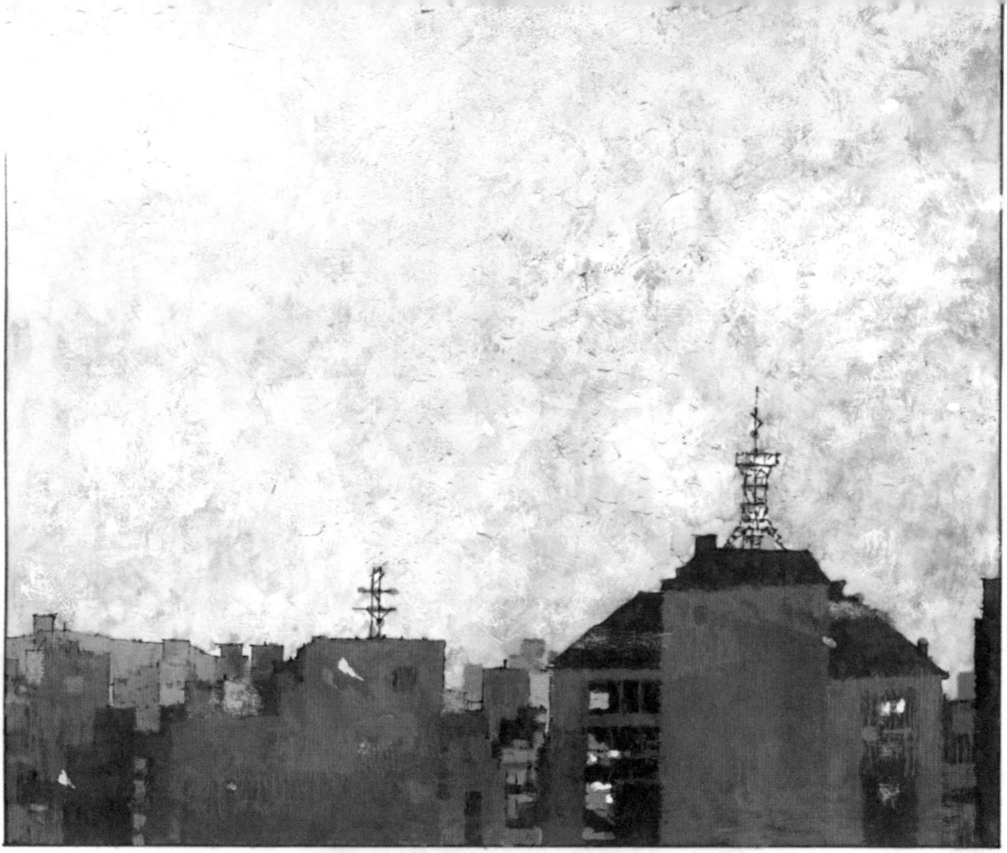

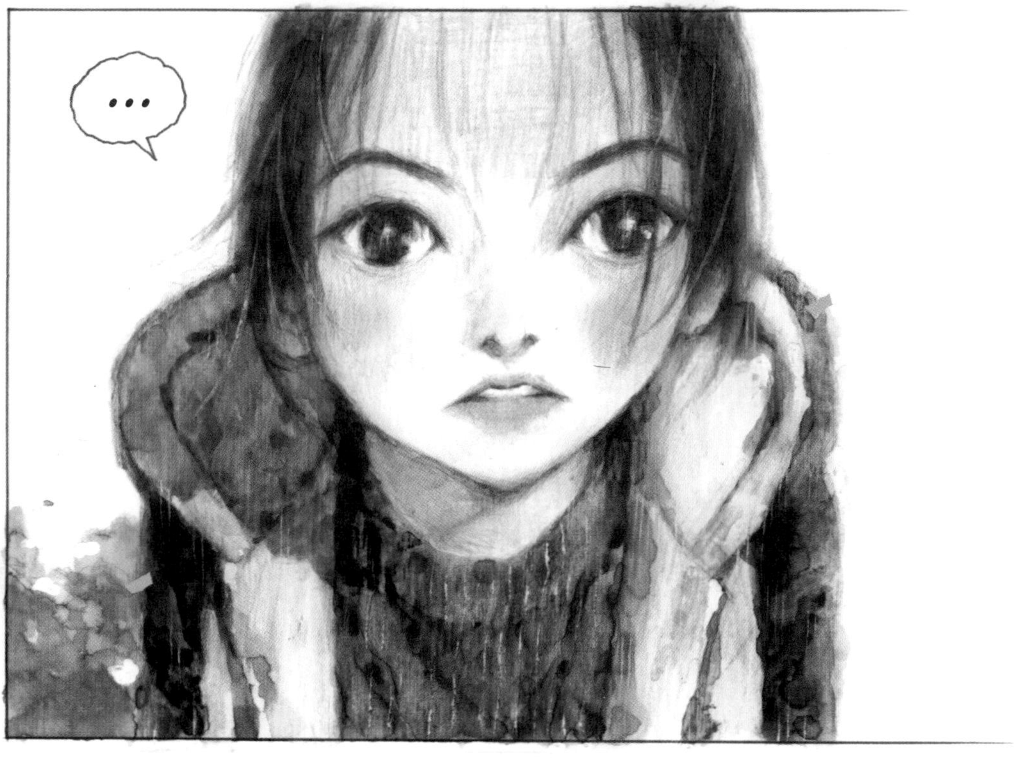
...

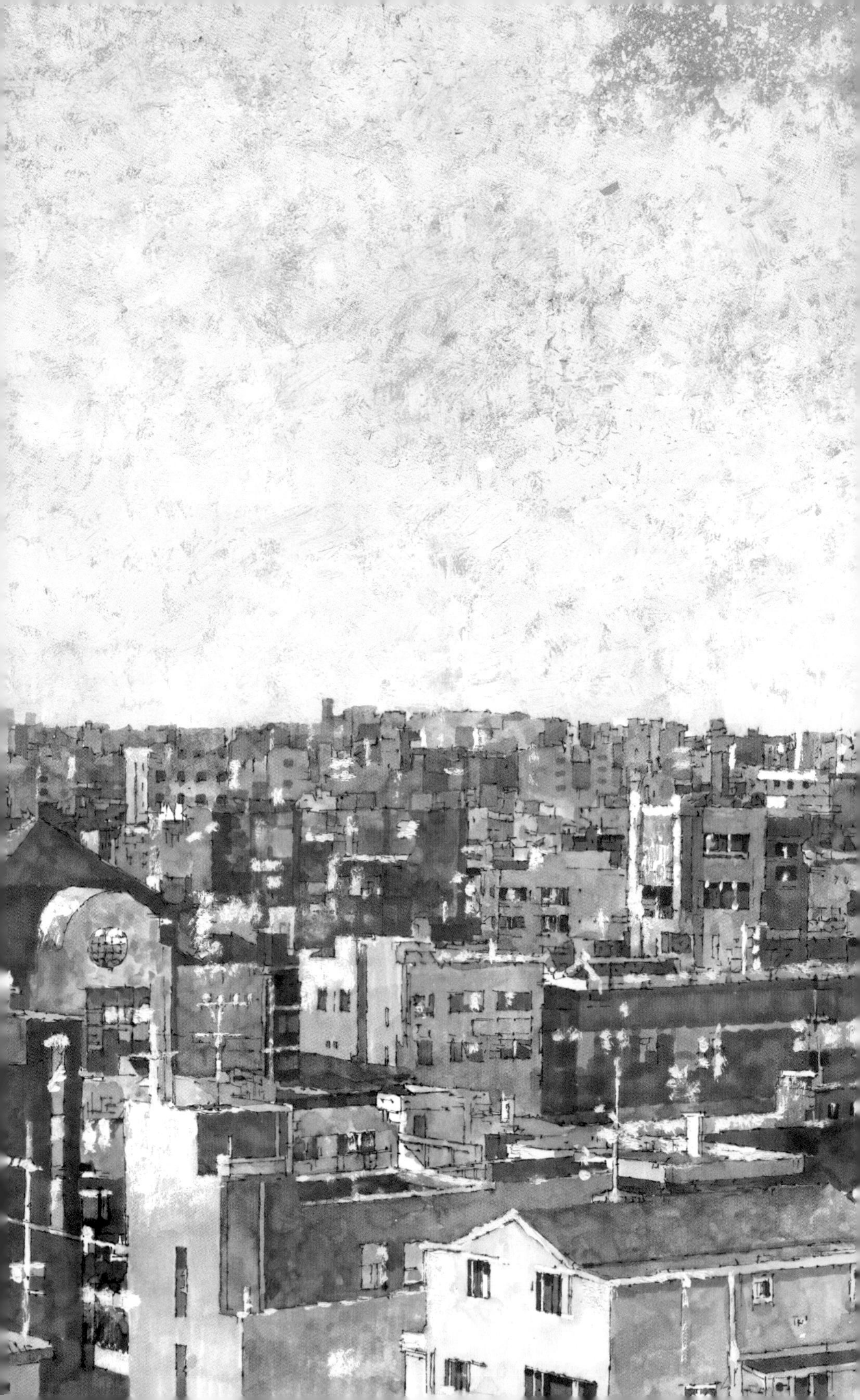

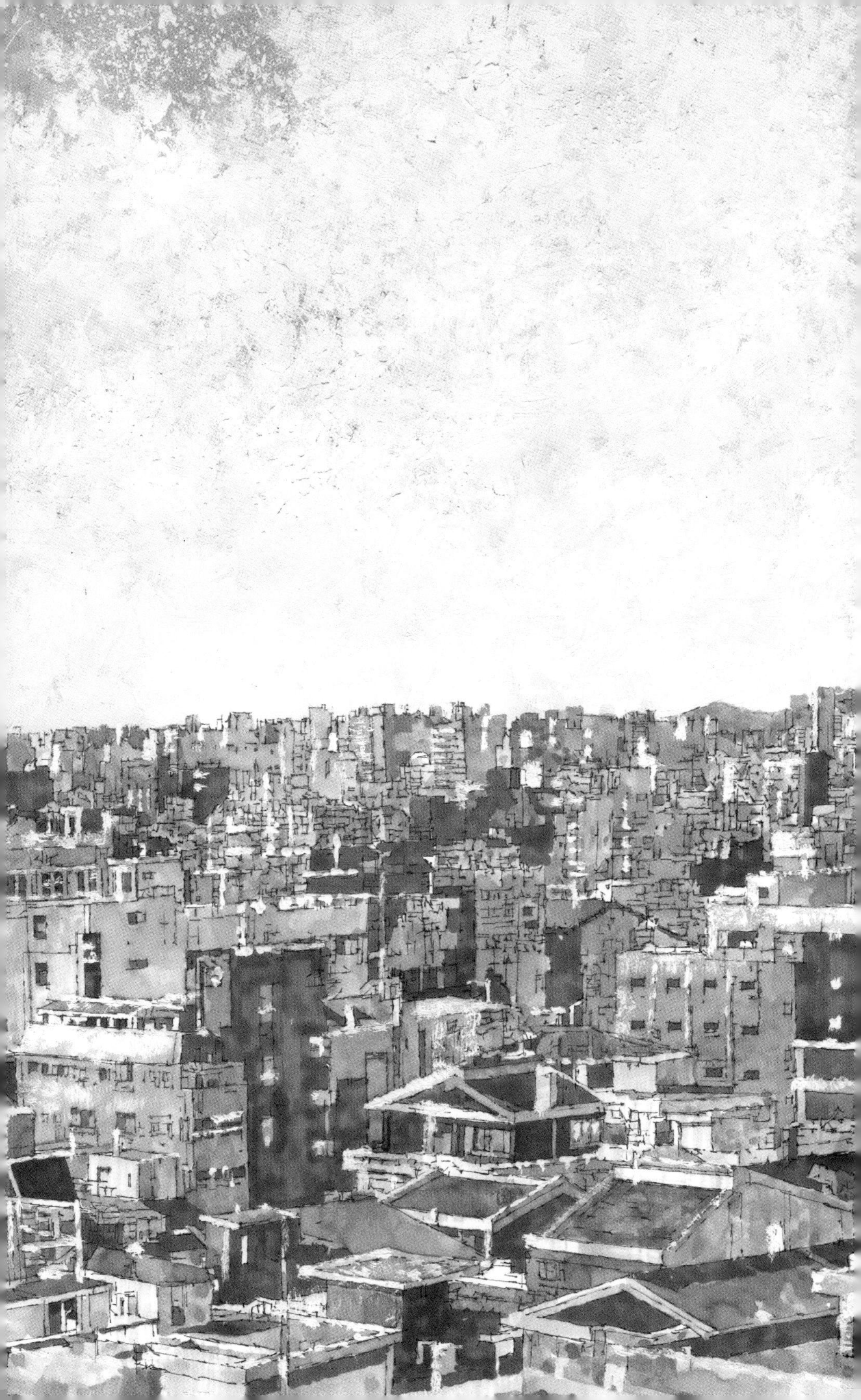

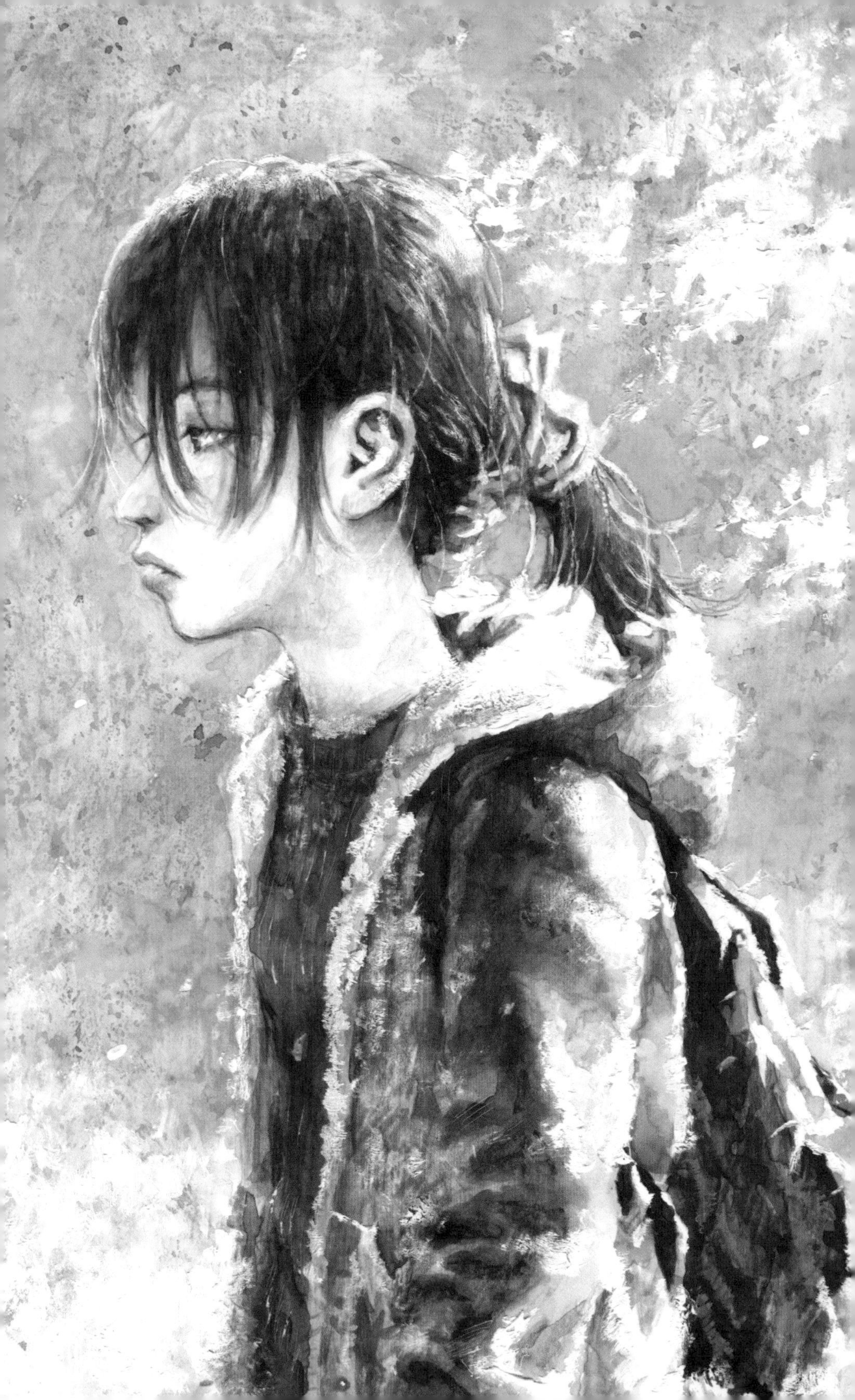

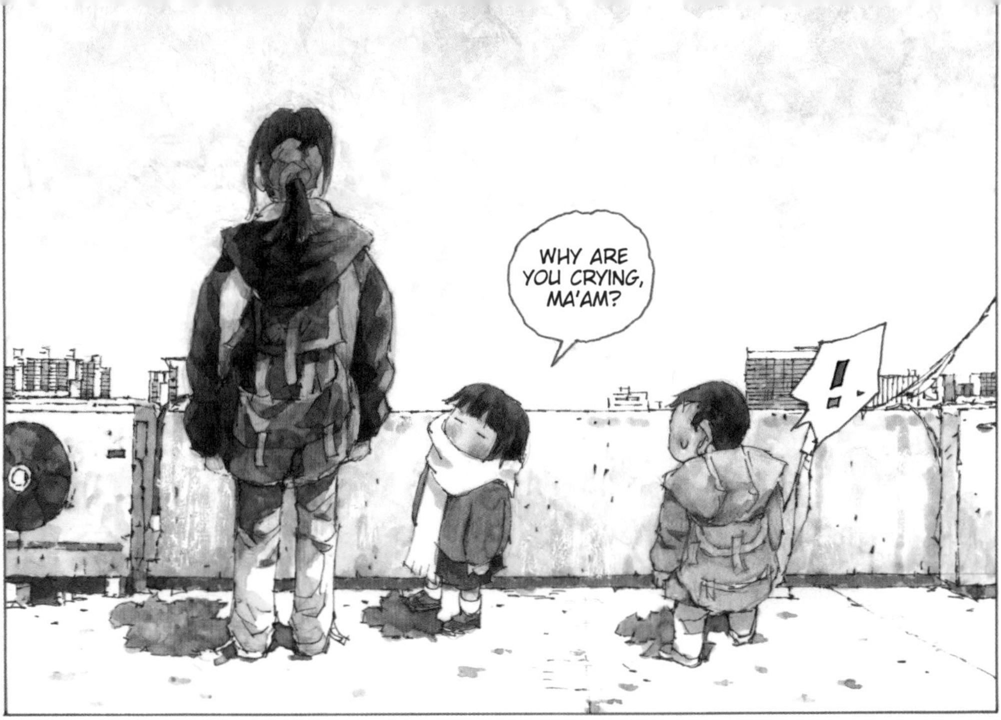
WHY ARE YOU CRYING, MA'AM?
!

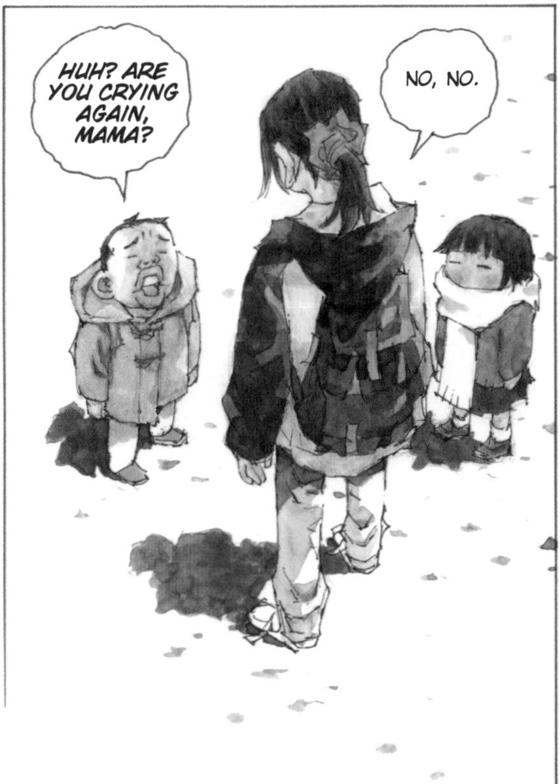
HUH? ARE YOU CRYING AGAIN, MAMA?
NO, NO.

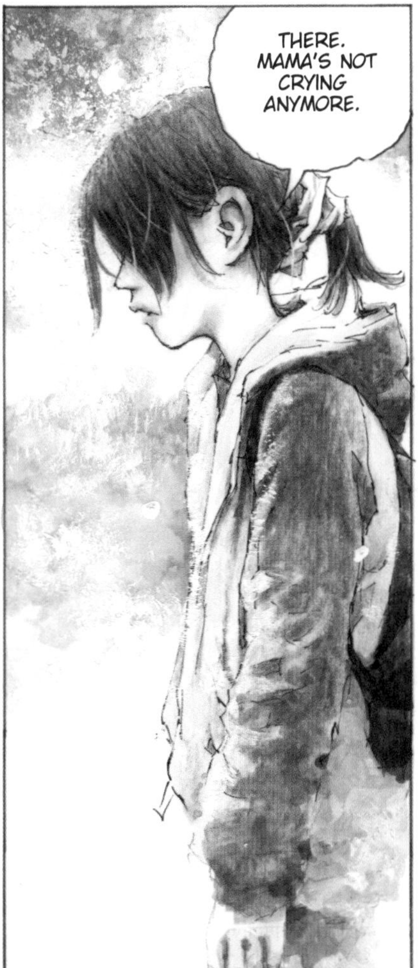
THERE. MAMA'S NOT CRYING ANYMORE.

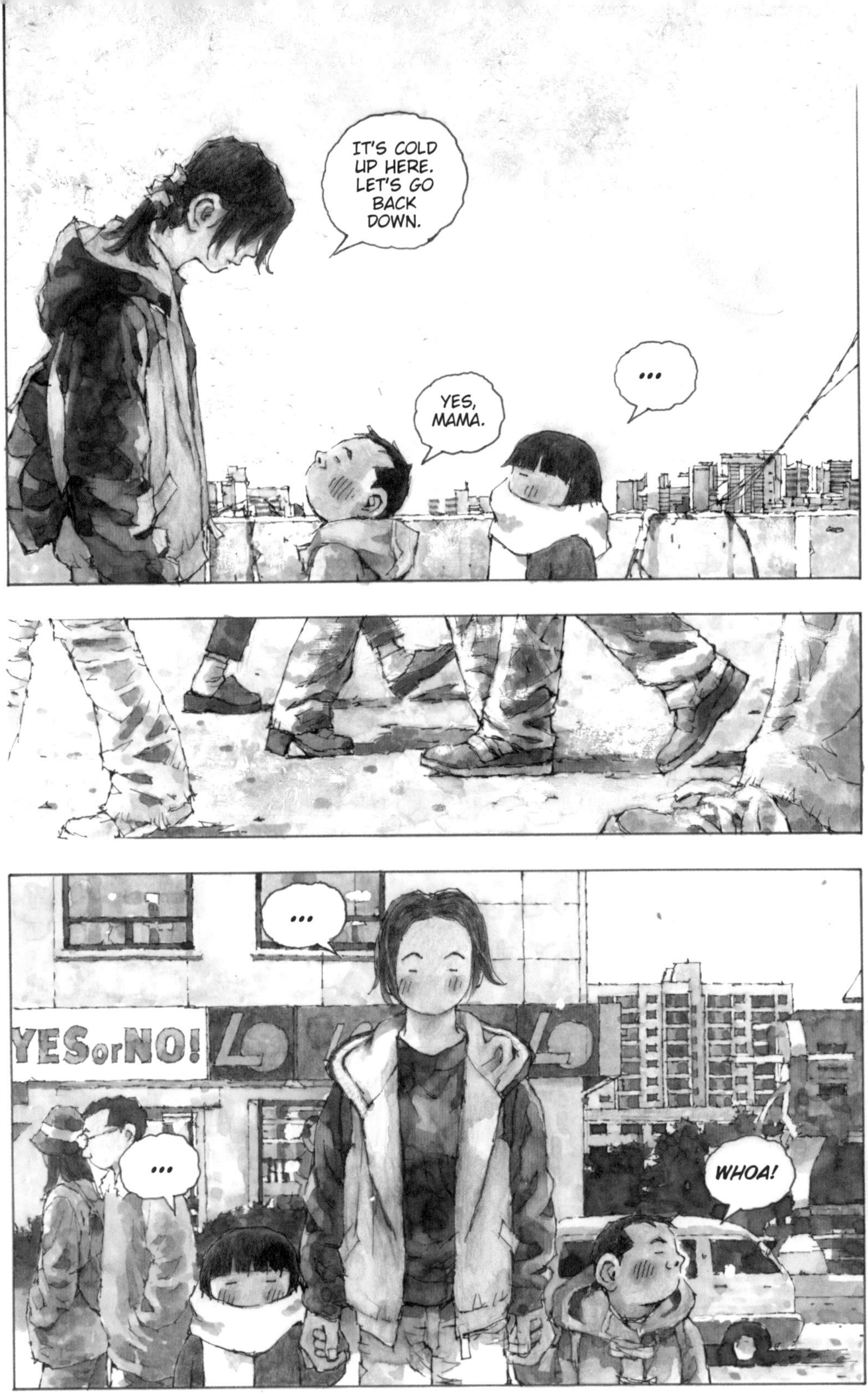
IT'S COLD UP HERE. LET'S GO BACK DOWN.
YES, MAMA.
...
...
...
WHOA!

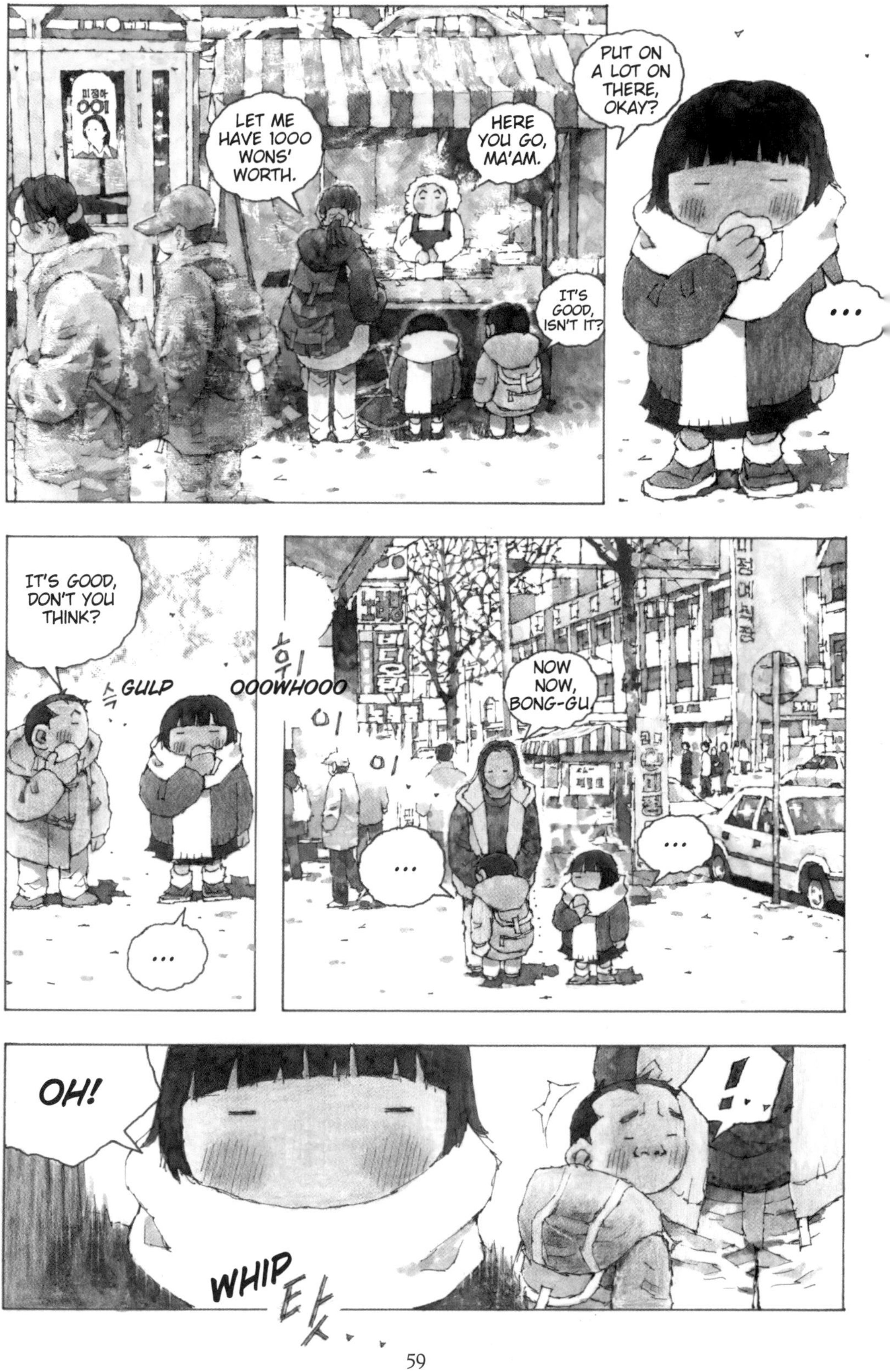
LET ME HAVE 1000 WONS' WORTH.
HERE YOU GO, MA'AM.
PUT ON A LOT ON THERE, OKAY?
IT'S GOOD, ISN'T IT?
...
IT'S GOOD, DON'T YOU THINK?
GULP
...
OOOWHOOO
NOW NOW, BONG-GU.
...
...
OH!
!
WHIP
탁

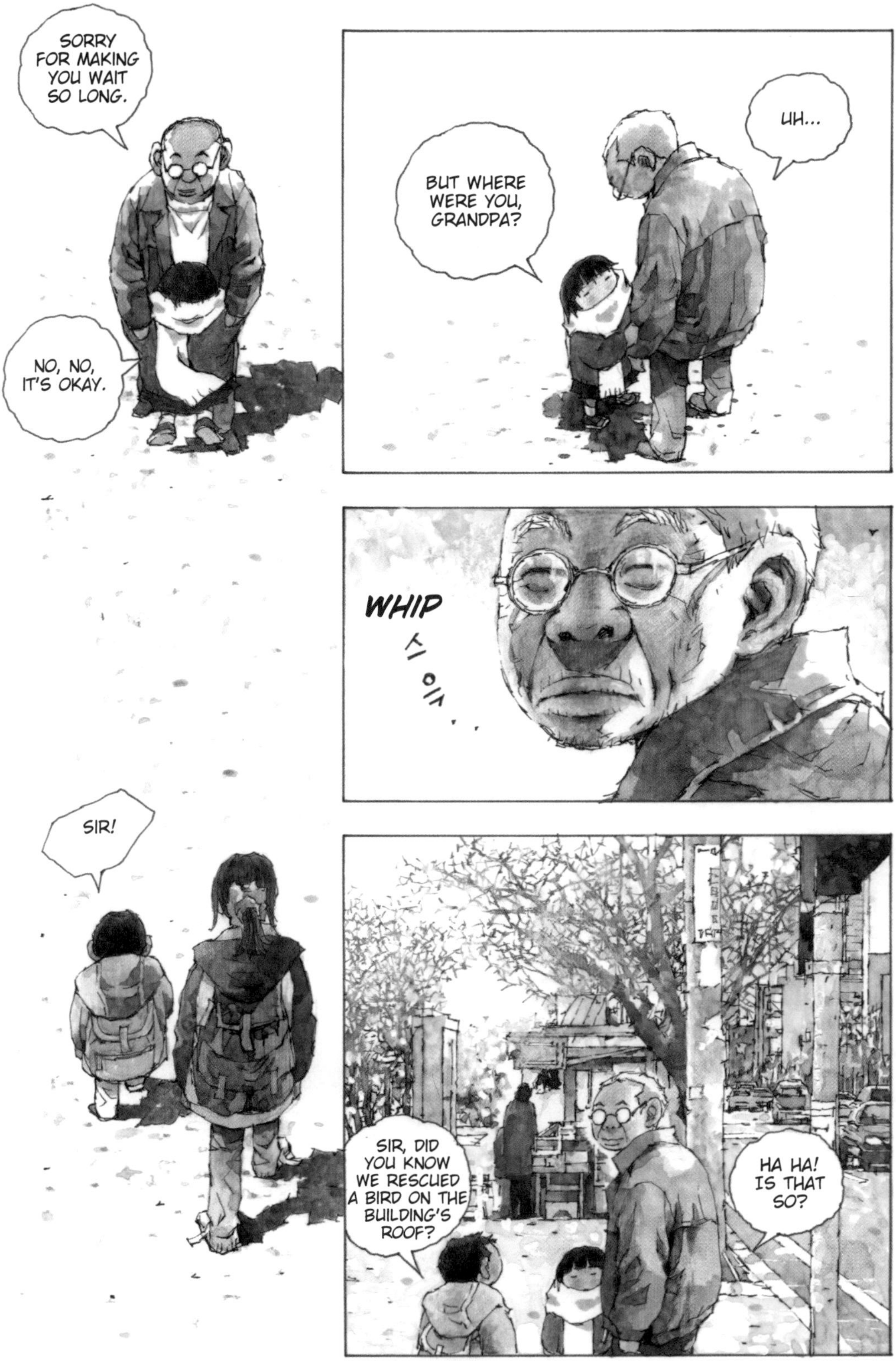
SORRY FOR MAKING YOU WAIT SO LONG.
NO, NO, IT'S OKAY.
BUT WHERE WERE YOU, GRANDPA?
UH...
WHIP
SIR!
SIR, DID YOU KNOW WE RESCUED A BIRD ON THE BUILDING'S ROOF?
HA HA! IS THAT SO?

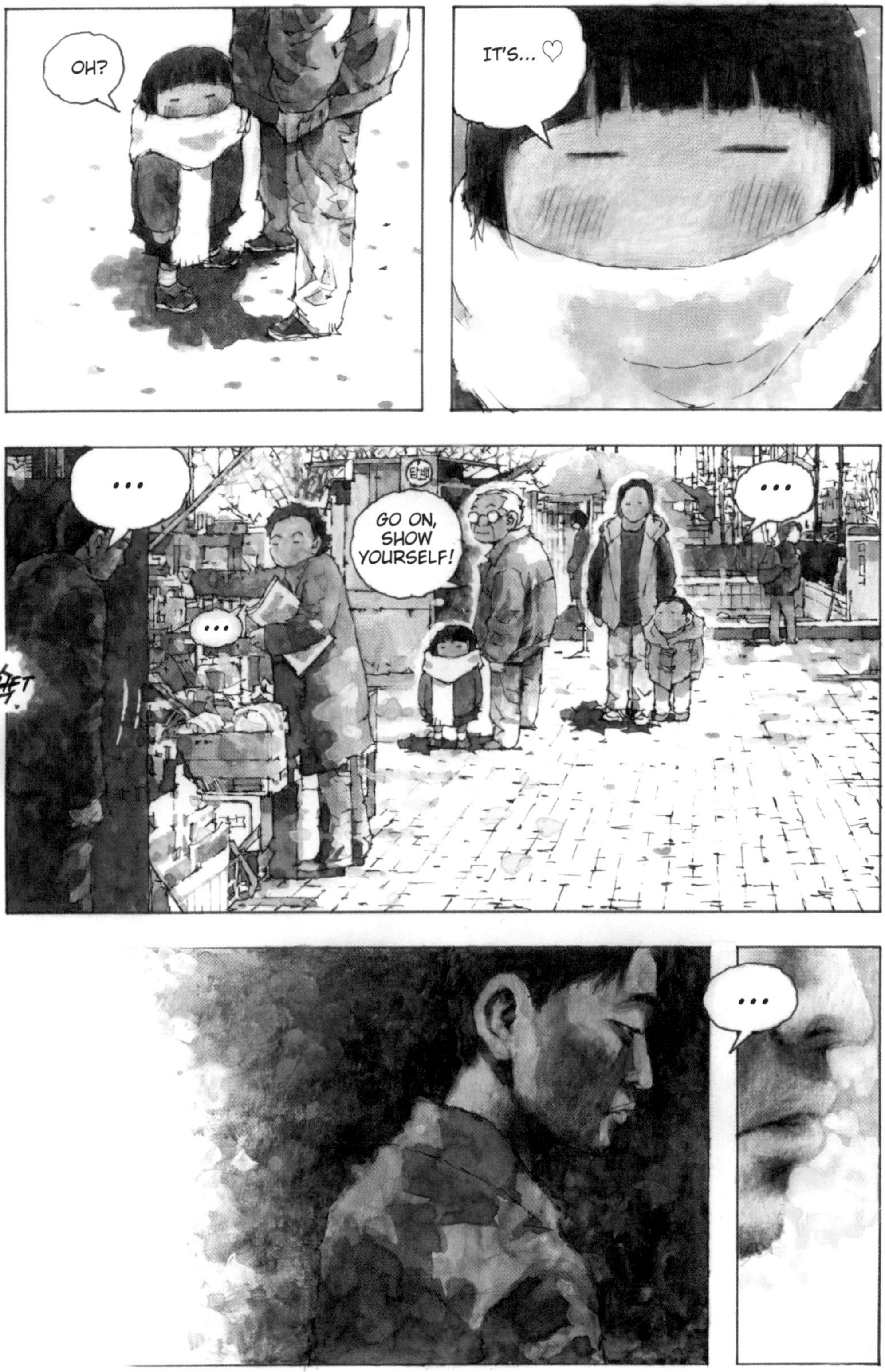
OH?
IT'S... ♡
...
...
GO ON, SHOW YOURSELF!
...
...

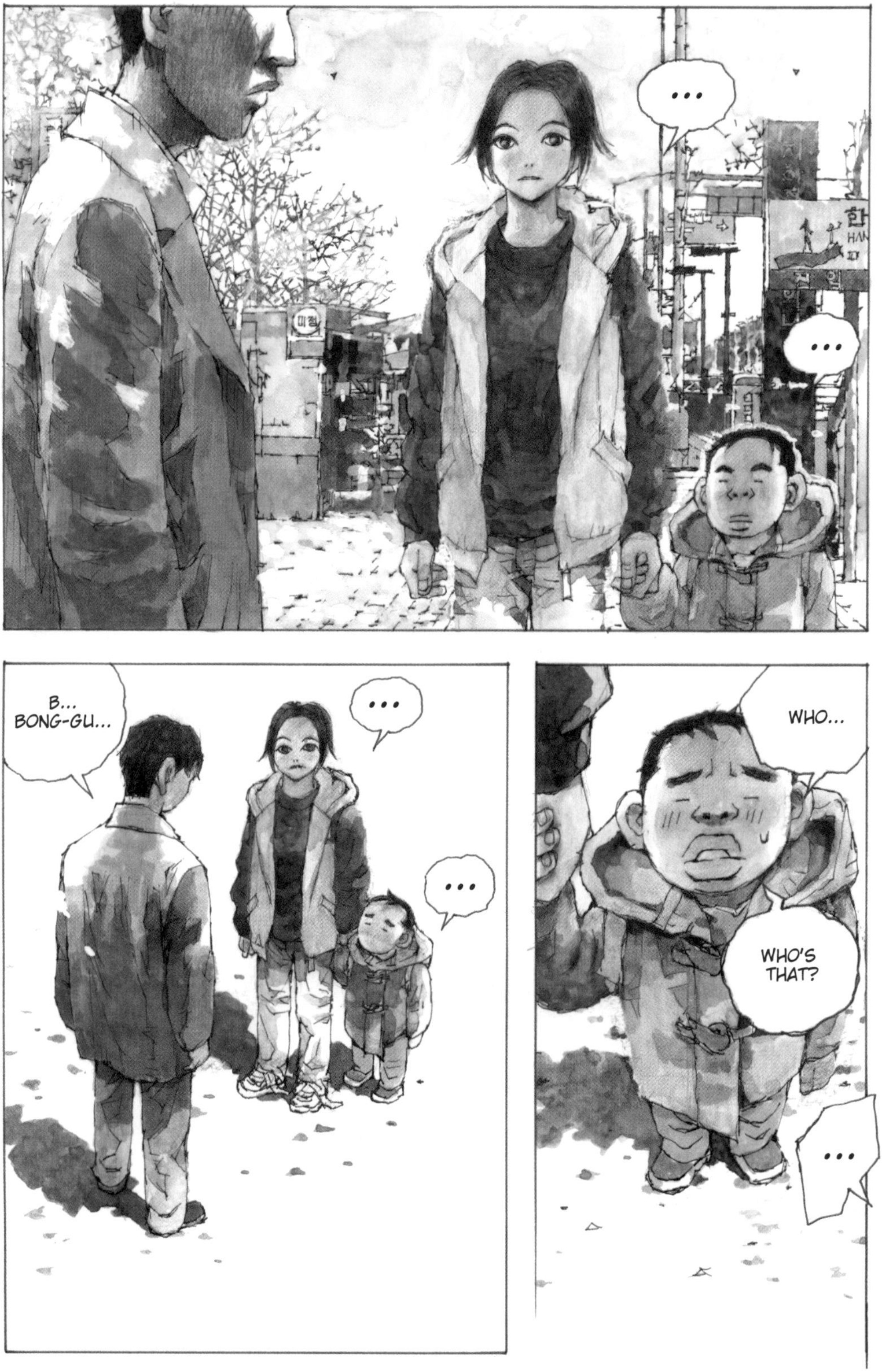
...
...
B... BONG-GU...
...
...
WHO...
WHO'S THAT?
...

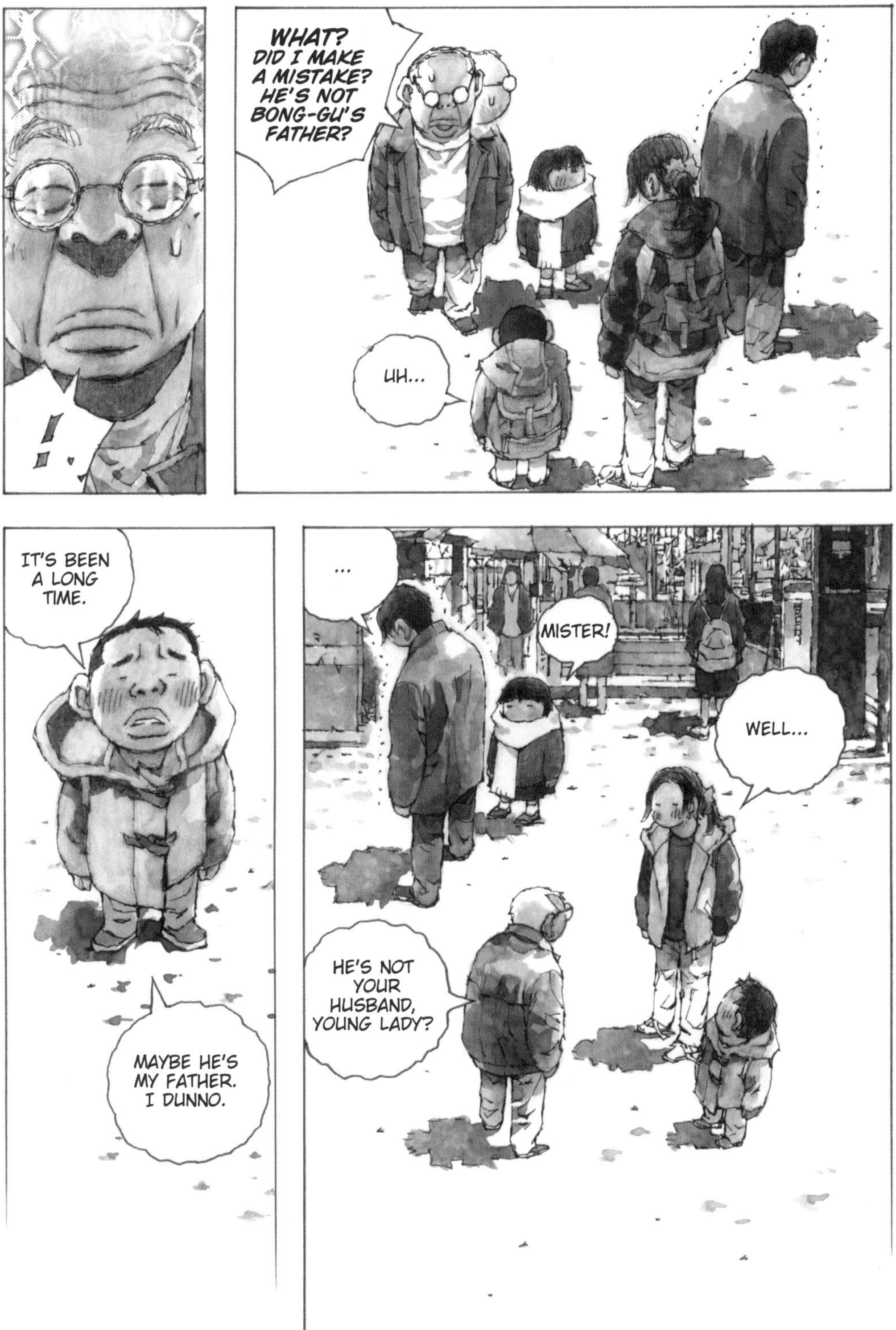
WHAT? DID I MAKE A MISTAKE? HE'S NOT BONG-GU'S FATHER?
UH...
IT'S BEEN A LONG TIME.
MAYBE HE'S MY FATHER. I DUNNO.
...
MISTER!
WELL...
HE'S NOT YOUR HUSBAND, YOUNG LADY?

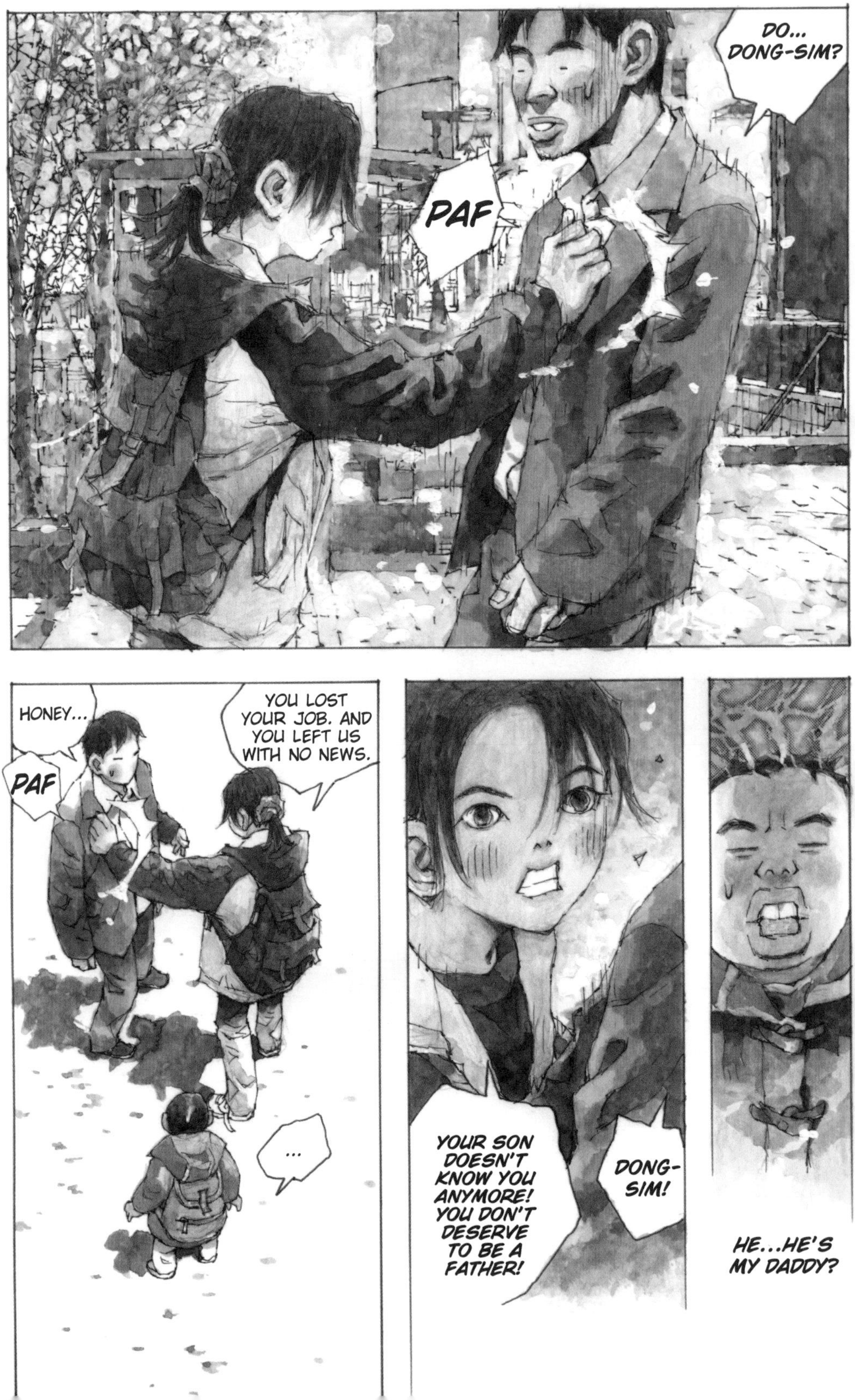
DO... DONG-SIM?
PAF
HONEY...
PAF
YOU LOST YOUR JOB. AND YOU LEFT US WITH NO NEWS.
...
YOUR SON DOESN'T KNOW YOU ANYMORE! YOU DON'T DESERVE TO BE A FATHER!
DONG-SIM!
HE...HE'S MY DADDY?

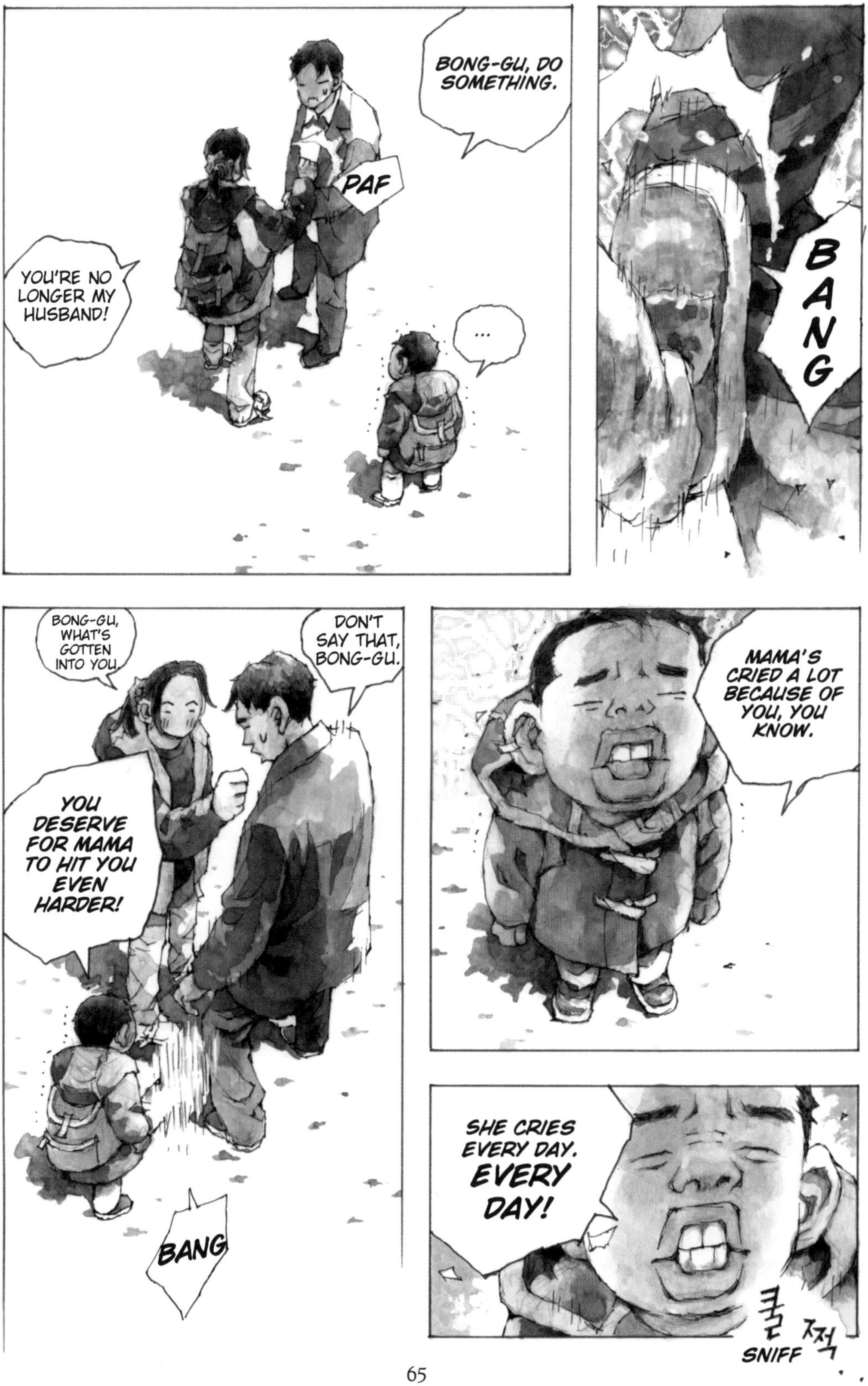
BONG-GU, DO SOMETHING.
PAF
YOU'RE NO LONGER MY HUSBAND!
...
BANG
BONG-GU, WHAT'S GOTTEN INTO YOU
DON'T SAY THAT, BONG-GU.
YOU DESERVE FOR MAMA TO HIT YOU EVEN HARDER!
BANG
MAMA'S CRIED A LOT BECAUSE OF YOU, YOU KNOW.
SHE CRIES EVERY DAY. EVERY DAY!
쿨적
SNIFF

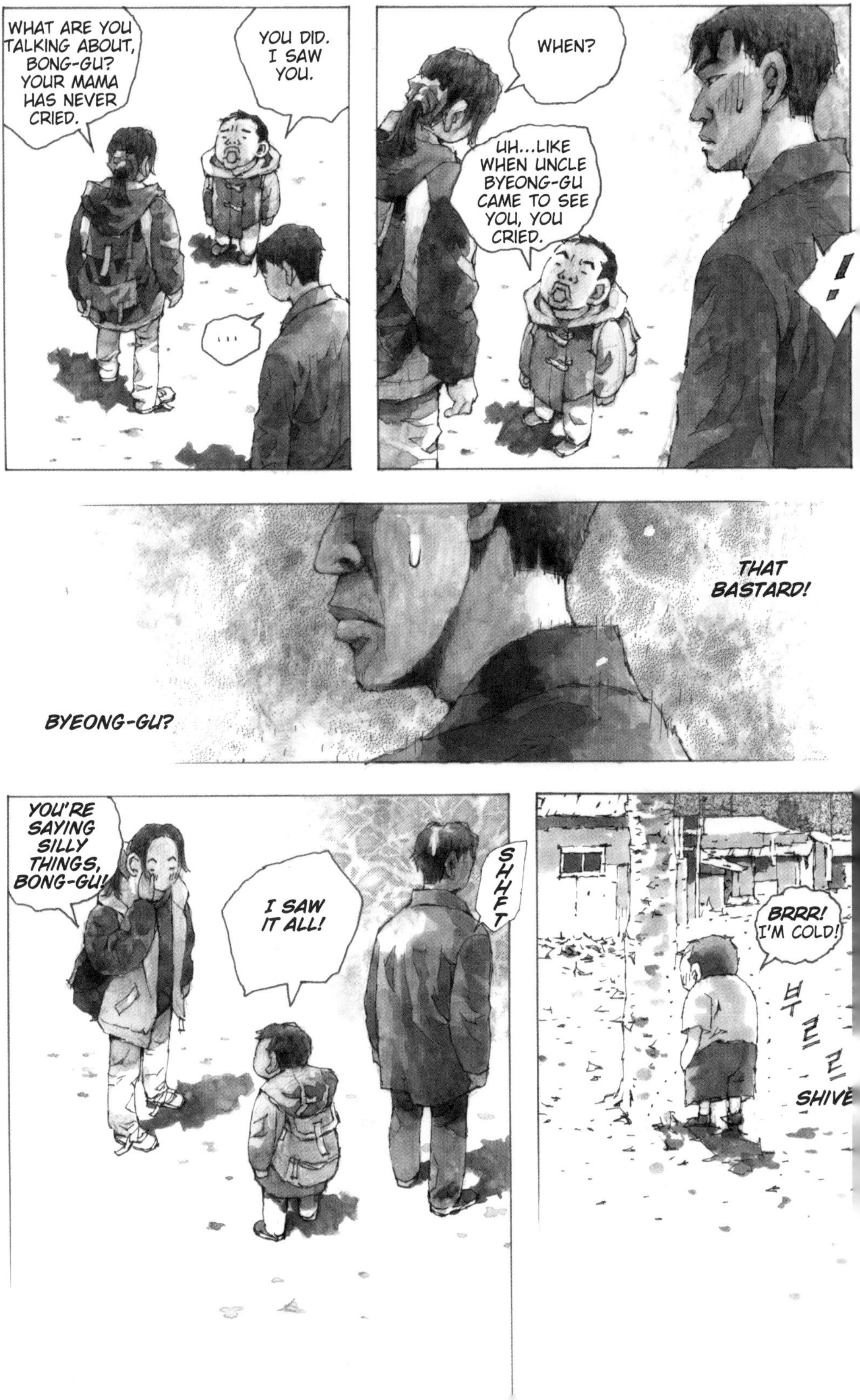

WHAT ARE YOU TALKING ABOUT, BONG-GU? YOUR MAMA HAS NEVER CRIED.
YOU DID. I SAW YOU.
...
WHEN?
UH...LIKE WHEN UNCLE BYEONG-GU CAME TO SEE YOU, YOU CRIED.
!
THAT BASTARD!
BYEONG-GU?
YOU'RE SAYING SILLY THINGS, BONG-GU!
I SAW IT ALL!
SHHFT
BRRR! I'M COLD!
부르르
SHIVE

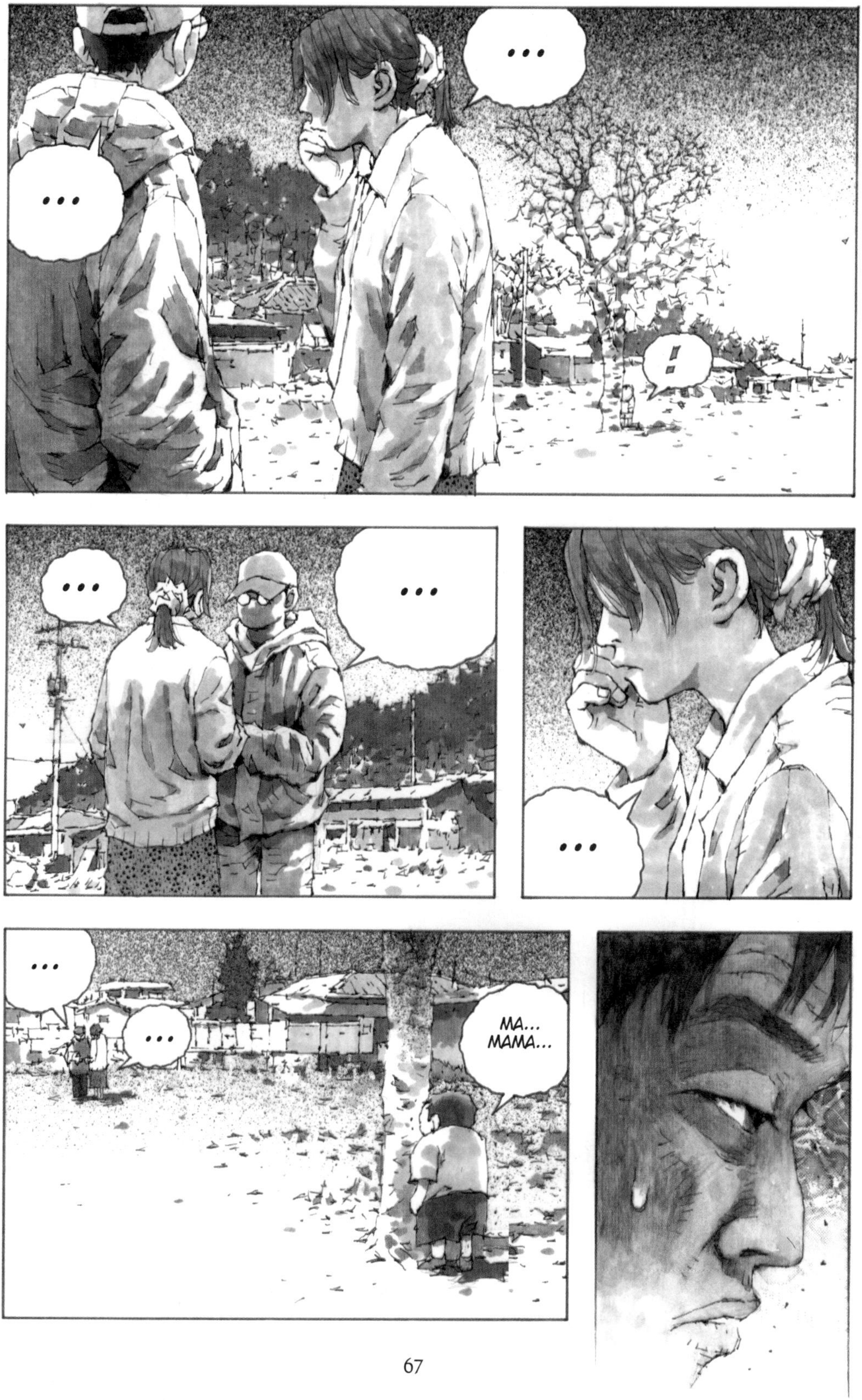
...
...
!
...
...
...
...
...
MA...
MAMA...

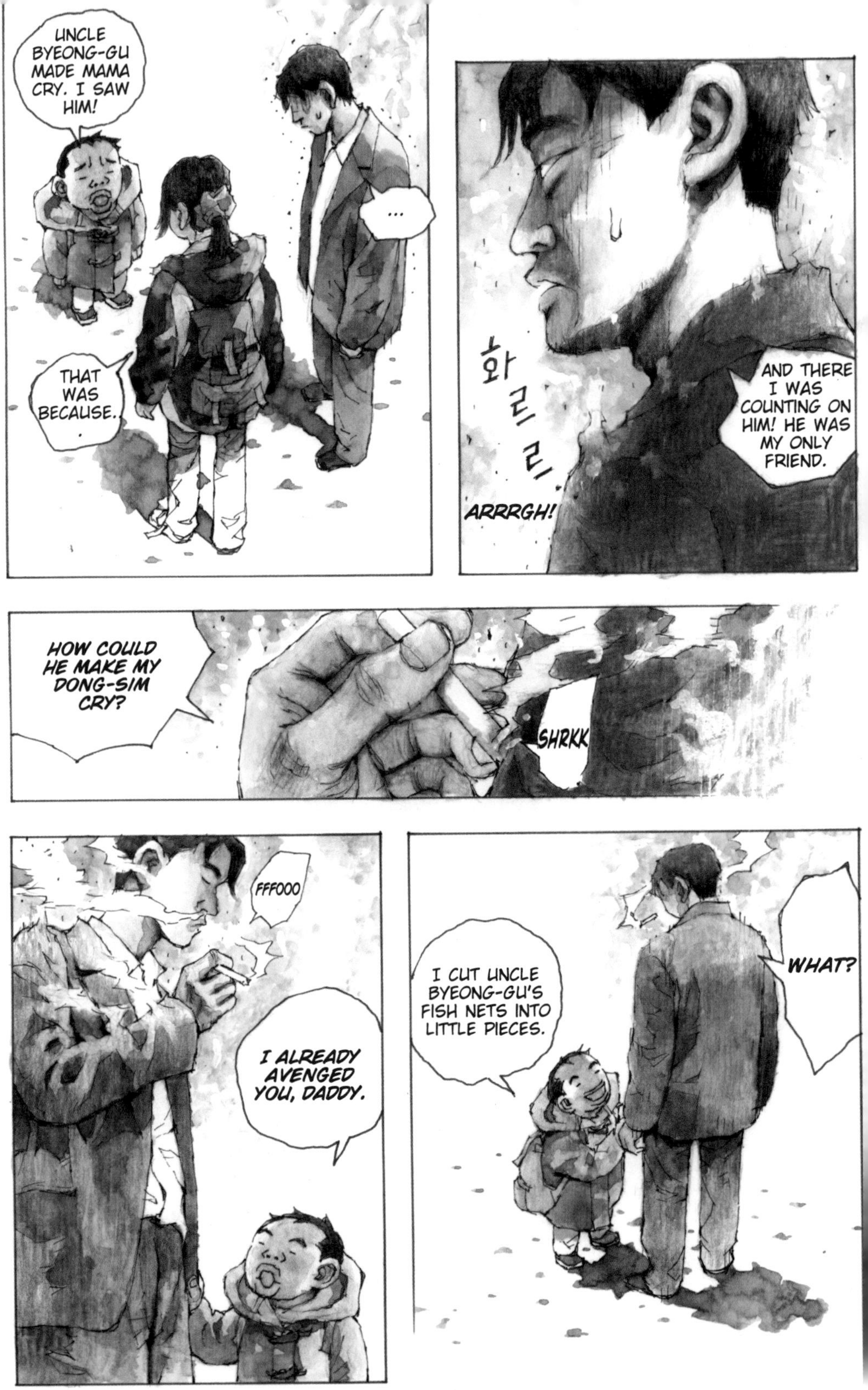
UNCLE BYEONG-GU MADE MAMA CRY. I SAW HIM!
...
THAT WAS BECAUSE...
화르르
ARRRGH!
AND THERE I WAS COUNTING ON HIM! HE WAS MY ONLY FRIEND.
HOW COULD HE MAKE MY DONG-SIM CRY?
SHRKK
FFFOOO
I ALREADY AVENGED YOU, DADDY.
I CUT UNCLE BYEONG-GU'S FISH NETS INTO LITTLE PIECES.
WHAT?

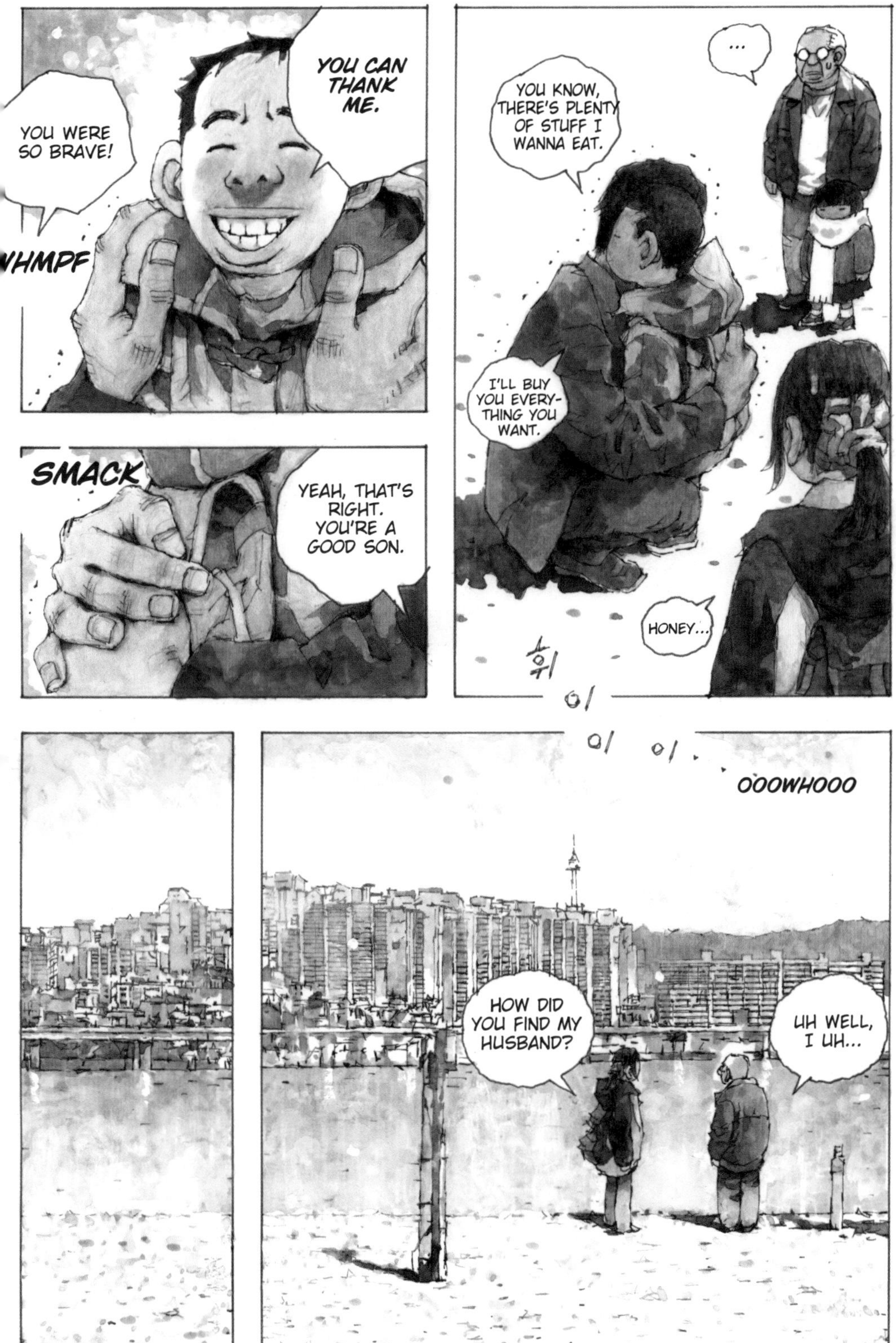
YOU WERE SO BRAVE!
YOU CAN THANK ME.
WHMPF
SMACK
YEAH, THAT'S RIGHT. YOU'RE A GOOD SON.
...
YOU KNOW, THERE'S PLENTY OF STUFF I WANNA EAT.
I'LL BUY YOU EVERYTHING YOU WANT.
HONEY...
슈위
이
이 이..
OOOWHOOO
HOW DID YOU FIND MY HUSBAND?
UH WELL, I UH...

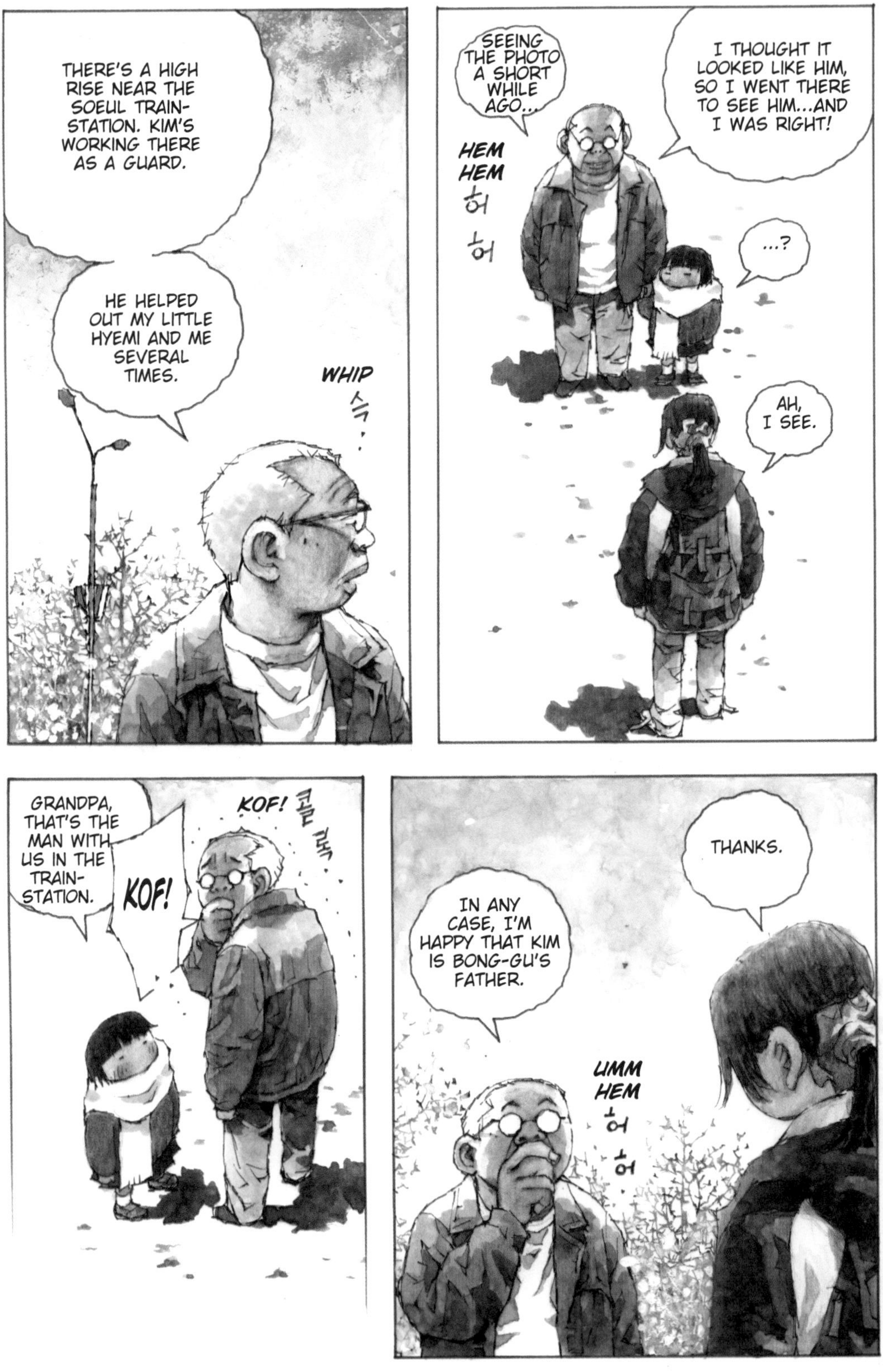
THERE'S A HIGH RISE NEAR THE SOEUL TRAIN-STATION. KIM'S WORKING THERE AS A GUARD.
HE HELPED OUT MY LITTLE HYEMI AND ME SEVERAL TIMES.
WHIP
슥
SEEING THE PHOTO A SHORT WHILE AGO...
I THOUGHT IT LOOKED LIKE HIM, SO I WENT THERE TO SEE HIM...AND I WAS RIGHT!
HEM HEM
허 허
...?
AH, I SEE.
GRANDPA, THAT'S THE MAN WITH US IN THE TRAIN-STATION.
KOF!
콜록
KOF!
THANKS.
IN ANY CASE, I'M HAPPY THAT KIM IS BONG-GU'S FATHER.
UMM HEM
허 허

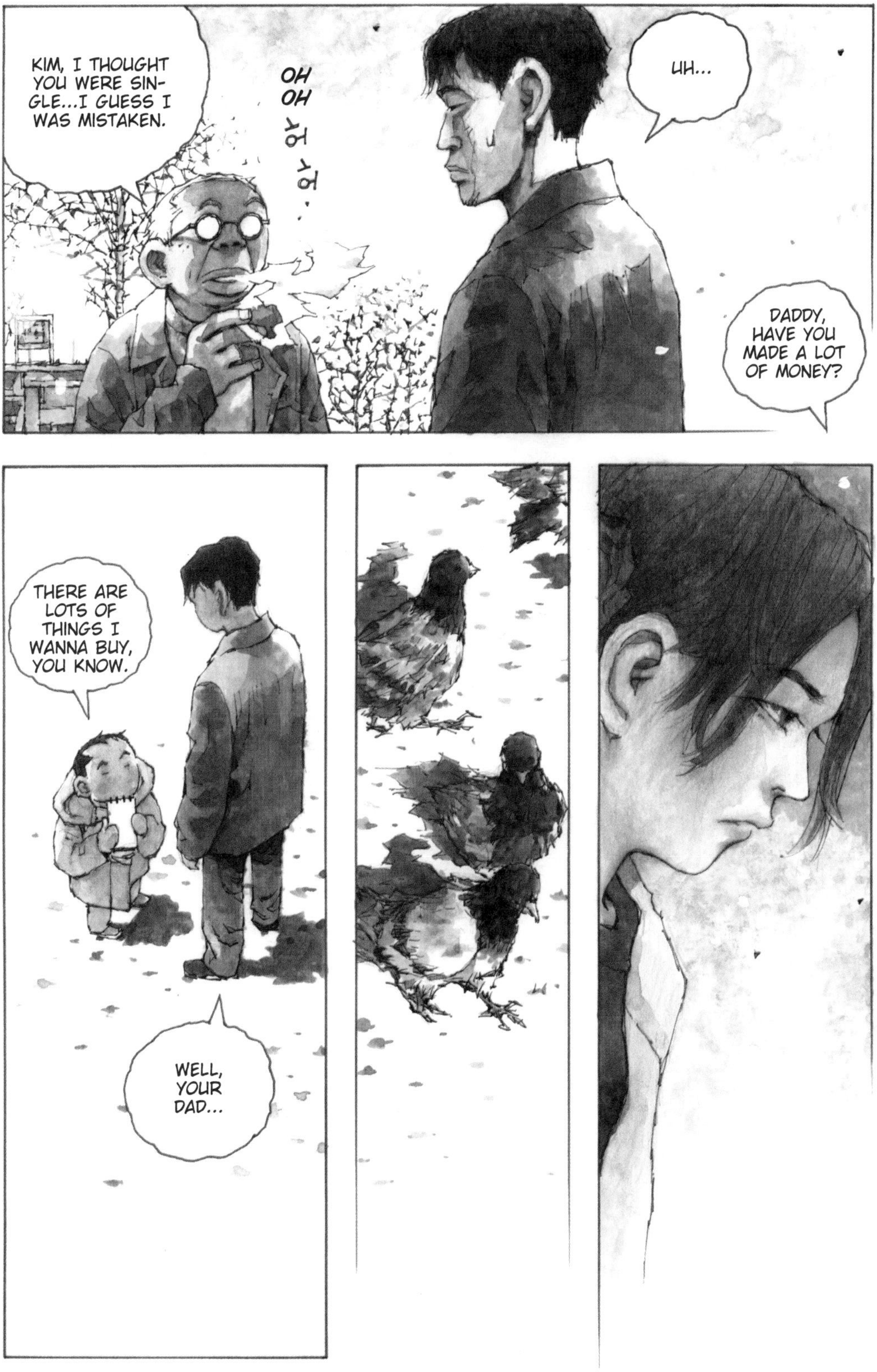
KIM, I THOUGHT YOU WERE SIN-GLE...I GUESS I WAS MISTAKEN.
OH OH
허 허.
UH...
DADDY, HAVE YOU MADE A LOT OF MONEY?
THERE ARE LOTS OF THINGS I WANNA BUY, YOU KNOW.
WELL, YOUR DAD...

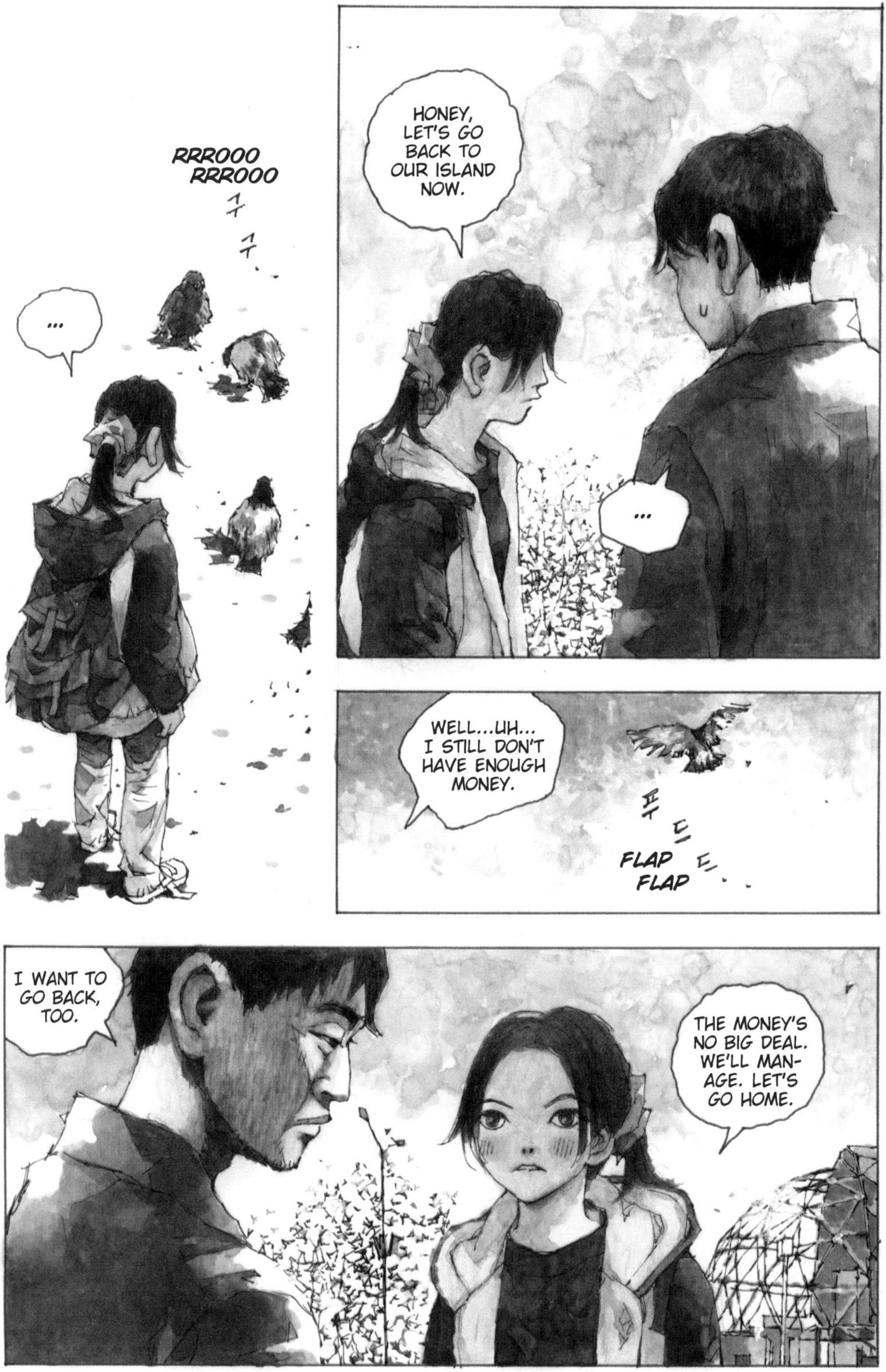
RRROOO
RRROOO
...
HONEY, LET'S GO BACK TO OUR ISLAND NOW.
...
WELL...UH... I STILL DON'T HAVE ENOUGH MONEY.
FLAP
FLAP
I WANT TO GO BACK, TOO.
THE MONEY'S NO BIG DEAL. WE'LL MAN-AGE. LET'S GO HOME.

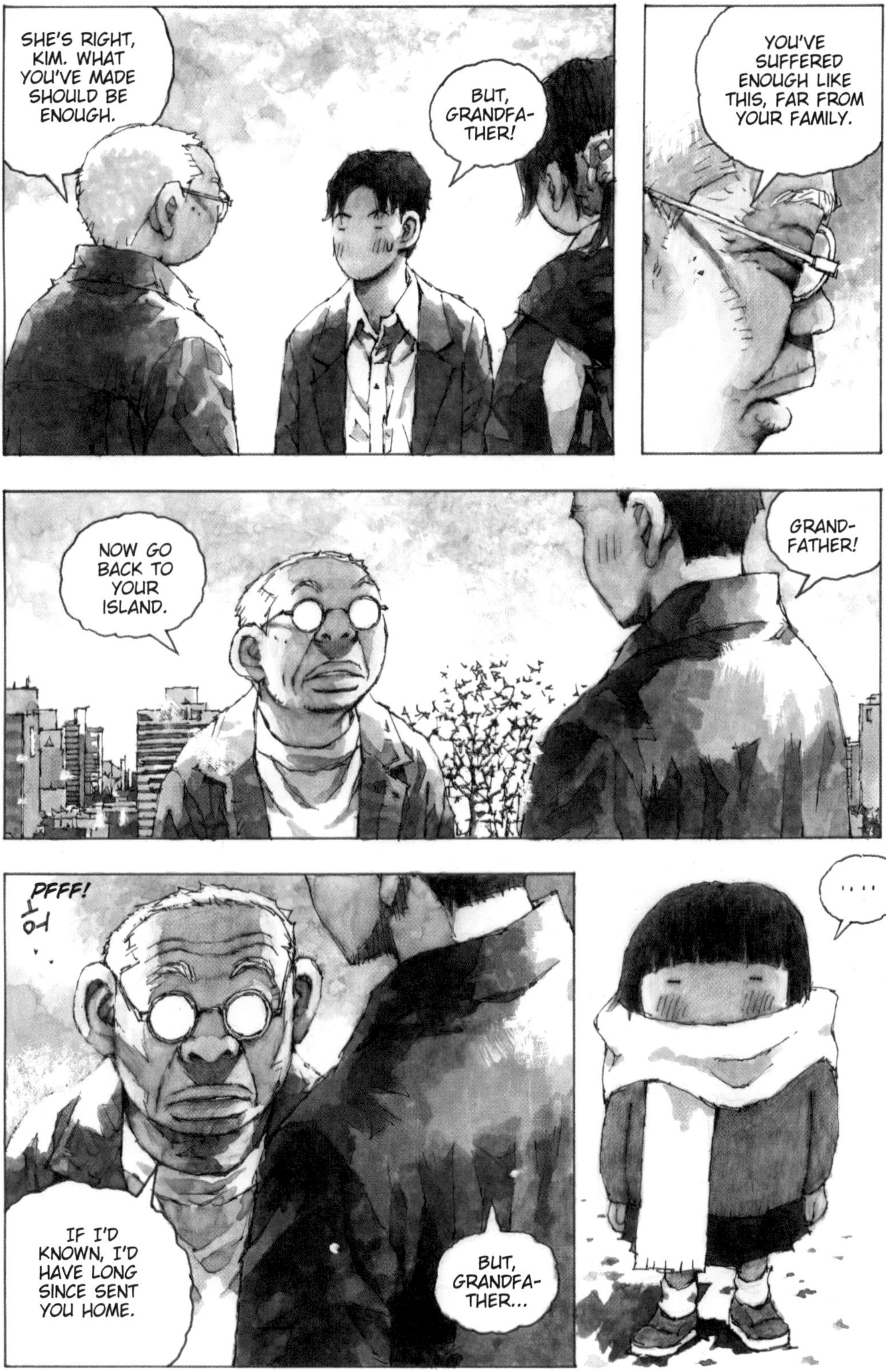
SHE'S RIGHT, KIM. WHAT YOU'VE MADE SHOULD BE ENOUGH.
BUT, GRANDFA-THER!
YOU'VE SUFFERED ENOUGH LIKE THIS, FAR FROM YOUR FAMILY.
NOW GO BACK TO YOUR ISLAND.
GRAND-FATHER!
PFFF!
IF I'D KNOWN, I'D HAVE LONG SINCE SENT YOU HOME.
BUT, GRANDFA-THER...
....

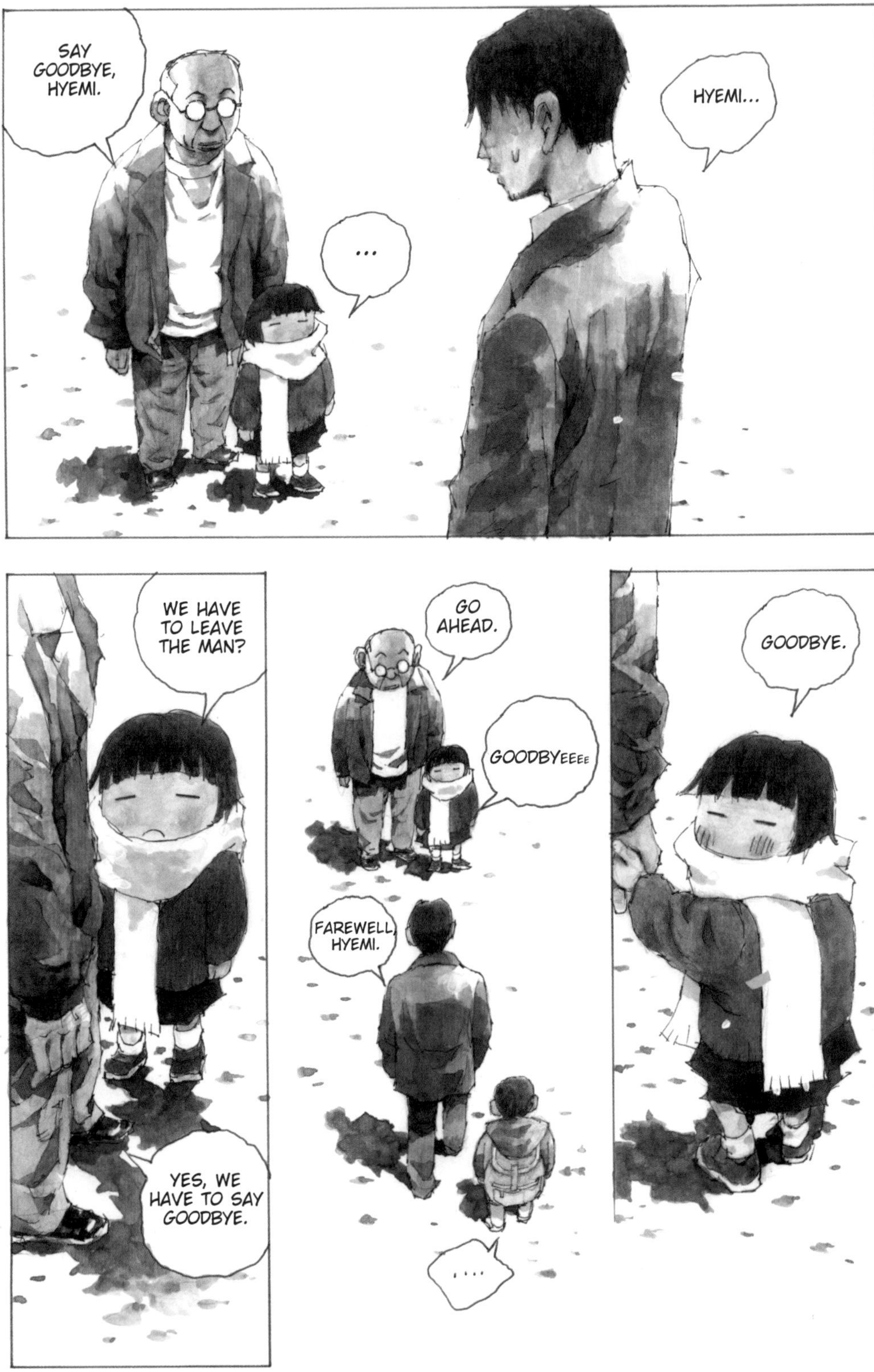
SAY GOODBYE, HYEMI.
...
HYEMI...
WE HAVE TO LEAVE THE MAN?
YES, WE HAVE TO SAY GOODBYE.
GO AHEAD.
GOODBYEEEEE
FAREWELL, HYEMI.
....
GOODBYE.

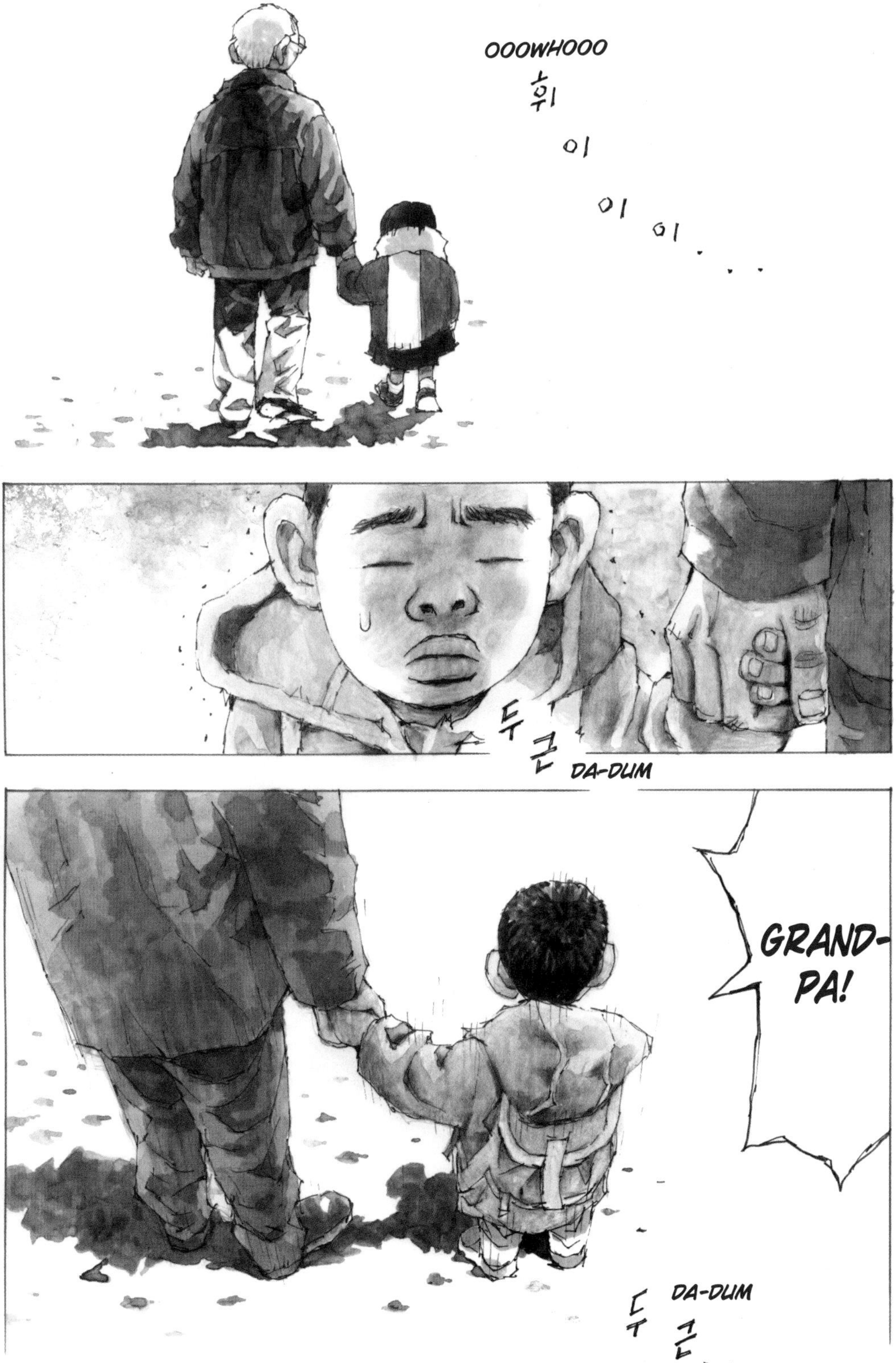
OOOWHOOO
휘이이이....
두근
DA-DUM
GRAND-PA!
DA-DUM
두근.

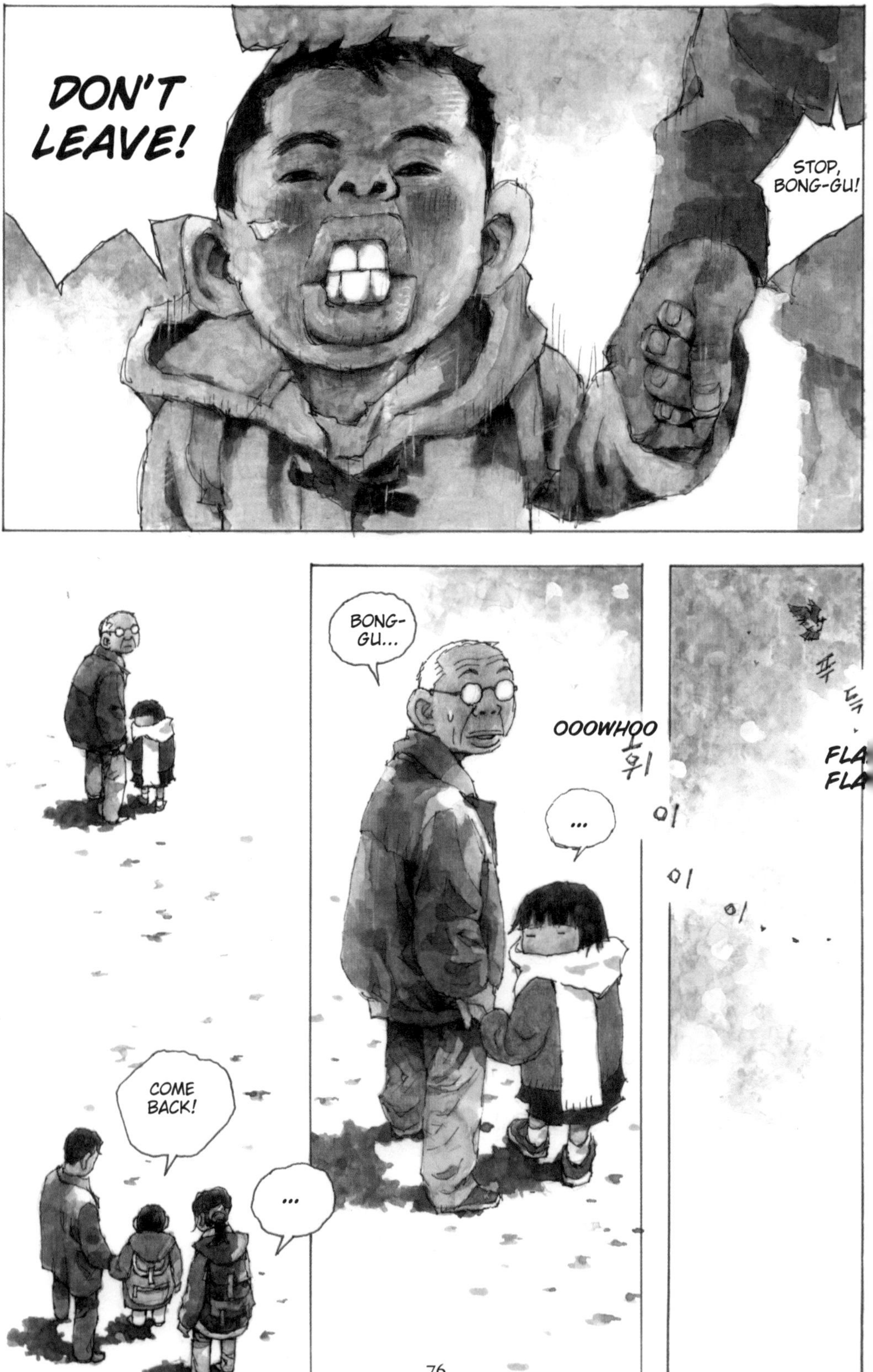
DON'T LEAVE!
STOP, BONG-GU!
COME BACK!
...
BONG-GU...
OOOWHOO
...
FLA
FLA

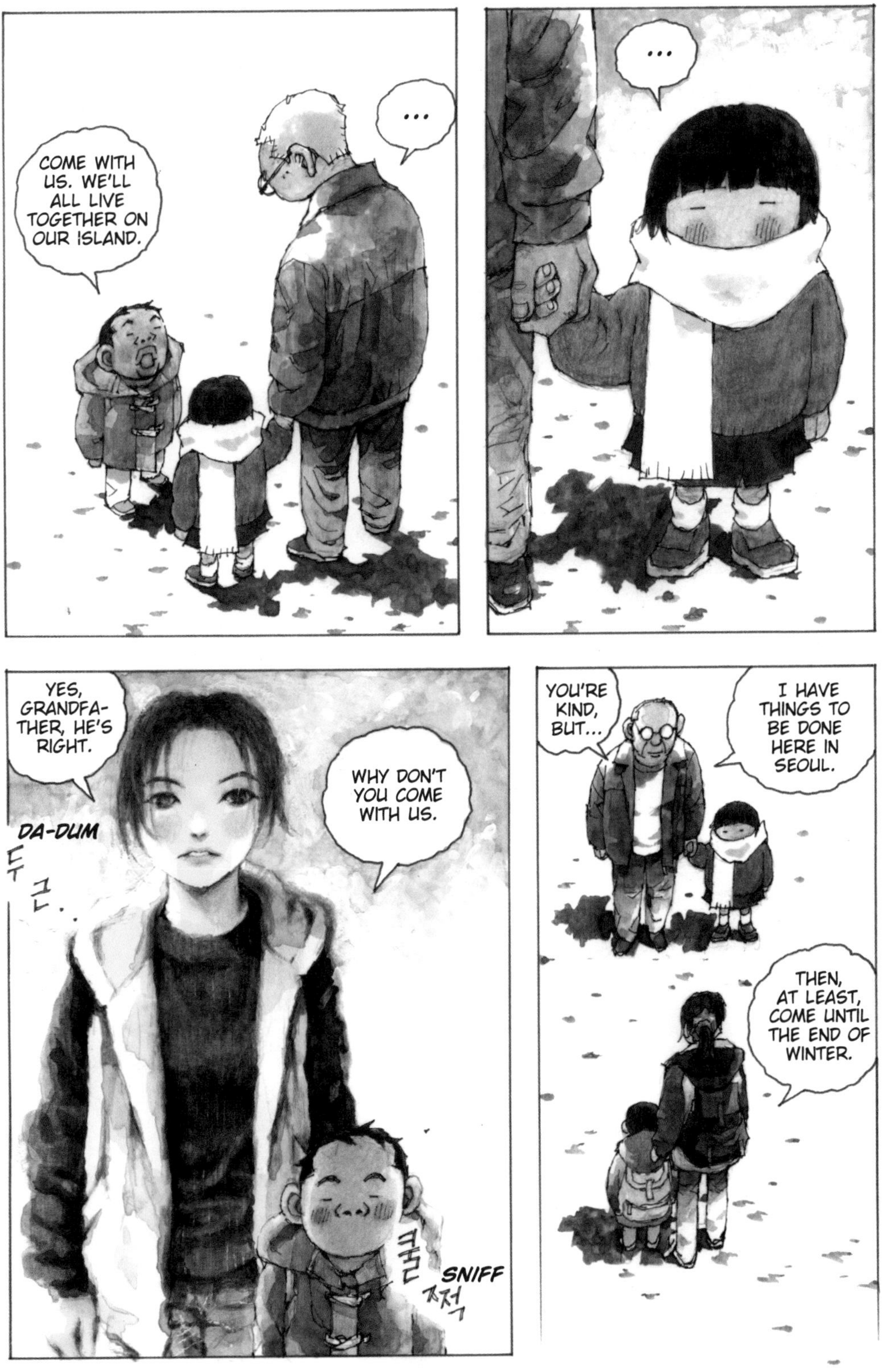
COME WITH US. WE'LL ALL LIVE TOGETHER ON OUR ISLAND.
...
...
YES, GRANDFA-THER, HE'S RIGHT.
WHY DON'T YOU COME WITH US.
DA-DUM
두근..
SNIFF
훌쩍
YOU'RE KIND, BUT...
I HAVE THINGS TO BE DONE HERE IN SEOUL.
THEN, AT LEAST, COME UNTIL THE END OF WINTER.

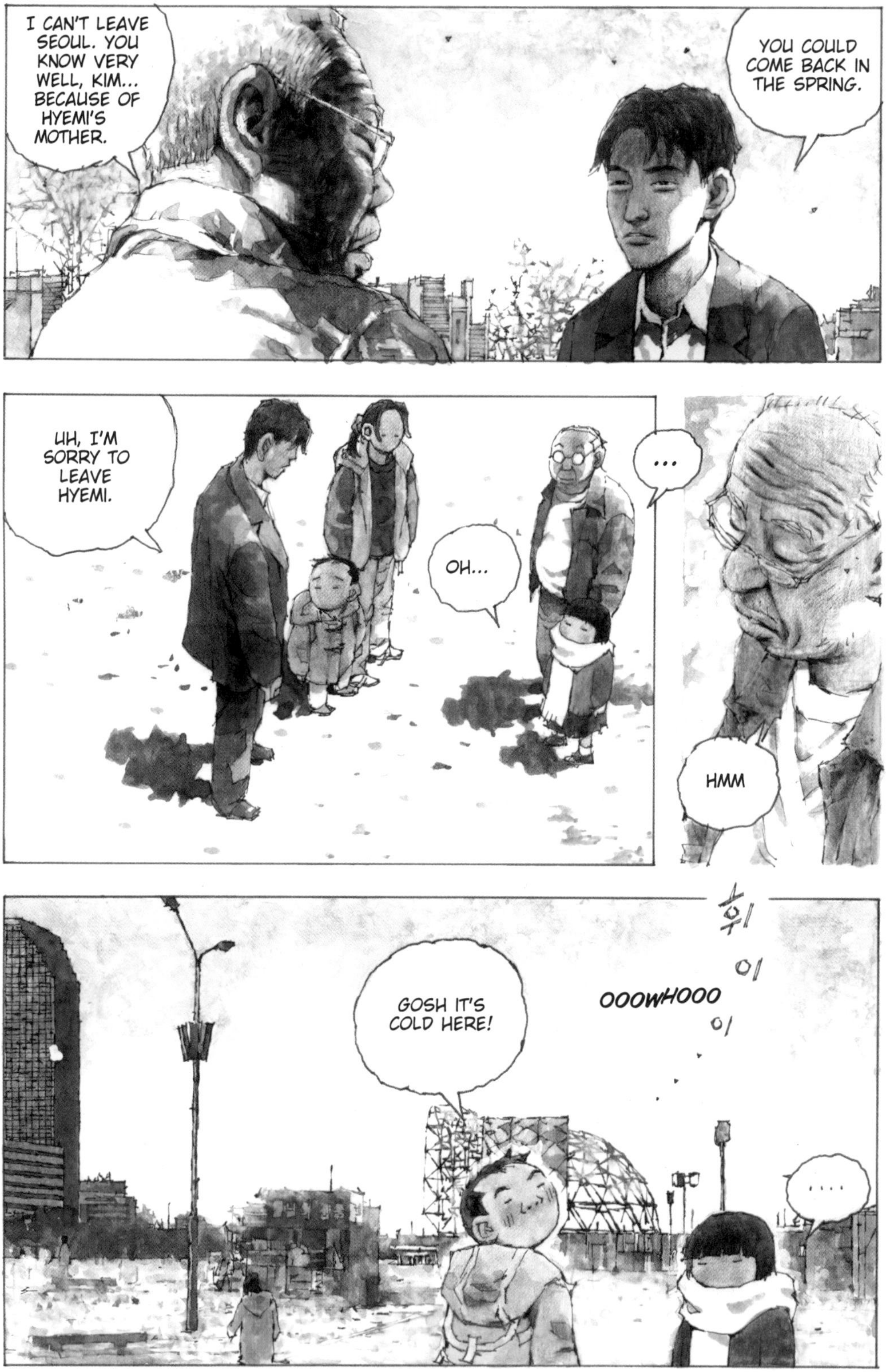
I CAN'T LEAVE SEOUL. YOU KNOW VERY WELL, KIM... BECAUSE OF HYEMI'S MOTHER.
YOU COULD COME BACK IN THE SPRING.
UH, I'M SORRY TO LEAVE HYEMI.
OH...
...
HMM
휘
이
OOOWHOOO
이
GOSH IT'S COLD HERE!
....

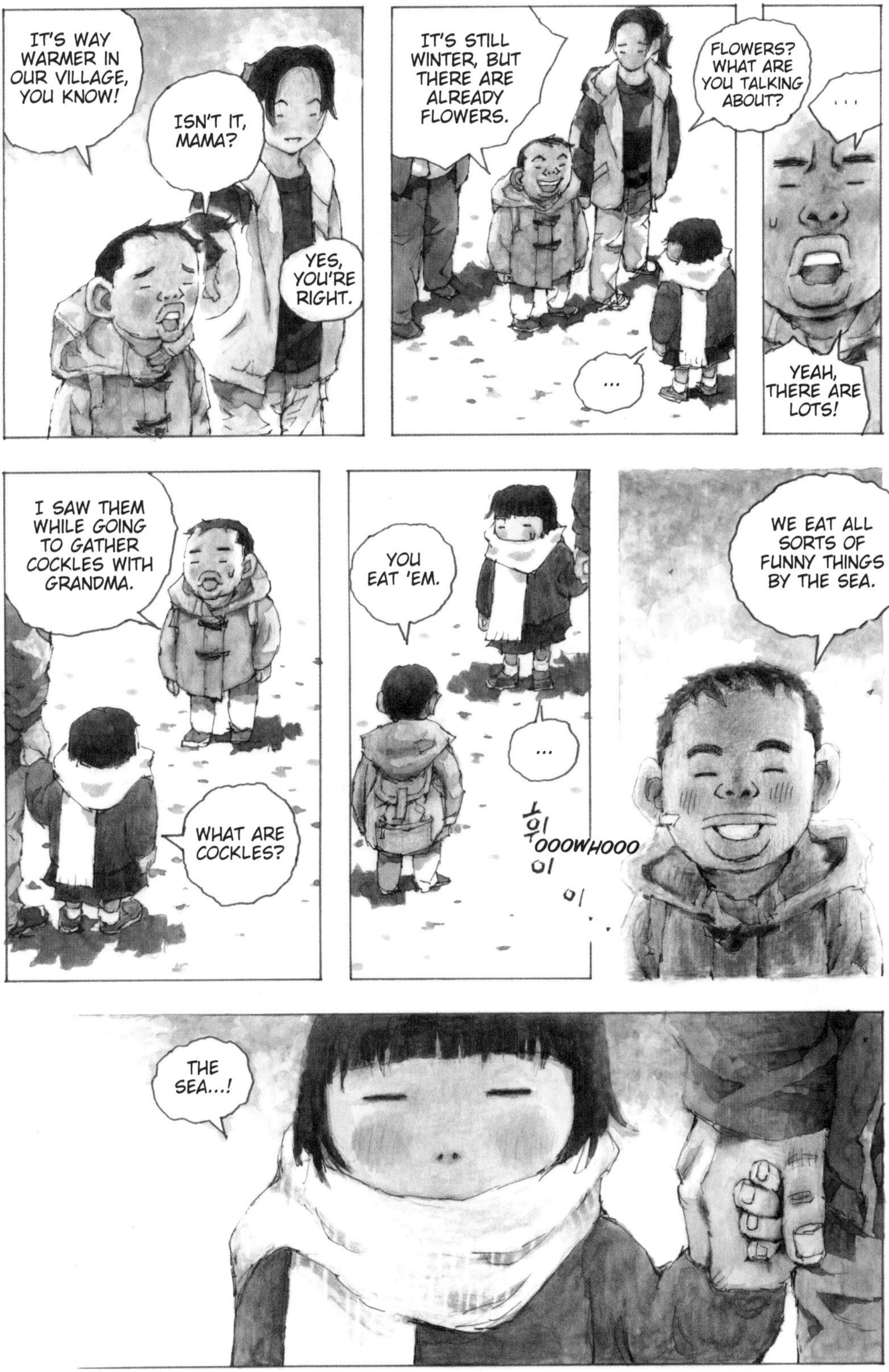
IT'S WAY WARMER IN OUR VILLAGE, YOU KNOW!
ISN'T IT, MAMA?
YES, YOU'RE RIGHT.
IT'S STILL WINTER, BUT THERE ARE ALREADY FLOWERS.
...
FLOWERS? WHAT ARE YOU TALKING ABOUT?
...
YEAH, THERE ARE LOTS!
I SAW THEM WHILE GOING TO GATHER COCKLES WITH GRANDMA.
WHAT ARE COCKLES?
YOU EAT 'EM.
...
OOOWHOOO
WE EAT ALL SORTS OF FUNNY THINGS BY THE SEA.
THE SEA...!

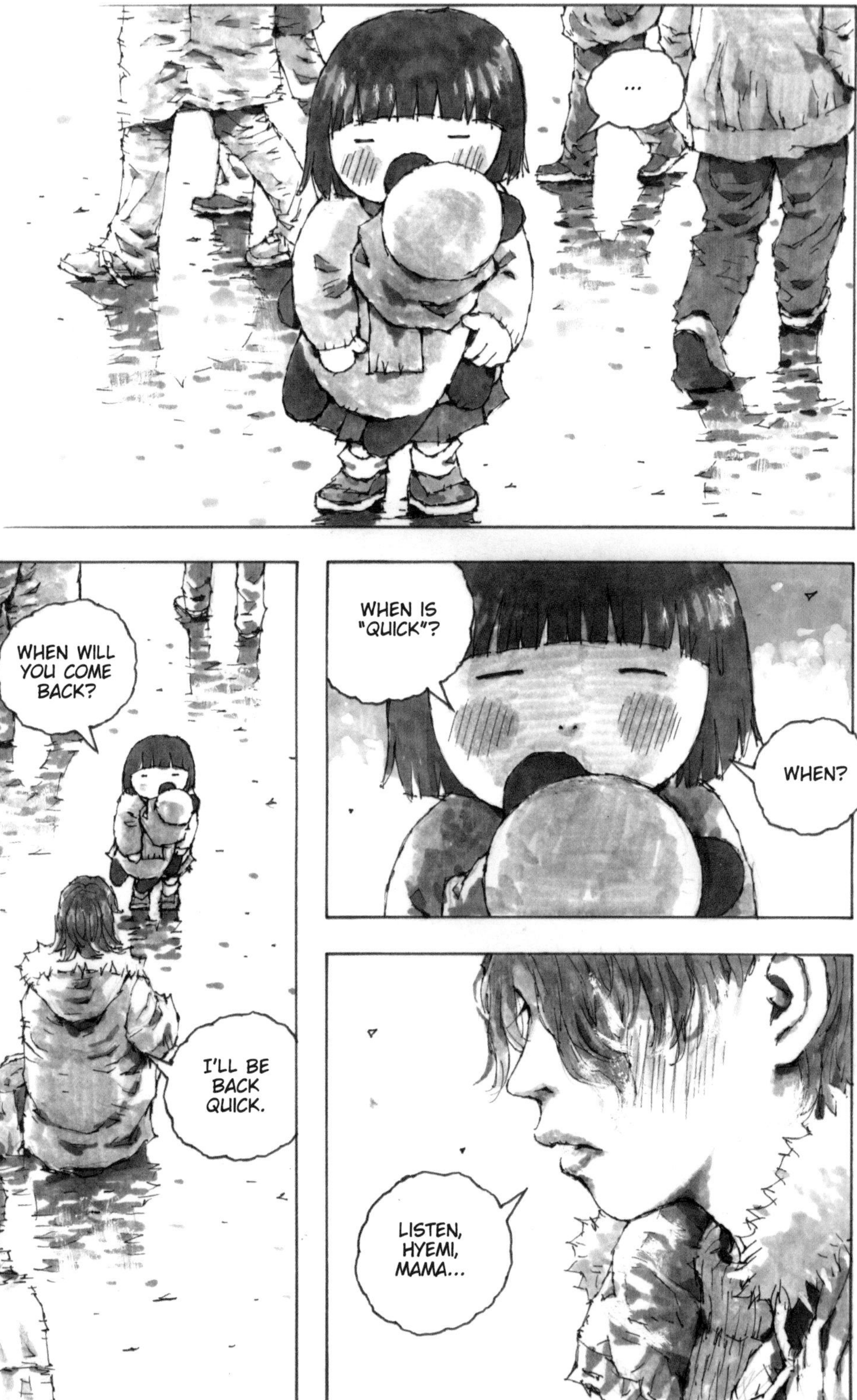
...
WHEN WILL YOU COME BACK?
I'LL BE BACK QUICK.
WHEN IS "QUICK"?
WHEN?
LISTEN, HYEMI, MAMA...

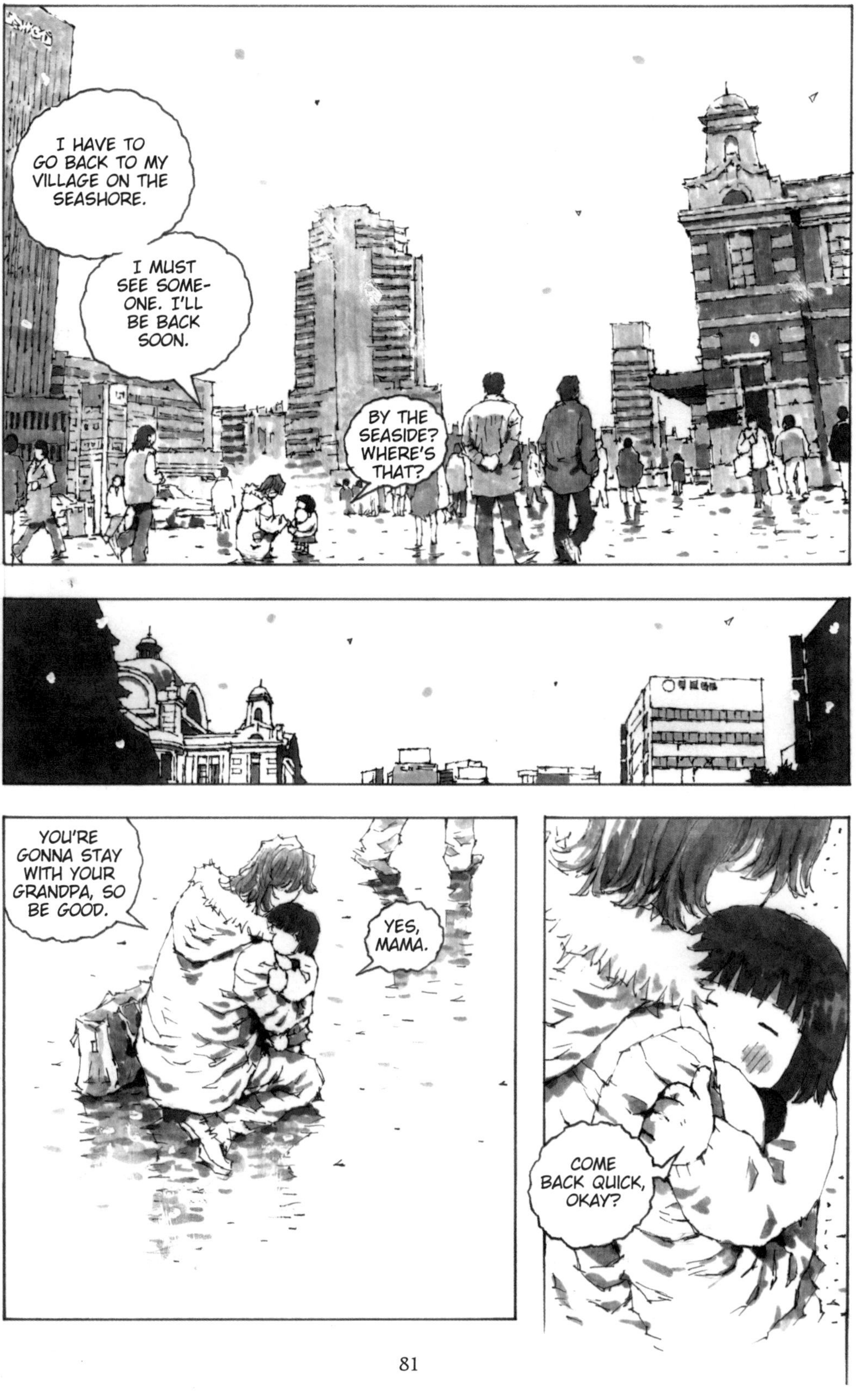
I HAVE TO GO BACK TO MY VILLAGE ON THE SEASHORE.
I MUST SEE SOME-ONE. I'LL BE BACK SOON.
BY THE SEASIDE? WHERE'S THAT?
YOU'RE GONNA STAY WITH YOUR GRANDPA, SO BE GOOD.
YES, MAMA.
COME BACK QUICK, OKAY?

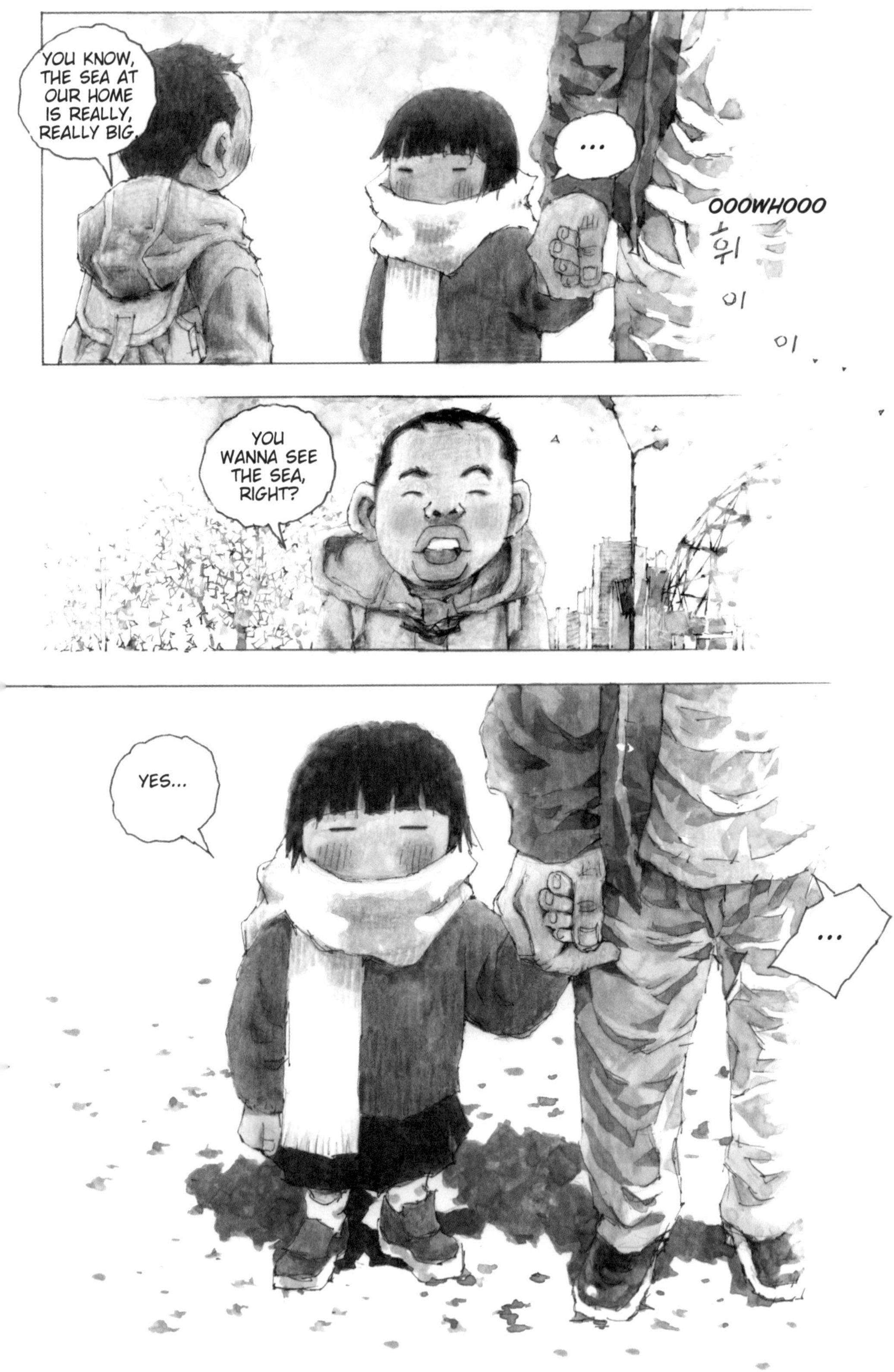
YOU KNOW, THE SEA AT OUR HOME IS REALLY, REALLY BIG.
...
OOOWHOOO
후위이이...
YOU WANNA SEE THE SEA, RIGHT?
YES...
...

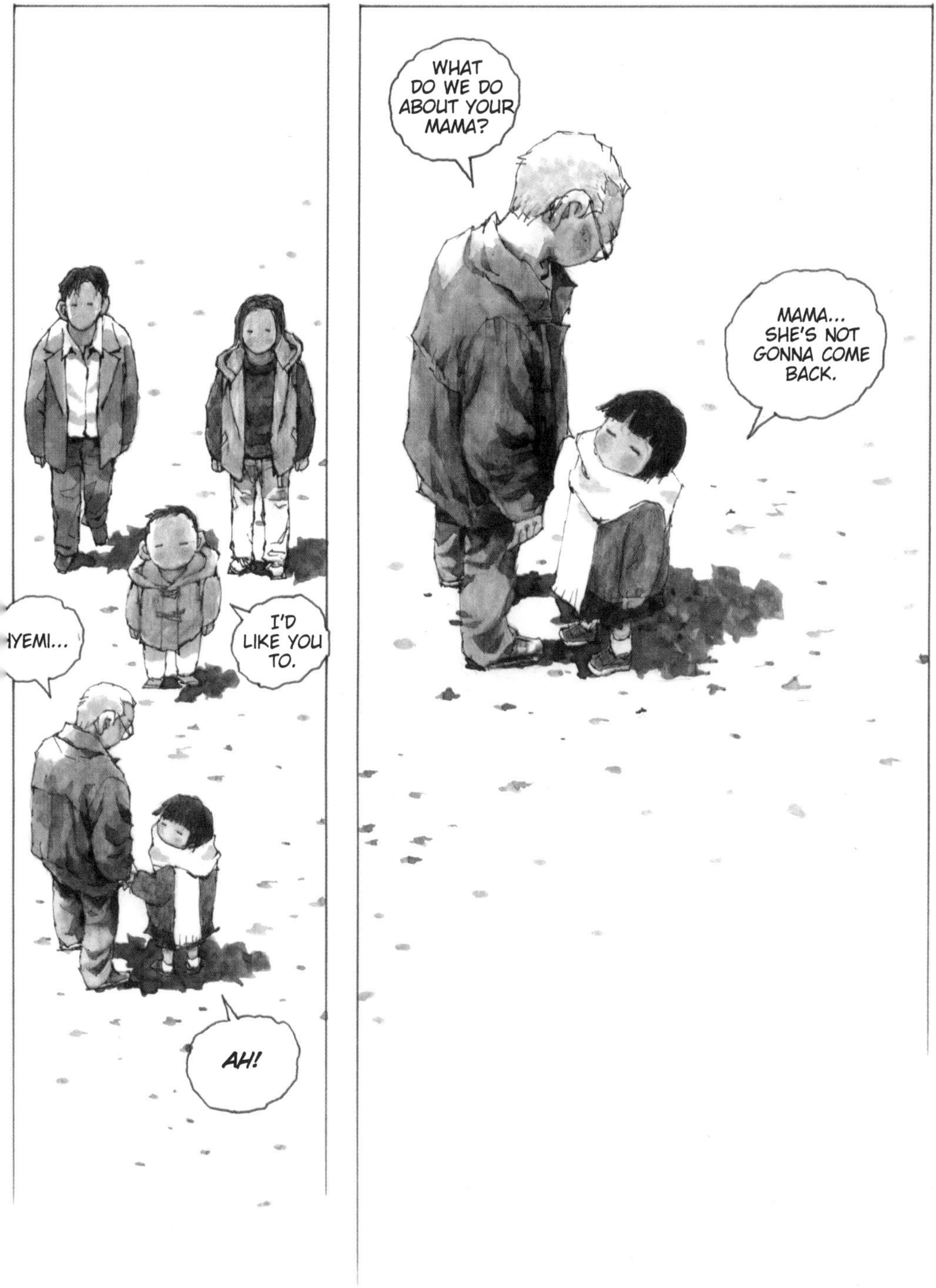
IYEMI...
I'D LIKE YOU TO.
AH!
WHAT DO WE DO ABOUT YOUR MAMA?
MAMA... SHE'S NOT GONNA COME BACK.

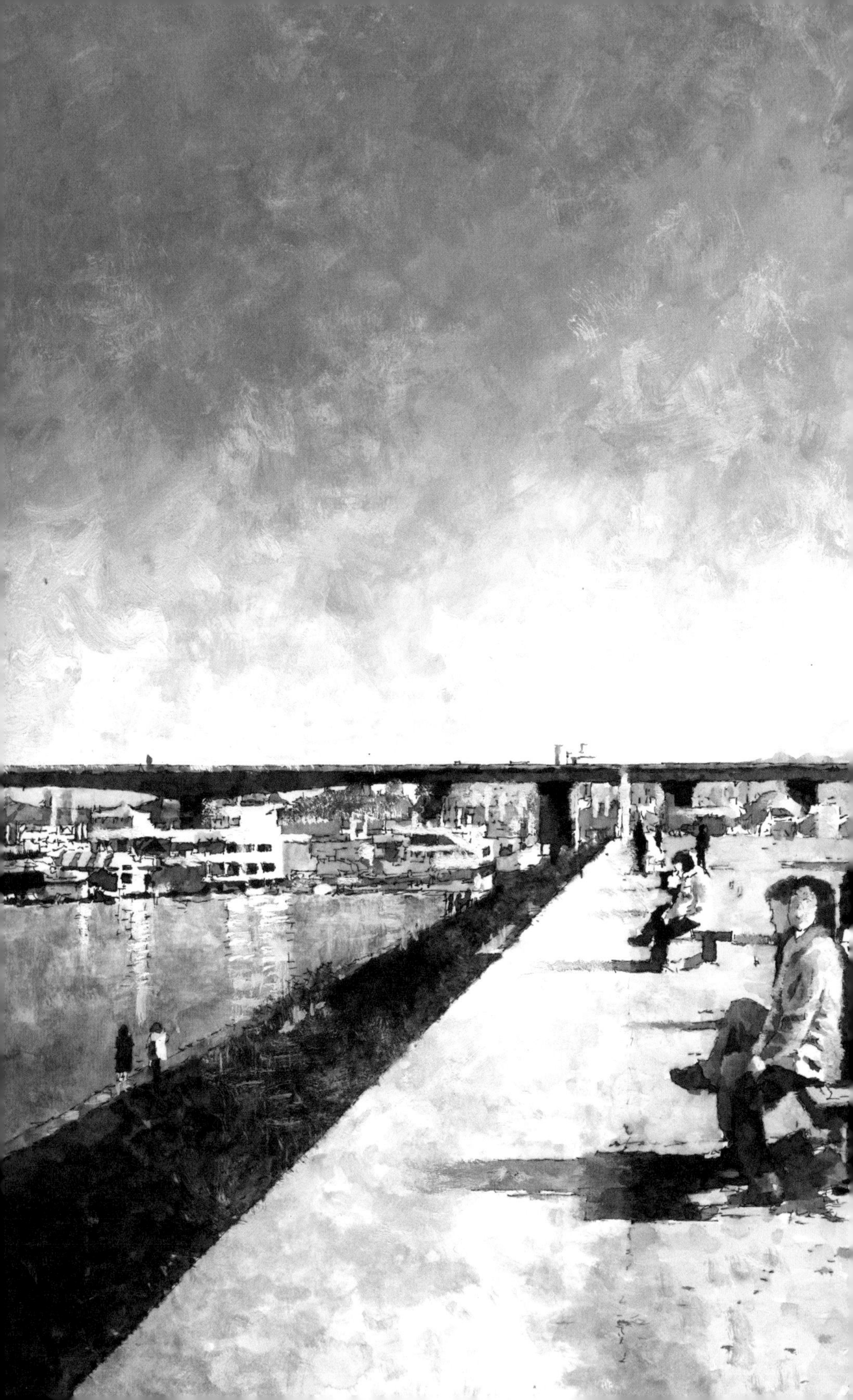

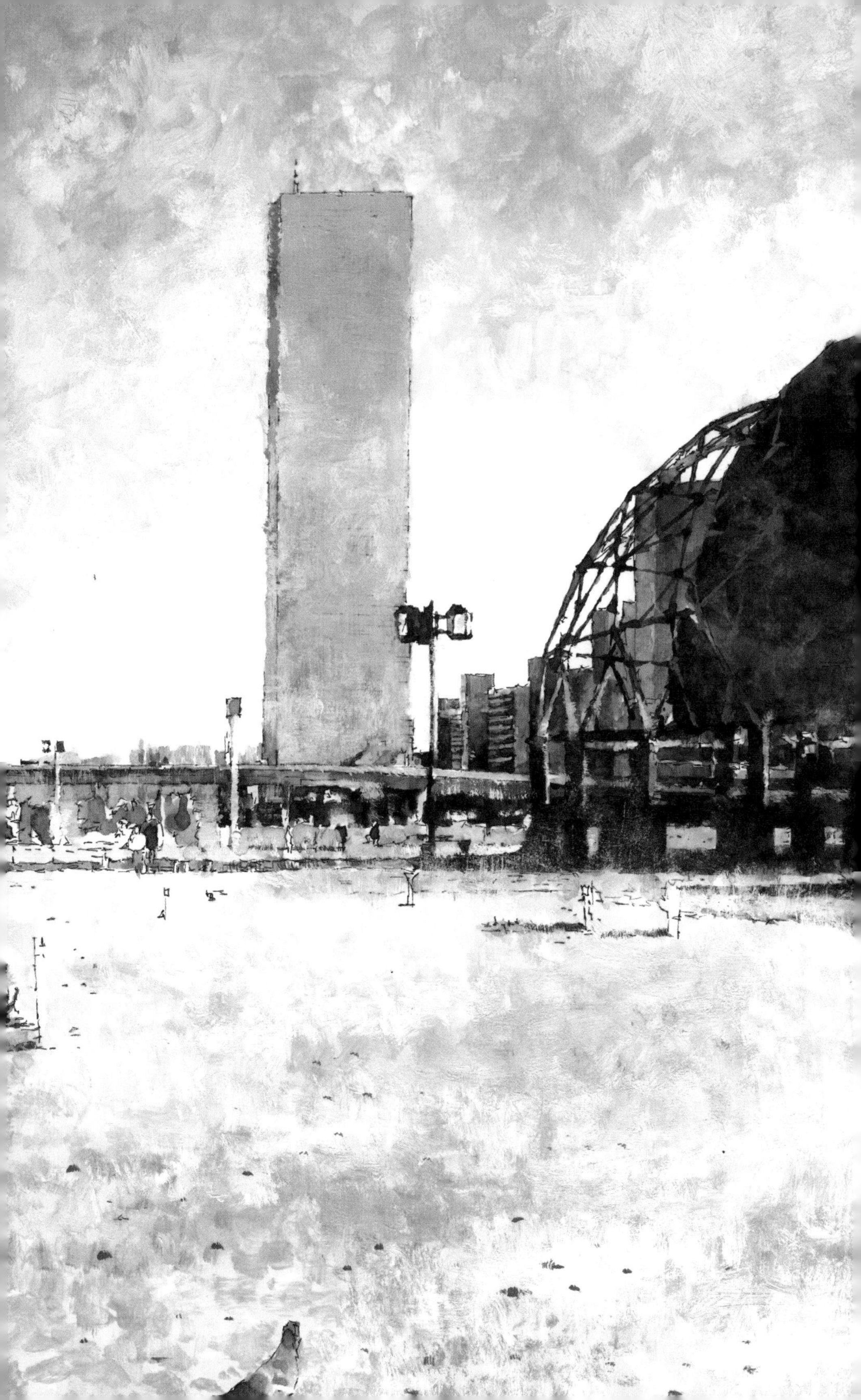

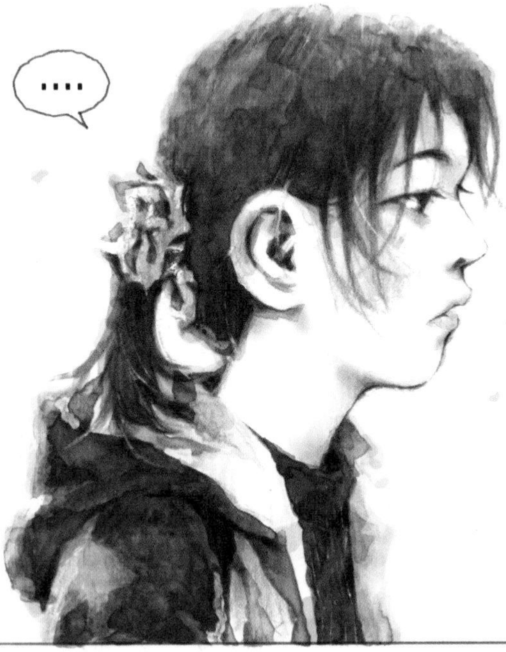
....

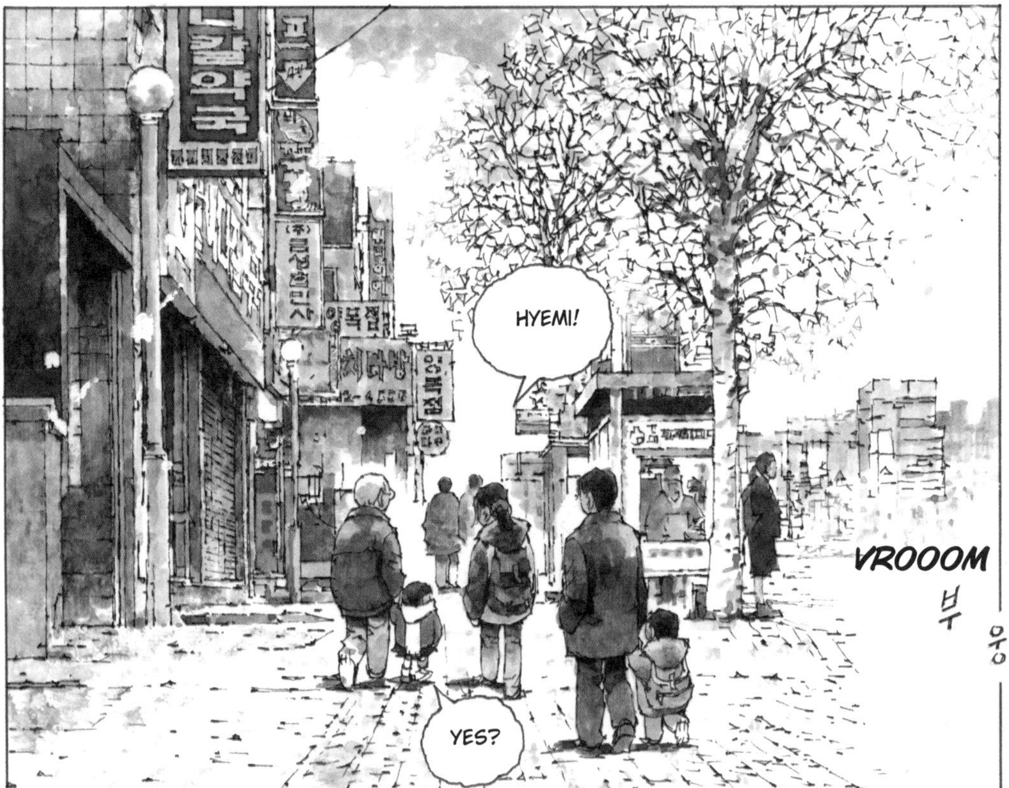
HYEMI!
YES?
VROOOM
부
웅

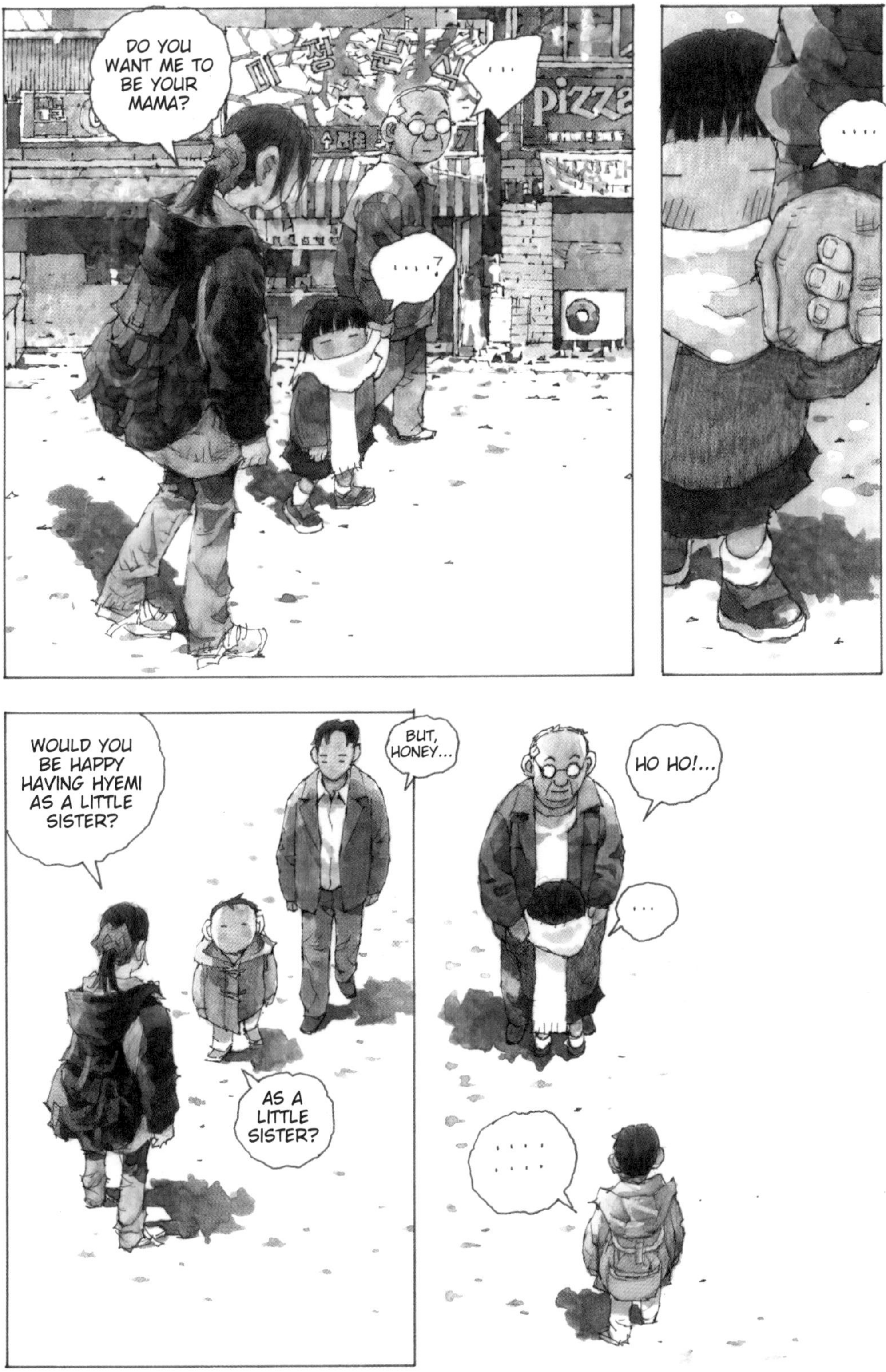
DO YOU WANT ME TO BE YOUR MAMA?
...
....?
pizza
....
WOULD YOU BE HAPPY HAVING HYEMI AS A LITTLE SISTER?
BUT, HONEY...
AS A LITTLE SISTER?
HO HO!...
...
....

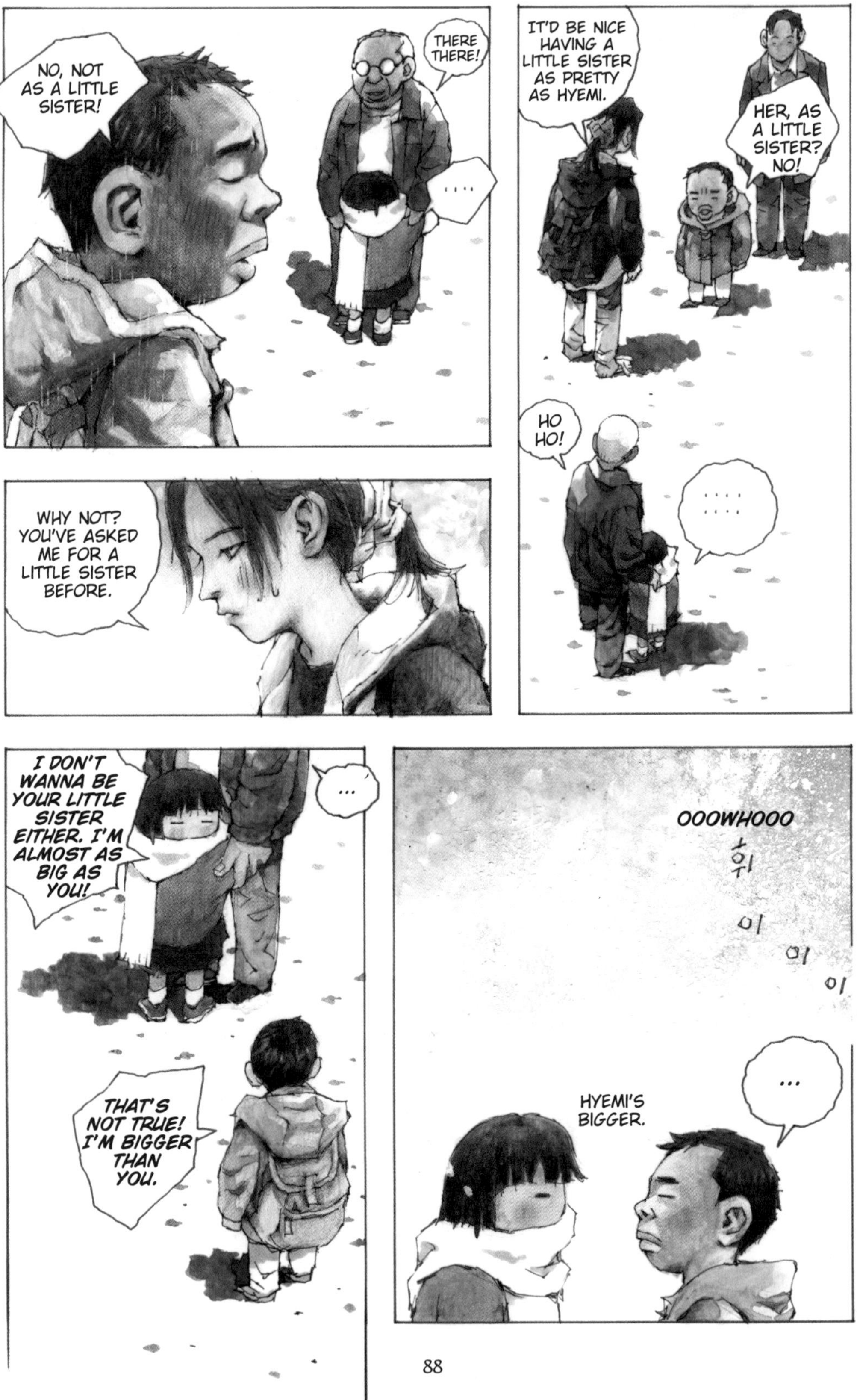
NO, NOT AS A LITTLE SISTER!
THERE THERE!
....
IT'D BE NICE HAVING A LITTLE SISTER AS PRETTY AS HYEMI.
HER, AS A LITTLE SISTER? NO!
WHY NOT? YOU'VE ASKED ME FOR A LITTLE SISTER BEFORE.
HO HO!
....
I DON'T WANNA BE YOUR LITTLE SISTER EITHER. I'M ALMOST AS BIG AS YOU!
...
THAT'S NOT TRUE! I'M BIGGER THAN YOU.
OOOWHOOO
후이 이 이 이
HYEMI'S BIGGER.
...

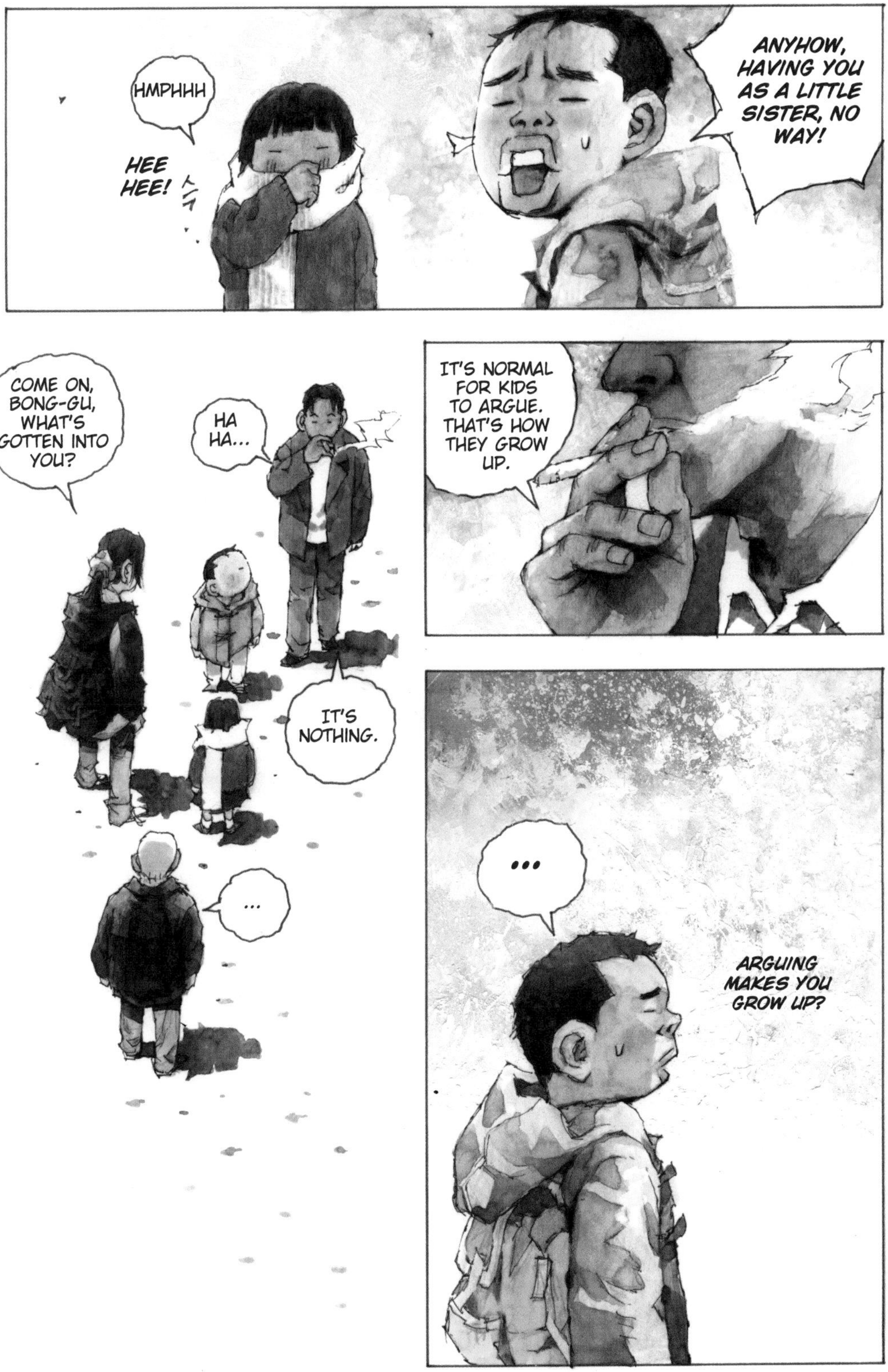
HMPHHH
HEE HEE!
ANYHOW, HAVING YOU AS A LITTLE SISTER, NO WAY!
COME ON, BONG-GU, WHAT'S GOTTEN INTO YOU?
HA HA...
IT'S NOTHING.
...
IT'S NORMAL FOR KIDS TO ARGUE. THAT'S HOW THEY GROW UP.
...
ARGUING MAKES YOU GROW UP?

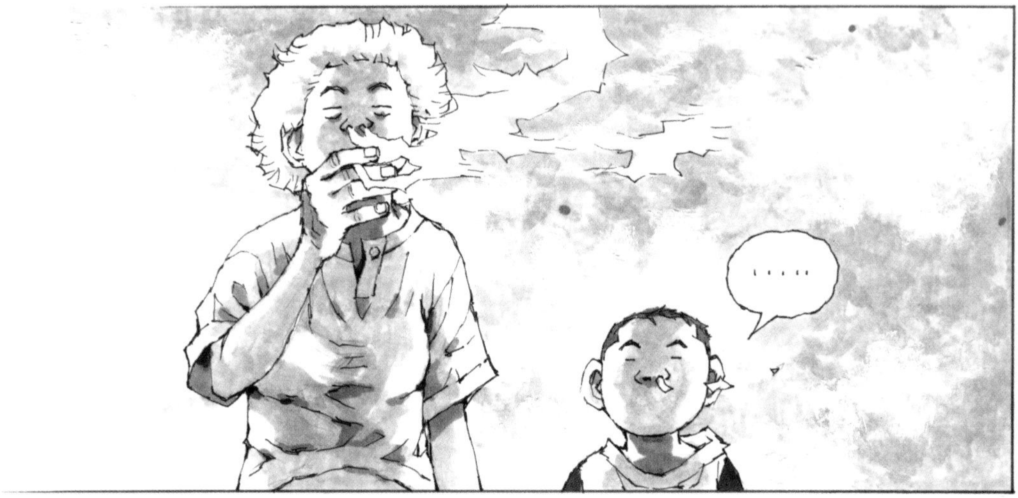
.....

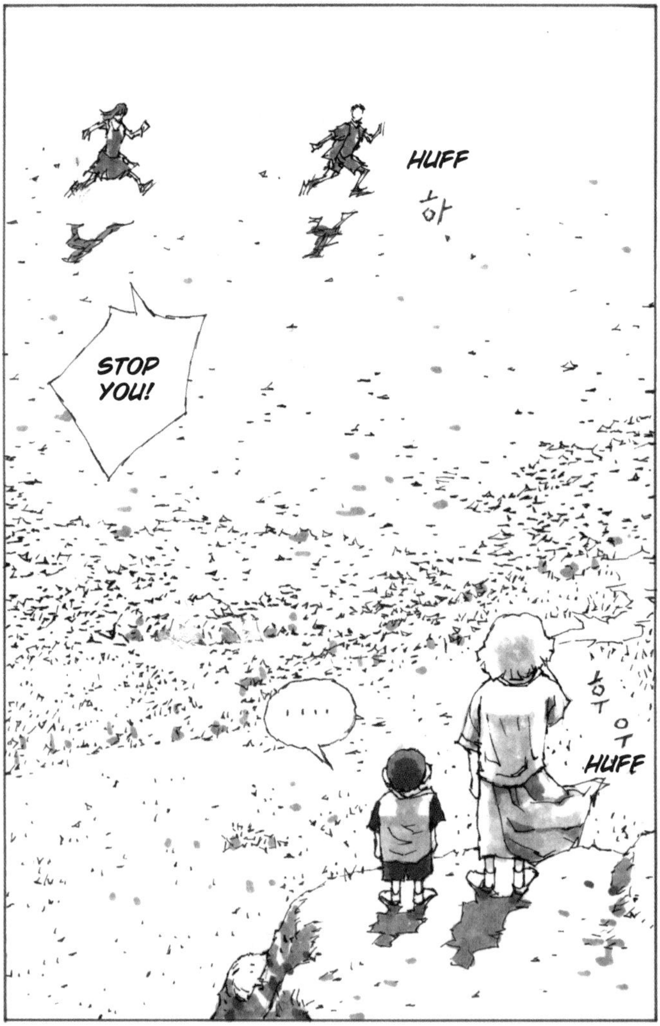
HUFF
하
STOP YOU!
....
HUFF

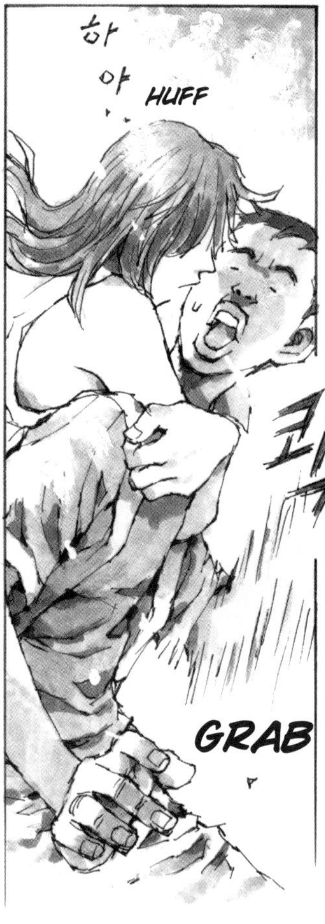
하
아
HUFF
GRAB

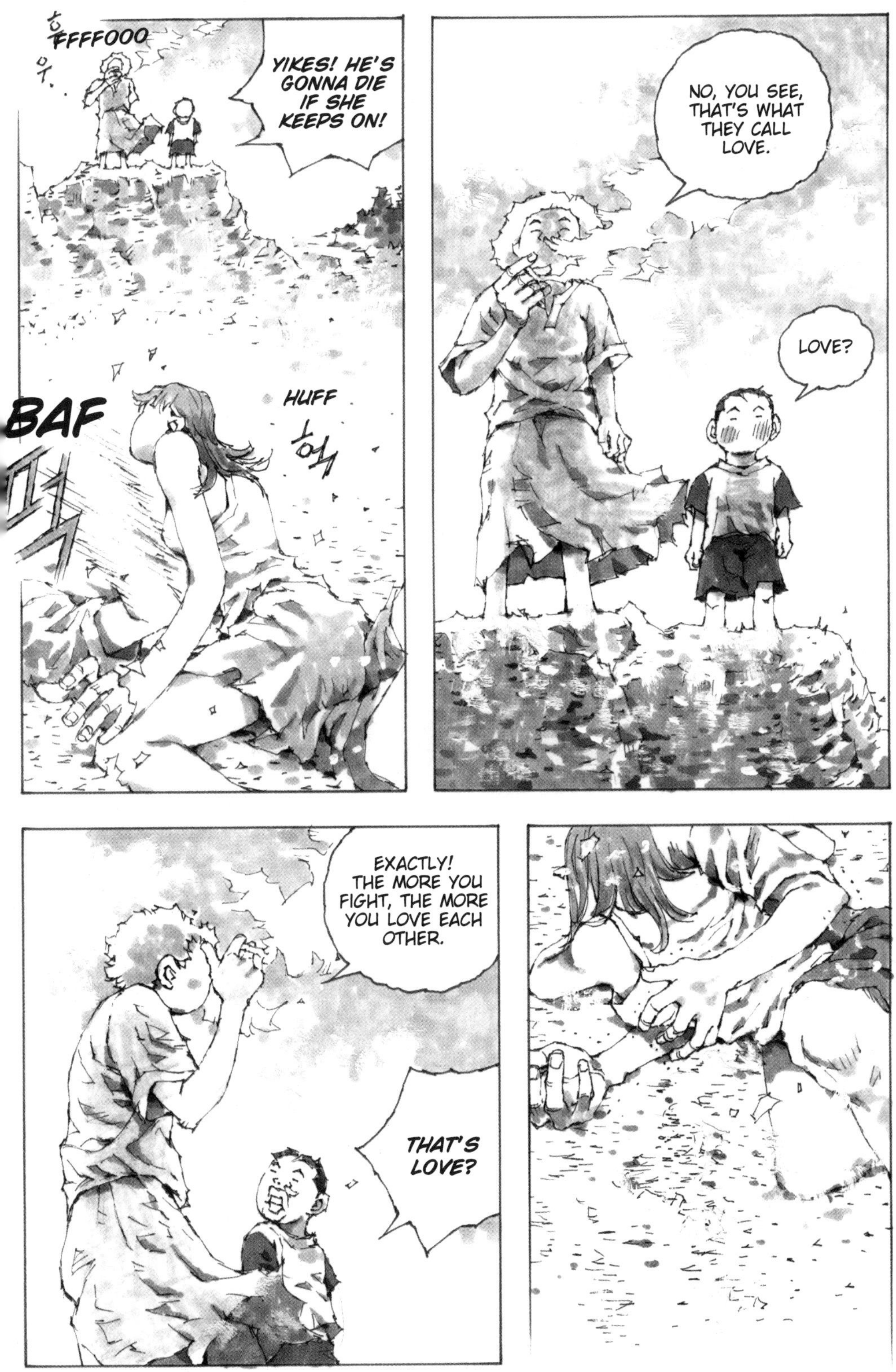
FFFFOOO
YIKES! HE'S GONNA DIE IF SHE KEEPS ON!
BAF
HUFF
NO, YOU SEE, THAT'S WHAT THEY CALL LOVE.
LOVE?
EXACTLY! THE MORE YOU FIGHT, THE MORE YOU LOVE EACH OTHER.
THAT'S LOVE?

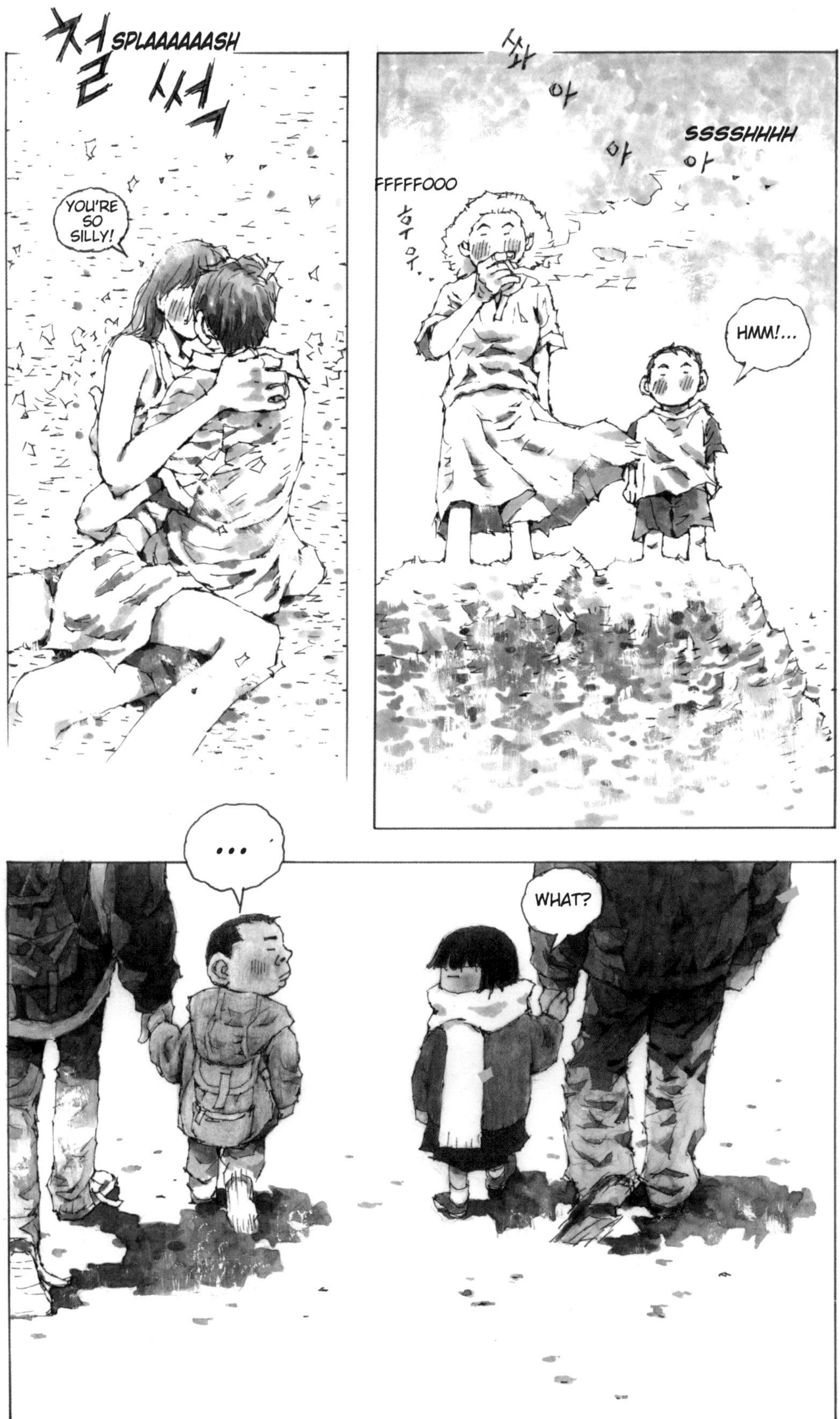
철썩
SPLAAAAAASH
YOU'RE SO SILLY!
쏴아아아
SSSSHHHH
FFFFFOOO
후우...
HMM!...
...
WHAT?

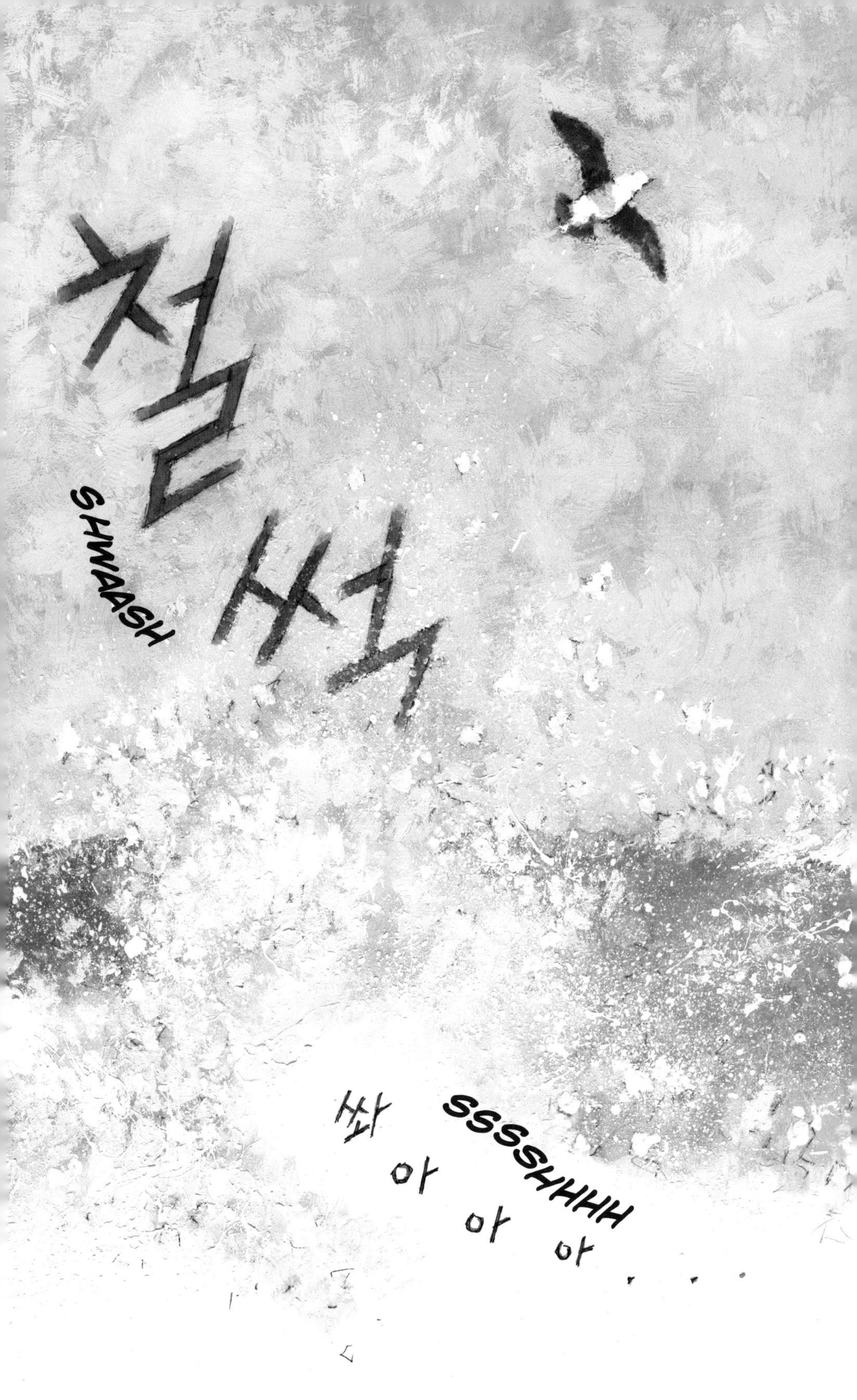
철썩
SHWASH
쏴아아아...
SSSSHHHH

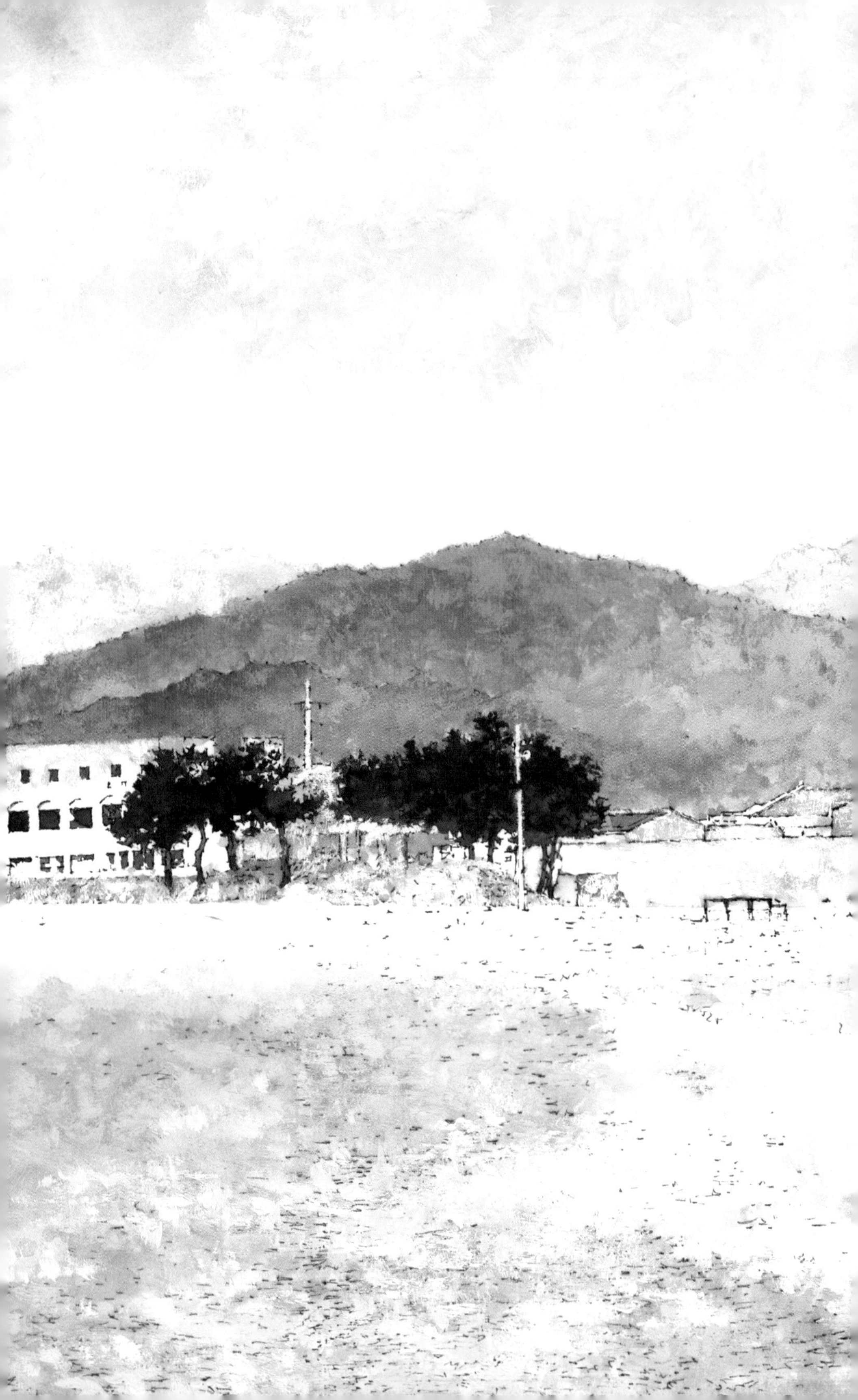

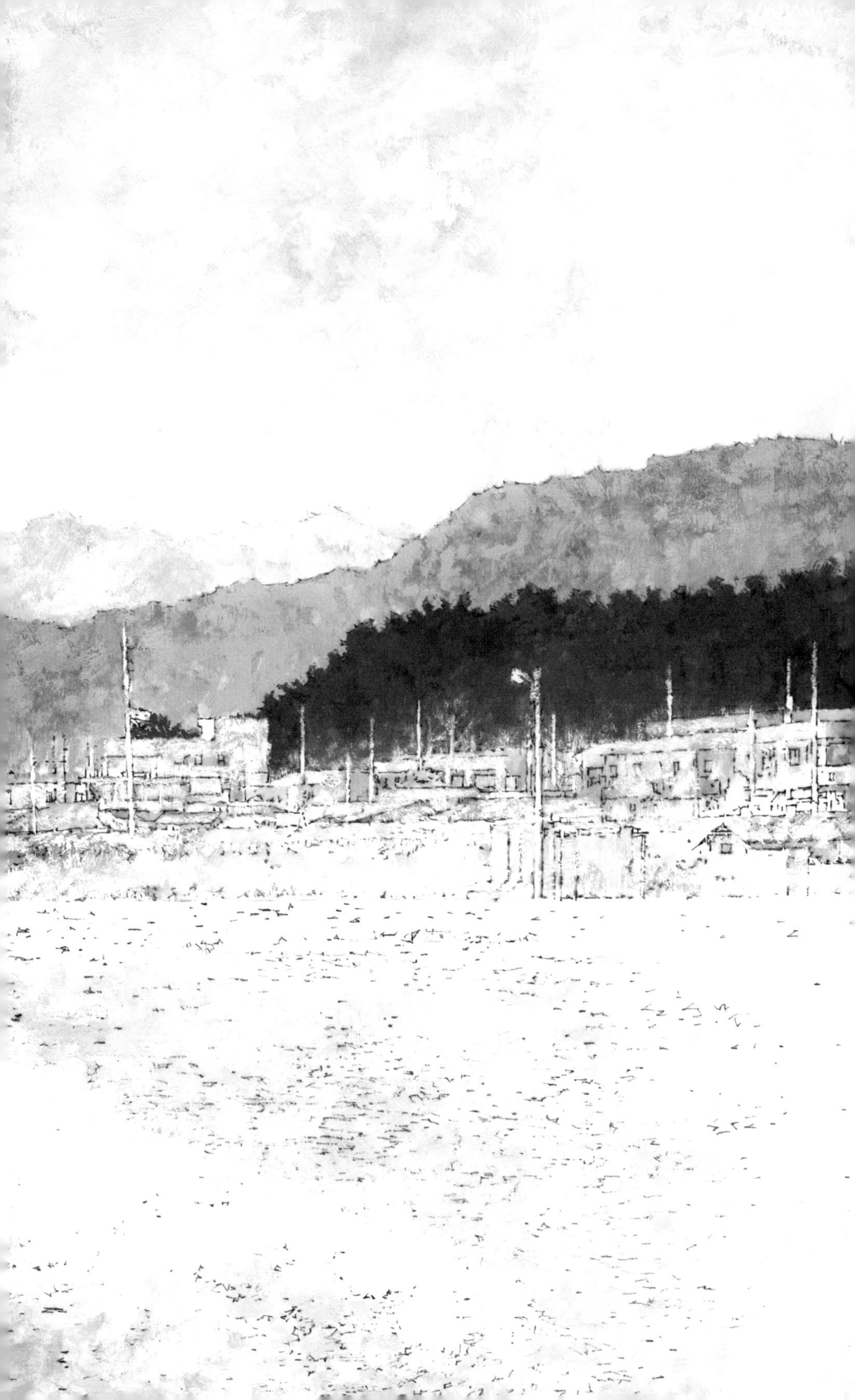

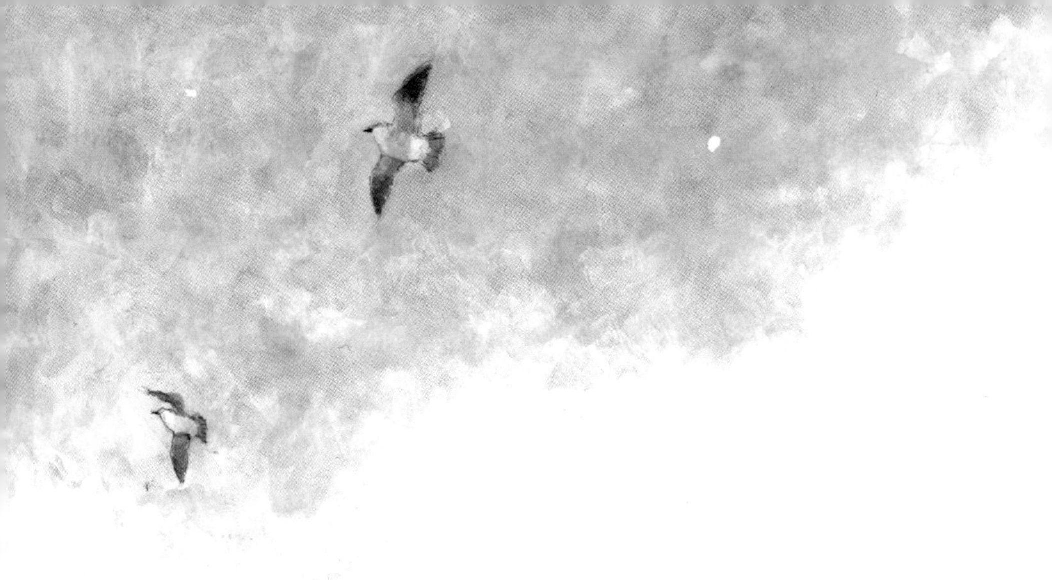

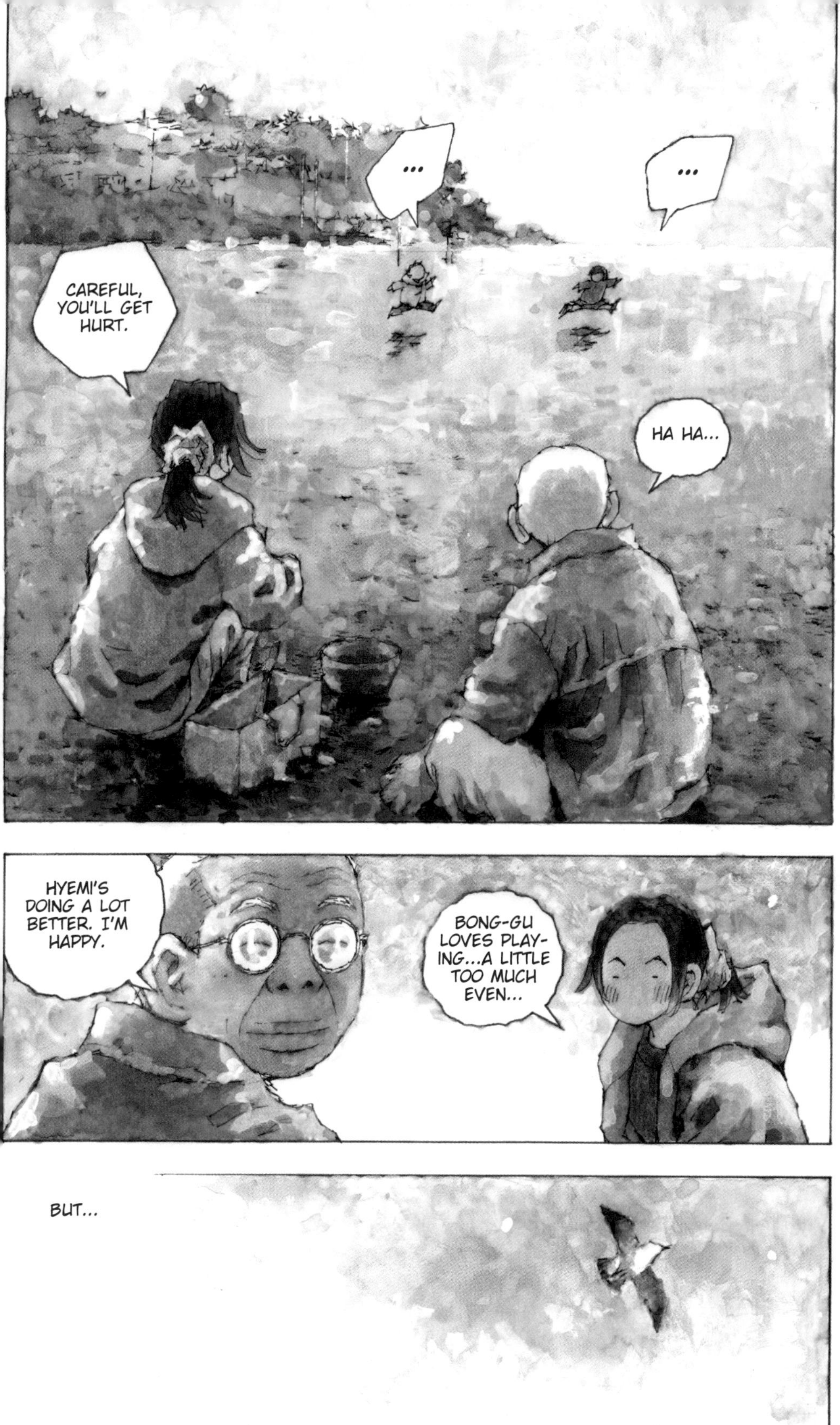
...
...
CAREFUL, YOU'LL GET HURT.
HA HA...
HYEMI'S DOING A LOT BETTER. I'M HAPPY.
BONG-GU LOVES PLAY-ING...A LITTLE TOO MUCH EVEN...
BUT...

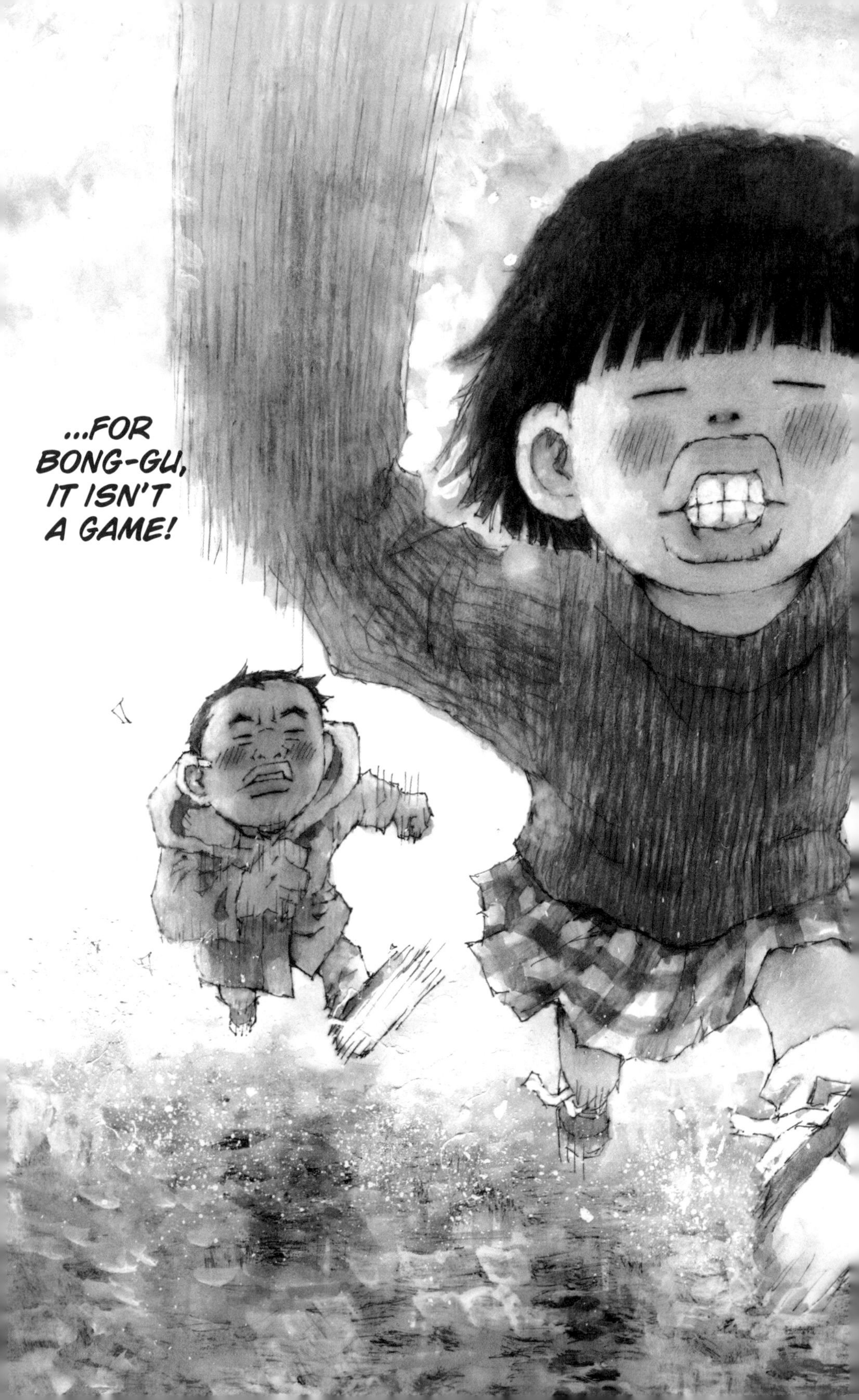
...FOR BONG-GU, IT ISN'T A GAME!

THE END

WINTER 2002, ON THE PLATFORM OF THE SEOUL TRAIN-STATION, IN FRONT OF THE TRAIN EN ROUTE TO MOKPO.

THE BEGINNING OF SPRING 2003.

AT THE PORT OF HAENAM, JEOLLA PROVINCE.

The Power to Touch Someone's Heart

Run, Bong-Gu, Run!
By Byun Byung-Jun

Pak Won-Sun
(lawyer and permanent member of the Beautiful Foundation)*
*a Korean foundation for the Public Interest

"A slightly insipid, rather frustrating story." Frankly speaking, that was my first impression upon reading this *manhwa*. No doubt, I was expecting a story full of humor and original characters, an arresting, lively story overflowing with gaiety.

But over time, my opinion of this little book has completely changed. It is true that, at first, I felt a sort of boredom, a touch of sadness even, but little by little, these feelings gave way to a more tender vision marked with hope.

I am no expert concerning *manhwa*. For reasons beyond my will, I don't often have occasion to read them. It would therefore be difficult for me to express any sort of opinion as to the quality of a graphic novel. Nonetheless, I must admit that this one impressed me particularly with its lyric style of drawing, its transparent, refined colors, its ordinary heroes, and even its story, which, in the end, I found moving.

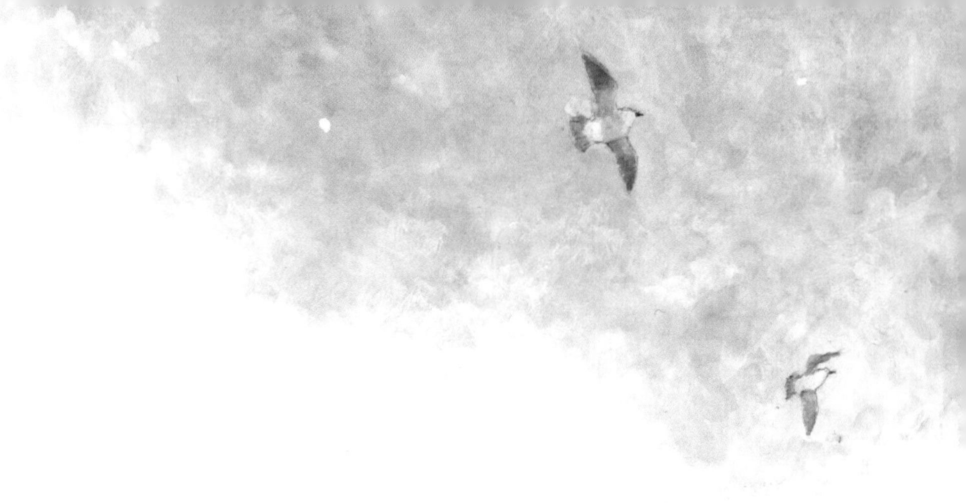

We're familiar with the coldness and indifference that reign in urban society, which our little hero Bong-Gu and his mother run smack into. These attitudes are part of our daily environment. The subway that they experience for the first time, the old man begging in order to feed his granddaughter, pigeons digging through trashcans in search of some crumbs of nourishment—none of that is particularly new, nor distant from our reality. You can see it all around you. And yet, this book invites us to reconsider our daily reality from a new perspective; it reminds us of the presence by our sides of society's forgotten.

Another good aspect of this *manhwa* is that it has a happy ending. Maybe I'm a little naive, but I love stories with happy endings. Bong-Gu and his mother come to Seoul to find the little boy's father. The latter, who had gone to take his chances in the capital, disappeared one fine day without sending any news. Reunited, they'll return to their island, taking with them the old beggar and his granddaughter Hyemi.

Without wallowing in realism or darkness, this story has the power to touch our hearts. It shows us that hope and love for humanity can melt away the coldness and indifference of our urban societies. Isn't that, after all, what constitutes the charm of this little book?

Each of us suffers,
Knows troubles,
A little more every day.
Birds with wounded feet,
Cities peopled with ailing hearts.

May there be less suffering!
Less troubles!

Drawing,
My friends, my family
Give my heart peace.

Byun Byung-Jun,
Winter 2002.

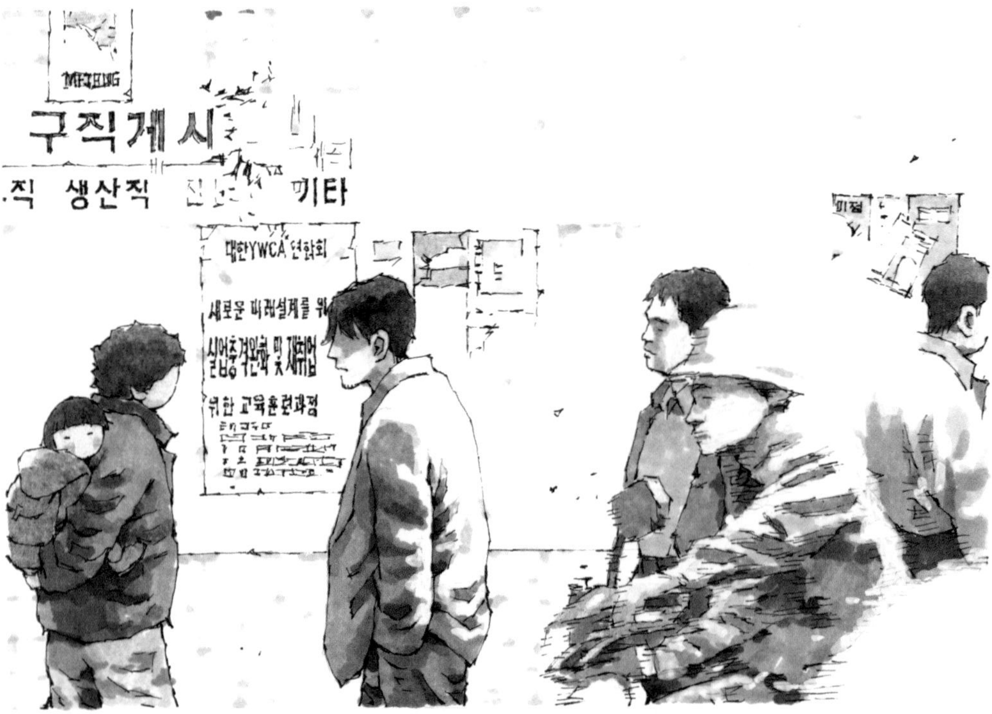
구직게시
생산직
기타
대한YWCA연합회
실업충격완화 및 재취업
위한 교육훈련과정

Run, Bong-Gu, Run!

A work of confluence

Kamakkui

(Editor of a webzine devoted to comics.)

1. Byun Byung-Jun's first works

Concerning *First Love*, the first collection of stories by Byun Byung-Jun, the critic Yi Jae-Hyeon opines:

> "[...] If you absolutely had to label him, one might say that Byun Byung-Jun belongs to the category of realist authors of *manhwa*. He's one of those authors of the new generation, heirs to Baek Seong-Min, Yi Hui-Jae and O Se-Yeong.* [...] Many readers dislike the lack of humor in realist comics. They blame it, moreover, for sidestepping daily realities of contemporary life, of trying to hold on too much to the past. But Byun Byng-Jun is striving to surpass this handicap by introducing into his work precisely what is missing from realist comics—gags, for example. [...] We'll be waiting impatiently to see how he'll cope with a longer story" (The Hankyoreh, January 15, 1999).

The new *manhwa* by Byun Byung-Jun, *Princess Anna*, an adaptation of a story by Bae Su-A, first published as a serial story in the magazine *Young Champ*, shows itself to be quite different from what Yi Jae-Hyeon was expecting. Instead of taking on modern life with a pleasant tone, the entire work reflects a melancholy that was already appearing in small touches in certain short stories by the author.

The story by Bae Su-A depicts the fantasies of a young girl suffering from melancholy and despair. In the *manhwa* version by Byun Byung-Jun, the sinister image of the city, which the author had already depicted in some of his stories, is remarkably in synch with the very feminine description of the melancholy imbuing the original work. But a good literary work doesn't necessarily translate into a good graphic novel. In his *manhwa*, Byun Byung-Jun, by depicting people and events in his own manner, nonetheless succeeds in this major feat.

* See his 'Buja's Diary' available from NBM ComicsLit

The urban landscape, rendered grotesque by a deformed vision, as well as the people who haunt it, like souls in pain, reflect that reality all too well in its details, all the while betraying the author's subjectivity. As for the large eyes and the vague gaze of the heroine, they seem to want to affect the reader to the depths of his being. Those who have read this *manhwa* certainly will not have failed to notice the quality of this work and its author's potential.

Consider an extract from a review by Ham Seong-Ho, which differs radically from that by Yi Jae-Hyeon.

"[..] Byun Byung-Jun's principal trait is in situating himself entirely outside of the realist school. His *manhwa Princess Anna* is more of an expressionist work. [...] He doesn't use his brush to express reality such as it is, but to express feelings [...]" (*Manhwadang Insaeng* Magazine, 2002).

Rare are the authors who relish being the object of polemics. It is equally unusual for critics to be diametrically opposed concerning an author. We have only to take a look with anticipation at the appearance of the following work by Byun Byung-Jun, all the more knowing that the author has gone off to study the art of comics in Japan.

2. Run, Bong-Gu, Run!

Here finally is the third book by Byun Byung-Jun. From the beginning of the story, one finds oneself thrust into the melancholic life imbuing the city of Seoul. That capital, where pigeons injure themselves digging through trashcans, where the father of the little hero drags along in wretched homelessness, resembles the sinister city described in *Princess Anna*, without, all the same, giving as tragic an image. Thanks, no doubt, to the colors used, the drawings seem happier. However, the author introduces a certain aridity in his portrait of the urban landscape, which, along with the mute dialogs, makes you feel a kind of discomfort that you cannot escape, like those heavy metals that accumulate in the body.

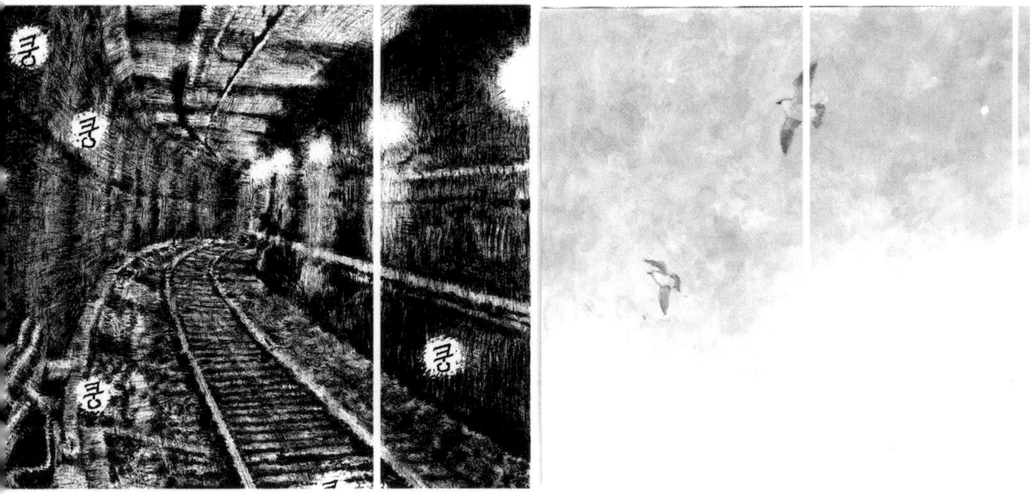
쿵
쿵
쿵
쿵

Through their absence of happiness, the characters of this story are related to those of *Princess Anna.* Nonetheless, they possess some candor and a touch of humor—where Anna feels nothing but hatred towards the tragedy of the world—and they still nourish within themselves hope and love for humanity.

Searching for her husband, who has come to Seoul to try to earn money, Dong-Sim, a provincial woman, disembarks in the capital along with her son. She meets an old homeless man who begs in the subway to meet the needs of his granddaughter. Together, they find Bong-Gu's father and will leave Seoul. Fleeing a solitude that weighs on them, all five of them will return to Bong-Gu's village of birth.

Run, Bong-Gu, Run! is a beautiful story, a pretty tale, against a backdrop of the sad, daily life of a great city. In this respect, the story fulfills the hopes expressed by Yi Jae-Hyeon after Byun Byung-Jun's first tales. But, at the same time, this work represents a change that did not escape Ham Seong-Ho. Finally, without getting too far away from the author's style, this *manhwa* is altogether an original.

3. A work of confluence

One could characterize *Run, Bong-Gu, Run!* as a confluence between two trends. The love stories of *First Loves* and *Princess Anna* can be categorized in the following manner:

Humorous stories	-"Thanks to the guts-fairy!" -"A Summer day's comedy" -"A Winter trip" -"A Cook's love" -"Streaking"
Country life and warm feelings	-"Jaenamli's first love" -"Story of an island village"
Melancholy brought about by the city	-"Surfing star" -"A Brave man's tears" -*Princess Anna*

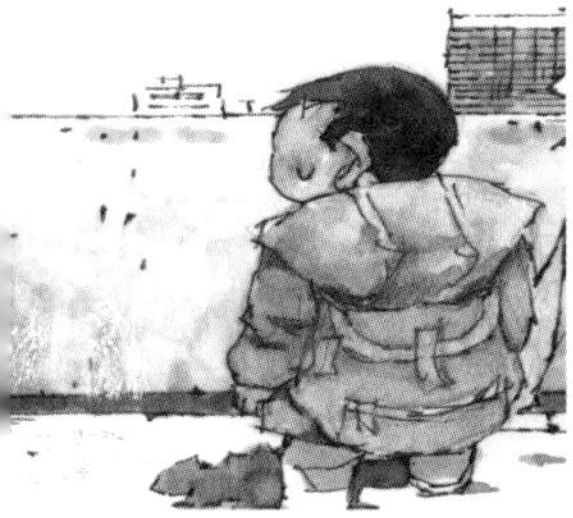

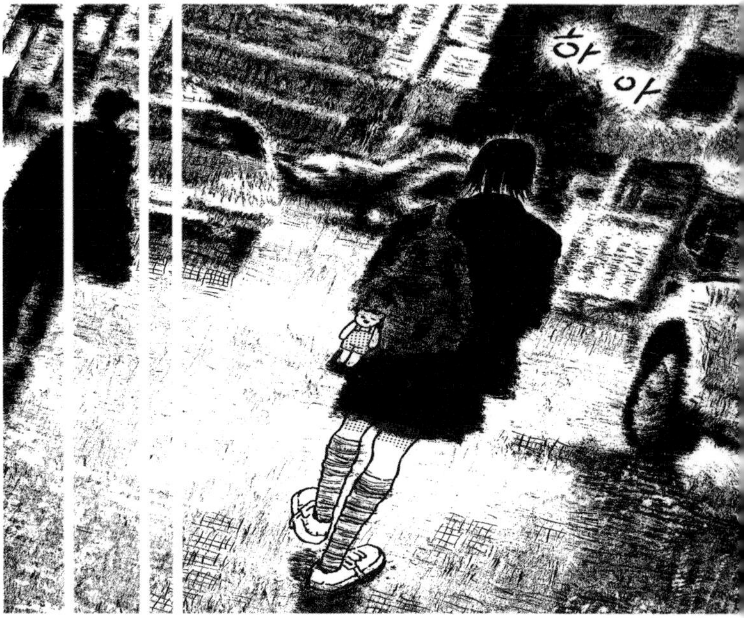

하
아

Among all these tales, humorous *manhwas* are not the major tendency in Byun Byung-Jun's works. They were particularly destined for easing his debut into the world of comics—in particular, in magazines marketed for teenagers. Little by little, the author no longer had recourse to humor except to lighten the mood.

The works where the countryside serves as the backdrop all involve warm feelings and are lightly marked with humor. On the other hand, those where the action takes place in cities describe in a poignant fashion the tragic marginalization of certain inhabitants of them. In sum, the former are beautiful, edifying stories, while the others are tragedies.

Run, Bong-Gu, Run! is situated at the confluence of these two tendencies. There is melancholy in the story, but discreetly so, as though attenuated. Humor and warmth of feelings are also expressed by the protagonists. The happy ending marks a change with respect to the melancholic image evoked in the aforementioned stories by a city without hope. As ocean currents mix together when the difference of water temperature declines, *Run, Bong-Gu, Run!* embodies the mixture of these two tendencies.

Did the author want to create a work of synthesis, by integrating all the elements—themes, images, characters—depicted up till then? In any event, it all can be found in *Run, Bong-Gu, Run!* Anna, the madonna of Byun Byung-Jun—a young woman with an unexpressive face, who curses the city—here becomes the country woman Dong-Sim, who comes to Seoul with his child, in search of her husband.

4. Photography, Literature, and *Manwha*

Byun Bung-Jun's work cannot be reduced to a simple portrait of country or city life. Let's consider the difference of opinions between Yi Jae-Hyeon and Ham Seong-Ho.

The almost photographic manner of representing the city, without any caricatured exageration, denotes, with this author, a desire for realism. The tales of the city and country are not very far from realist comics, themselves influenced by realist literature. It's in that sense that Yi Jae-Hyon is correct in characterizing Byun Byung-Jun as an heir to realism, especially concerning his collection *First Love*. However, although Byun Byung-Jun draws his landscapes like photos, it's not with the intention of making all the details appear in it. For a photographer, the problem of faithfulness to the real does not arise. The question lies uniquely in the manner of taking a photo in order to express one's state of mind through colors, composition, regulating exposure time and contrast. A photo thus taken must transmit to the person looking at it both the feelings of the photographer, as well as the spirit of the object. Byun Byung-Jun's drawing can be viewed in this sense. If he paints with a photographic faithfulness, it's not out of a care for realism, but from a desire to express his impressions of the moment. He transmits the reality of the landscape in a fantastic manner. This originality reached its acme with *Princess Anna*, adapted from a story at the polar opposite of realism. It's all of that which abounds in the sense of Ham Seong-Ho.

Likewise, from the perspective of these two critics, one can say that *Run, Bong-Gu, Run!* marks a junction, the one between realism and subjective expression. In this work, the two tendencies are present, while, at the same time, the author attempts to harmonize them.

In his descriptions of landscapes, Byun Byung-Jun allows his feelings to filter through thanks to the photographic quality of his drawing, and for the action scenes, he uses the frames peculiar to comics in a magical way. And as for the content of his stories, he seems to have inherited the realism of his predecessors. It will be of interest to the reader to observe how Byun Byung-Jun continues to conflate photography, literature, and *manhwa* in his future works.

Byun Byung-Jun started in manhwa in 1995 and, armed with both passion and talent, is one of its most promising rising stars. His works, mostly lyrical short stories for which he draws the backgrounds based on his own photographs, has garnered him many awards both in Korea and in Japan where he studied comics for a few years.

Another fine manwha from ComicsLit:
Buja's Diary by Seyeong O, $19.95

P&H: $3 1st item, $1 each addt'l.

We have over 200 titles, write
for our color catalog:
NBM
40 Exchange Pl., Suite 1308,
New York, NY 10005
see our website at
www.nbmpublishing.com

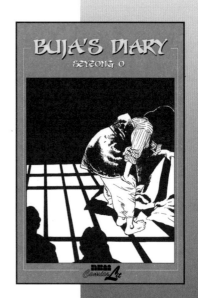

BUJA'S DIARY
SEYEONG O